HISTORY AND

C. B. F. W...
Thomas Pattie
Prudence Jones
N. Kollerstrom
Annabella Kitson
Nicholas Campion
John Heath-Stubbs
Derek Appleby
Patrick Curry

A
L
A

Annabella Kitson was educated at St Paul's, London, and Girton College, Cambridge. As writer and lecturer her interests have focused on the history of ideas both in the arts and in various symbolic systems. Papers given at the annual history of astrology seminars which she initiated in 1984 at the Astrological Lodge of London form the basis of this book.

The Astrological Lodge of London is a registered educational charity holding weekly lectures in term-time. Its work embraces the study of the history, philosophy and symbolism of astrology. Its address is BM Astrolodge, London, WC1N 3XX.

HISTORY AND ASTROLOGY

Clio and Urania Confer

Edited by ANNABELLA KITSON

MANDALA
UNWIN PAPERBACKS
London Boston Sydney Wellington

First published in paperback by Unwin Paperbacks, an imprint of Unwin Hyman Limited, in 1989

Unwin Hyman Limited
15–17 Broadwick Street
London W1V 1FP

Unwin Hyman Inc.
8 Winchester Place
Winchester
Mass 01890
USA

Allen & Unwin Australia Pty Ltd
8 Napier Street, North Sydney, NSW 2060, Australia

Allen & Unwin New Zealand Pty Ltd with the Port Nicholson Press
Compusales Building, 75 Ghuznee Street, Wellington,
New Zealand

British Library Cataloguing in Publication Data
History and astrology: Clio and Urania confer.
1. Astrology, history
I. Kitson, Annabella
133.5'09
ISBN 0-04-440522-7

Printed and bound in Great Britain by
Richard Clay Ltd, Bungay, Suffolk

CONTENTS

ACKNOWLEDGEMENTS

This book is based on contributions to the history of astrology seminar held each autumn since 1984 by the Astrological Lodge of London. The material reflects the interests of the historians and astrologers who take part.

The Astrological Lodge of London is a registered educational charity whose work embraces the study of the history, philosophy and symbolism of astrology.

The publication of this book has been assisted by a grant from the Twenty-Seven Foundation. The Twenty-Seven Foundation is a registered private charity which gives grants for research and publishing in history. Its address is: care of the Institute of Historical Research, Senate House, Malet Street, London, WC1 7HU.

We would like to express our thanks to the Twenty-Seven Foundation for its generous help.

Figures 9 and 10 on pages 158 and 165 are reproduced by courtesy of the Trustees of the Science Museum.

Quotations from Manilius are reprinted by permission of the publishers and the Loeb Classical Library from Manilius, *Astronomica*, trans. G. P. Gould (Cambridge, Mass.: Harvard University Press, 1977).

Quotations from Elias Ashmole are reprinted by permission of the publisher from *Elias Ashmole (1617–1692), His Autobiographical and Historical Notes*, edited with a biographical introduction by C. H. Josten (Oxford University Press, 1966).

INTRODUCTION

Annabella Kitson

> History is a desirable part of everybody's mental furniture . . . The man whose interests are bounded by the short span between his birth and death has a myopic vision and a limitation of outlook which can hardly fail to narrow the scope of his hopes and desires.
>
> Bertrand Russell, *History as an Art*

The history of astrology is long, varied and fascinating. The study of it provides astrologers with rewarding insights into the nature and philosophy of their craft. But it also confronts historians with the complexities inherent in the subject.

A variety of scholarly approaches have been made with astronomical, mathematical and observational methods in mind, or within the framework of philosophical, social or political concerns. Literary critics have naturally wished to gloss and elucidate texts containing astrological allusions; however, they have focused on the literary characteristics of those texts rather than upon astrological subtleties.

The problem for the historian is that the subject is intricate and multifarious. The grammar of its language is not rapidly grasped even when the validity of that language for its time is acknowledged. Thus historical areas which demand an intimate knowledge of the craft of astrology tend to be ignored or skirted around. Meanwhile astrologers – including those interested in the history of the subject – are often unaware of the antiquity of notions they ascribe to early modern invention.

The analogy which comes to mind and may be helpful is the study of art history. Artists as a group may feel themselves to be uniquely capable of understanding their subject. They may regard historical assumptions as unwarranted intrusions by those who do not understand the craft or its philosophy as practitioners do. Historians, on the other hand, may sometimes have found the technicalities of that craft less absorbing than the social, political and aesthetic views they wished to support.

Where ways of dealing with this unfruitful situation have been found in the art history world, they seem to have come from willingness on both sides to acknowledge the validity of the other's discipline and to learn from it.

In this book Nicholas Campion, both an historian and an astrologer, presents an extensive study of the work of Jean Bodin and Louis Le Roy in relation to astrological historiography in the Renaissance. He welcomes the recent revision of historians' views of the function of astrology as a philosophy of history, but argues that this has to be taken further and to be based on a better understanding of the nature and practice of astrology in the past. This underlines what has often been a very real lack.

This book is concerned with astrological ideas which have flowed into Europe over the centuries from Babylonian, Greek and Arabic traditions. During the twentieth century various modified and diluted versions of these ideas have been transmitted to a wider public and are current in the English-speaking world.

Broadly speaking, the modern emphasis has been on the horoscopes of individuals (natal astrology), sometimes with the addition of synastry (the comparison of horoscopes when considering personal relationships). What follows exemplifies – amongst much else – various different categories: mundane, electional, horary and natal astrology – this last was not the earliest kind. Mr C. B. F. Walker, of the Department of Western Asiatic Antiquities at the British Museum, sketches the development of Mesopotamian astrology. Evidence is sparse and all the more precious for that reason. He shows, for example, how the observations of Venus made in Babylon in the seventeenth century BC were interpreted in relation to the country as a whole – that is in mundane terms.

Greek astrologers worked on the basis of Babylonian mathematical procedures and astronomical observations. Mr Pattie, of the Department of Manuscripts of the British Library, emphasizes astrology's central place in the intellectual debate of ancient times. He exemplifies the kinds of question clients asked their astrologers, to be resolved sometimes by horary and sometimes by electional means; and he presents two horoscopes from British Library papyri, dating from the first century AD.

In her contribution 'Celestial and Terrestrial Orientation', Prudence Jones considers the derivation of House systems. The division of the heavens into – usually – twelve Houses, with their attributed significances, tends to be discussed today in rather empirical terms. Her approach is very much more radical.

Nicholas Kollerstrom, an historian of science with a special interest in planetary metals, discusses the temples dedicated to planetary gods in Harran, a ruined ancient city in modern Turkey, near Urfa, which was medieval Edessa. These temples are known of from ancient records. Nicholas Kollerstrom deals with the association between planetary deities, days of the week, and the metals which were used to build the temples where Sabian priests invoked the cosmic powers. This theme is taken up again, in my own discussion of the temples of Venus and Mars in Chaucer's 'Knight's Tale' and in some of his shorter poems.

Electional astrology, as a genre, has been somewhat neglected. This may be because neither in ancient nor medieval times was it very clearly distinguished from horary astrology as a technique for answering questions. It is a technique for choosing a propitious moment for the beginning of a process, or for any act where importance is attached to the outcome. I discuss a range of matters for which elections have been thought appropriate, particularly in the seventeenth century.

Derek Appleby, a distinguished practitioner and writer on traditional techniques, demonstrates electional astrology in relation to an historic moment, the laying of a foundation stone. To resume my art history analogy, we are like students watching an artist demonstrating the known seventeenth-century methods of preparing a canvas, or applying tinted glazes – a normal part of art education. Derek Appleby enters into the historical circumstances, and into the craft of an astrologer of the period.

Mundane astrology was of great importance from early times, its technique providing the basis for predictions of a general kind, political and otherwise. These techniques are specially relevant to the study of Bodin and Renaissance historiography.

Pursuing the theme of astrology concerned with a whole society, Derek Appleby considers the historic moment after the 'Glorious Revolution' of 1688 in England, when the Declaration of Rights was signed by William III and Mary II (both grandchildren of Charles I), who accepted the crown as joint monarchs. William's nativity is analysed and a range of astrological techniques deployed, demonstrating the traditional style. The declaration marked an important moment on the road to parliamentary government. The 1689 map is related to various horoscopes including the one for William I's coronation in 1066, which is regarded as having a continuing significance for the life of the country.

The reputations of the planets and their supposed influences have varied over the centuries – for reasons which are perhaps interesting to anthropologists and social historians. There has, for example, been a complex interaction between mythology and astrology, not confined to early times. (Indeed, Pluto, most recently discovered planet, named by a child after a cartoon-character dog, attracts even today the attributes of Hades–Pluto, god of the underworld.) This interaction had a remarkable expression in Chaucer's *Complaint of Mars*, where gods and a goddess are presented as planets; they behave like human beings, their movements limited by astronomical constraints; and they are possibly identifiable with historical personages. Chaucer's works, both prose and poetry, form an attractive repository of astrological ideas and instructive material – by no means limited to his *Treatise on the Astrolabe*, which I discuss; other themes are his presentation of Mars, Venus and Saturn, related to their reputations in some other texts.

The symbolism of planets and signs pervades the poetry of Edmund Spenser, Chaucer's Elizabethan admirer. John Heath-Stubbs, himself a distinguished poet and scholar, illustrates this in relation to *The Shephearde's Calender*. Astrology in poetry endures as the poetry endures, available to successive generations in a context of enjoyment.

Johannes Kepler's belief in astrology in the seventeenth century is significant. We know that he and other astrologers were employed by Wallenstein during the Thirty Years' War to give astrological guidance as to the timing of military affairs. Apart from his great importance as an astronomer, Kepler experimented with and introduced several minor aspects for use in astrology. William Lilly mentions these rather coolly in *Christian Astrology*, saying that 'of late one Kepler, a learned man, hath added [to the major aspects Lilly previously recommended] some new ones . . . I only acquaint you with these, that finding them anywhere you may apprehend their meaning.' About 500 pages later he demonstrates their use in the direction of nativities.

Patrick Curry, who wrote his doctoral thesis on the history of English astrology at London University, was responsible for organizing the history of astrology conference which took place at the Warburg Institute in London in 1984. In this book he contributes accounts of astrological periodical literature in the late eighteenth century; and of John Worsdale, a little known but significant astrologer of the time. He sets both in the context of a period during which sales of *Vox Stellarum* (*Old Moore's Almanac*) were rising, to reach 300,000 copies a year by 1800.

Worsdale prided himself on his predictive techniques, and data he used survives. A method of researching his techniques would be to set up horoscopes on which he based forecasts he claimed proved accurate. In this way one might analyse his methods. Research of this kind – returning to my earlier analogy – would correspond to the investigation of pigments and glazes in an eighteenth-century painting.

To illustrate eighteenth-century periodical literature I have included some horoscopes from *The Conjuror's Magazine* (later *The Astrologer's Magazine*). These show the keen interest of contributors in contemporary events such as the 'murder' of Louis XVI. The analysis of Nicholas Culpeper's nativity provides an example of contemporary natal interpretation.

The arrangement of the material in this book is very roughly chronological. Certain themes recur in an interesting way: for example, the recommended behaviour of the astrologer, in Firmicus and in William Lilly; or again, attitudes to Saturn in various texts, also appearing in Kepler's self-analysis. Some cross references have been included so that such themes may be pursued.

Because a good deal is now known about seventeenth-century practice, a number of themes from other times have been related to it for purposes of comparison. Lilly's *Christian Astrology*, published in the middle of the century, is a convenient focus for this purpose. In its modern edition it is perhaps the most readily available and comprehensive textbook of traditional astrological practice, 'A most easie Introduction to the whole Art of Astrology'. It gives insight into the mentality of those who think in terms of symbolism.

It was in Florence in 1980 that I first saw Clio, muse of history, conferring with Urania, who was muse of astrology in days when it was one with astronomy. The engraving, which illustrates this book and hints at some of its intentions, was displayed at the magnificent exhibition, 'Astrologia, Magia e Alchimia nel Rinascimento fiorentino ed europeo'. This picture, with harmonious Libra rising, may stand as a paradigm of fruitful discussion.

NOTE ON TRADITIONAL ASTROLOGY

Broadly speaking this means an emphasis on the sun, moon, Mercury, Venus, Mars, Jupiter and Saturn, which are regarded as rulers of the appropriate signs, rather than on the outer planets – Uranus, Neptune and Pluto – which were discovered from 1781 onwards and are considered by modern astrologers.

Traditionalists consider mutual reception, Fortuna and some other Arabic parts, and the fixed stars. The planet (lord or lady) ruling the sign on the cusp of a House is significant and its condition and placing are taken into account. At different periods Regiomontanus, Campanus or Placidus cusps tended to be used in preference to Equal House. The term 'traditional' is sometimes used in this book to denote 'not modern' with respect to the period discussed; if the usage is elastic alternatives would certainly be cumbersome.

The moon's nodes (Caput and Cauda Draconis) are given importance and such terms are explained in the Glossary. Detailed explanations of traditional technicalities are to be found in the 1985 facsimile edition of William Lilly's *Christian Astrology* [1647].

Publisher's Note: Annabella Kitson was invited to provide a commentary, introducing and linking the various subjects and tracing some of the recurrrent themes.

I

A SKETCH OF THE DEVELOPMENT OF MESOPOTAMIAN ASTROLOGY AND HOROSCOPES

C. B. F. Walker

Commentary

The first four subjects to be addressed adumbrate major astrological themes: the zodiac, Greek horoscopes, the beginnings of House systems, and the planetary attributes as exemplified in records of the Harran temples.

First of all Mr Walker describes – amongst much else – the very early notions of celestial influence on earthly events, and types of predictions made on the basis of planetary phenomena. He discusses early evidence of the concept of the zodiacal sign and the way it was used.

A. L. K.

Our knowledge of the astronomy and astrology of Sumer, Babylon and Assyria is still fragmentary and dependent very much on the accidents of preservation and archaeological discovery. There are large gaps in the record, and it happens that the bulk of the evidence comes from Babylonia. Whether there really was in Sumerian times anything that we would understand as astronomy or astrology remains obscure. For Assyria we only have useful information from a period of not more than a hundred years from the late eighth to the late seventh centuries BC, but it gives us the only tantalizing glimpse of astrology in action. Much of what we know from Assyria plainly derives from Babylonian tradition and practice, and it is only from Babylonia that we have, at a later date, the detailed astronomical observations and mathematical procedures on which the later Greek astronomers and astrologers built.

Apart from some fragmentary lists of star names which may go back as early as the Sumerian period (third millennium BC), the earliest list of star names from Mesopotamia is that given in the Old

Babylonian 'Prayer to the gods of the night', which is datable to about 1800 BC:

> May the great gods of the night: shining Fire-star, heroic Irra, Bow-star, Yoke-star, Šitaddaru, Mušḫuššu-star, Wagon, Goat-star, Goatfish-star, Serpent-star – stand by and put a propitious sign on [the extá of] the lamb I am blessing [now] for the extispicy I will perform [tomorrow].

This prayer does not give us the means to identify particular Babylonian constellations in the sky, but it does show that already at this early date the concept existed that the stars or constellations were regarded as (or represented) gods who were able to influence events on earth.

The slightly later Venus observations contained in the so-called 'Venus tablets of Ammiṣaduqa' (who was King of Babylon from 1702 to 1682 BC) record the dates of first and last sightings of the planet Venus as morning or evening star and make predictions based on the time intervals between these observations. Thus, 'If in the eighth month on the eleventh day Venus disappeared in the east, and stayed away from the sky for two months and seven days, and Venus became visible in the west again in the tenth month on the nineteenth day, the harvest will prosper'. Other omens on the tablet are of the same character. No omens concerning other planets are known from this period, but lunar eclipse omens confirm what we find from the Venus omens that astrology was regarded as relating to the fortunes of either the country as a whole or the person of the king, but not to private individuals. Thus from a tablet of lunar eclipse omens, 'If an eclipse of the moon occurs in the eleventh month on the fourteenth day then the enemy will capture a party going out from the city gate. The king will go out with his troops and will be defeated. After the death of that king the land will prosper and there will be peace.'

The next documented stage in the development of Babylonian astronomy is represented by the two-tablet series Mul-Apin, 'the Constellation of the Plough', which in its present form is thought to date from about 1000 BC, although elements of the text may well go back to the Old Babylonian period. Among other matters this text lists the constellations of the Babylonian sky in three broad bands (known as the ways of Enlil, Anu and Ea) running more or less parallel to the equator. The planets are also listed among the constellations:

Transliteration	*Transcription*	*Translation*	*Planet*
MUL.SAG-ME-GAR	nēberu	The ferry	Jupiter
dele-bat	delebat	(unknown)	Venus
UDU-IDIM-GU_4-UD	šiḫṭu	Jumping	Mercury
UDU-IDIM-SAG-UŠ	kayamānu	Constant	Saturn
ṣal-bat-a-nu	ṣalbatānu	(unknown)	Mars

The text then specifies those eighteen constellations which lie in the ecliptic, 'These are the gods standing on the path of the moon, [the gods] through whose sectors the moon passes every month and whom he touches'.

Sumerian/Babylonian name	*Translation*	*Equivalent*
MUL.LÚ.ḪUN-GA	The hired man	Aries
MUL-MUL	The stars	Pleiades
MUL.GU_4-AN-NA	The bull of heaven	Taurus
MUL.SIPA-ZI-AN-NA	The true shepherd of Anu	Orion
MUL.ŠU-GI	The old man	Perseus
MUL.ZUBI	The hooked staff	Auriga
MUL.MAŠ-TAB-BA-GAL-GAL	The great twins	Gemini
MUL.AL-LUL	The crab	Cancer
MUL.UR-GU-LA	The lion	Leo
MUL.AB-SÍN	The barley-stalk	Virgo
MUL.zi-ba-ni-tum	The balance	Libra
MUL.GÍR-TAB	The scorpion	Scorpius
MUL.PA-BIL-SAG	Pabilsag (a god)	Sagittarius
MUL.SUḪUR-MÀŠ.KU_6	The goat-fish	Capricornus
MUL.GU-LA	The giant	Aquarius
MUL.KUN.MEŠ	The tails	Pisces
MUL.SIM-MAḪ	The swallow	SW Pisces
MUL.a-nu-ni-tum	Anunitum (a goddess)	NE Pisces

Apart from the fact that more constellations are listed than we are accustomed to see in the modern zodiac, it is also apparent that some of these constellations, for example, Orion, Perseus, Auriga, are only just touched by the path of the moon. That fact and the number of constellations shows that we are not dealing with equal divisions of the zodiac but with actual visible constellations.

This assumption is confirmed by study of the surviving astrological reports from Assyria of the early seventh century BC, found in the royal archives at Nineveh. For instance: 'To the king my lord, [from] your servant Mār-Ištar: . . . As regards the planet Jupiter about which I previously wrote to the king my lord: "It has appeared on the way of the Anu stars, in the area of Orion." [As] it was low, it was not clearly recognizable in the haze, [and] they said: "It is on the way of the Anu stars." Now it has risen [and] become clearly recognizable; it stays under the constellation Auriga on the way of the Enlil stars.' Modern calculations based on the known date of the letter show that the planet was moving in the narrow space between Taurus and Gemini, but clearly the Assyrian observers divided this space into a part belonging to Orion and a part belonging to Auriga.

On this occasion the astrologers offered the king a variety of interpretations of the planetary phenomena: 'If Jupiter approaches Orion, the [pest] god will consume [the land]. If Jupiter enters into Orion, the gods will consume the land. If Jupiter appears on the way of the Anu stars, a crown prince will rebel against his father [and] seize the throne.' This is typical of Assyrian practice, to judge by the royal correspondence. Study of such predictions in the Assyrian letters shows that they were derived from a variety of sources, including both oral and written traditions, the opinions of contemporary experts and the prescriptions of the great astrological series Enuma Anu Enlil (named after its opening words, 'When the gods Anu and Enlil . . . '). The correspondence shows a pattern of an astrology still applied only to the fortunes of king and country. How the Assyrian 'man in the street' reacted to astrology we do not know.

The canonical astrological series Enuma Anu Enlil, which runs to some sixty tablets and is known primarily from copies preserved in the royal libraries at Nineveh, is still slowly being reconstructed. Like Mul-Apin it may in part date back to the Old Babylonian period. It contains a wide diversity of omens taken from astronomical observations, together with scholarly comments and interpretations. Much of the series deals with the sun and moon, their appearance and disappearance, the circumstances of eclipses, etc. Weather phenomena, halos, strange cloud formations, thunderstorms, etc., are discussed at length; for obvious reasons the weather remains of significance to astrologers almost to the end of the cuneiform tradition. There is briefer treatment of the movements and appearance of the planets, especially Venus, and of the appearance and ominous significance of the constellations. By contrast with modern astrology the series shows an apparent lack of systematization of astrological science, and the details of planetary positions in the sky are of minor importance.

At about the same time in Babylonia was beginning a process of the greatest significance for the history of both astrology and astronomy. From the mid-seventh century BC (or perhaps a little earlier) the official astrologers kept a regular official day-by-day record of their astronomical observations, which was subsequently compiled into monthly and annual summaries. The earliest surviving record in this series (known to modern scholars as Astronomical Diaries) dates to 652 BC, and the latest to 47 BC. The following extract, taken from the Diary for 652 BC, gives an idea of the character of these texts:

> The 14th, one god was seen with the other [i.e. sun and moon]. The river level receded. Mercury's last appearance in the east behind Pisces, and Saturn's last appearance behind Pisces; I did not watch because the days were overcast. The 17th, in the morning, overcast. Thunder, gusty south wind, rain, small [hail]-stones. Mars became stationary in the area of the Lip of the Scorpion, it came close to the Scorpion's head. The 25th, Mars was east of the star to the right of the Scorpion.

Apart from the perennial concern with the weather, the essential point to note is that the Babylonian concern with the planets now centres on the dates of their first and last visibility and with their precise positions in the sky with relation to fixed stars or visible constellations. The first evidence for placing planets in theoretically calculated zodiacal signs as opposed to visible constellations comes from the mid-sixth century BC; for instance a Diary for 464 BC contains monthly summaries of the zodiacal positions of the planets, such as: 'At that time, Jupiter was behind Cancer in the beginning of Leo; Venus was in Pisces; Mars . . . ; Saturn was in Capricorn; Mercury was in Aquarius.' From then on such monthly summaries become a regular feature of the Diaries, but in observation texts the concept of the zodiacal sign is restricted to such summaries; observations continue to be related to fixed stars and the visible constellations.

These mid-sixth century Diaries are the earliest evidence for the concept of the zodiacal sign, and for the division of the zodiac into twelve equal parts of 30 degrees each. Curiously enough modern calculations from the Babylonian records show that the Babylonian zodiac system does not start at the first point of Aries, but about

5 degrees earlier, and this difference extends through the whole zodiac. The further development of Babylonian mathematical astronomy suggests that the concept of the zodiac sign was developed not out of astrological theory but for practical reasons in order to meet the need for a precise framework for calculating solar, lunar and planetary movements. Detailed mathematical procedures allowed for the calculation of solar and lunar longitudes and velocities, conjunctions and eclipse magnitudes, etc.; and similar calculations were attempted for the planets. The goal was the production of ephemerides predicting the timing of the lunar calendar and periodic phenomena. But once the mathematical concept of the zodiac sign was established it was quickly also taken over for astrological purposes.

What astrological development had been taking place in the interval since the fall of the Assyrian Empire in 612 BC we do not know; but the appearance of the first Babylonian horoscopes in the late fifth century BC marks a significant change. For the first time in Mesopotamia astrology is related to the fortunes of private individuals and is dependent not on observed events but on theoretical calculations. The intellectual and social forces behind this change remain totally obscure to us. The earliest known example of the genre, a horoscope for 29 April 410 BC (dated by calculation based on the astronomical data), has been translated as follows:

> Month Nisan, night of the 14th, . . . son of Shuma-usur, son of Shuma-iddina, descendant of Deke, was born. At that time the moon was below the 'horn' of the Scorpion, Jupiter in Pisces, Venus in Taurus, Saturn in Cancer, Mars in Gemini. Mercury, which had set (for the last time), was invisible. [There follow precise details of the lunar month.] (Things?) will be good for you. (Written in) month Du'uz, year 12.

The deduction drawn from the horoscope is remarkably brief, but the majority of the Babylonian horoscopes contain no predictions at all.

The following text recently published, and almost contemporary with the previous text, illustrates a preliminary stage in the preparation of horoscopes. Having established the child's date of birth the scribe then collects, no doubt by consulting the Diaries, the relevant data for the planets during that year.

> Ṭebētu, the 24th, on the morning (preceding the evening) of the 25th, year 13 of Darius, the child was born [24/25 X 13

Darius (II)=12 Jan 410 BC]. Kislīmu, on the 15th Mercury's first morning visibility . . . ; Ṭebētu, the 9th, solstice; 26 . . . ; Šabāṭu . . . on the 2nd, Mercury's last morning visibility in Capricorn; Šabāṭu, the 14th, Venus's last morning visibility at the beginning of Aquarius; Addaru was intercalary. Tašrītu, the 22nd, Jupiter stationary in Aquarius; in Addaru, the 2nd, [Jupiter's] last visibility in Pisces; Du'ūzu, the 30th, Saturn's first visibility in Cancer, a little high, [hence theoretical] first visibility on the 26th; Kislīmu, the 7th, [Saturn's first] stationary point [this date is in error by nearly a month]; Tebēṭu, the 17th, [Saturn's] acronychal rising; Addaru was intercalary.

If it were not for the statement, 'the child was born', one would hardly have imagined that such a text belonged in the earliest literature of horoscopy. The latest example of the type currently known dates to 142 BC, and with that our knowledge of the practice of Babylonian astrology comes to an end.

Selected Bibliography

Aaboe, A. (1980), 'Observation and theory in Babylonian astronomy', *Centaurus*, vol. 24, pp. 14–35.

Hodson, F. R. (ed.) (1974), 'The place of astronomy in the ancient world', *Philosophical Transactions of the Royal Society of London* A 276, (British Academy and OUP).

Huber, P. J. (1958), 'Ueber den Nullpunkt der babylonischen Ekliptik', *Centaurus*, vol. 5, pp. 192–208.

Neugebauer, O. (1951), *The Exact Sciences in Antiquity*, 2nd edn (1957), (University Press of New England; New York: Harper Torchbooks, 1962).

Oppenheim, A. L. (1959), 'A new prayer to the "gods of the night"' *Analecta Biblica*, vol. 12, pp. 282–301 (Rome).

Oppenheim, A. L. (1969), 'Divination and celestial observation in the last Assyrian empire', *Centaurus*, vol. 14, pp. 97–135.

Parpola, S. (ed.) (1970–83), *Letters from Assyrian Scholars to the Kings Esarhaddon and Assurbanipal*, Parts 1 and 2 (Alte Orient und Altes Testament 5/1 and 5/2), (Kevelaer and Neukirchen-Vluyn). These two volumes contain many of the observations and astrological interpretations of the Assyrian court astronomers.

Reiner, E. with Pingree, D. (1981), *Enûma Anu Enlil, tablets 50–51* (Babylonian planetary omens 2=Bibliotheca Mesopotamica 2/2, Malibu).

Rochberg-Halton, F. (1984), *Journal of Cuneiform Studies*, vol. 36, pp. 127–144. Canonicity in cuneiform texts. (On the tradition of the astronomical omen literature.)

Sachs, A. (1948), *Journal of Cuneiform Studies*, vol. 2, pp. 271–90. A classification of the Babylonian astronomical tablets of the Seleucid period.

Sachs, A. (1952), *Journal of Cuneiform Studies*, vol. 6, pp. 49–75. Babylonian horoscopes.

Thompson, R. Campbell (1900), *The Reports of the Magicians and Astrologers of Nineveh and Babylon in the British Museum*, 2 vols (London).

Van der Waerden, B. L. (1952–3), *Archiv für Orientforschung*, vol. 16, pp. 216–230. History of the zodiac.

Van der Waerden, B. L. (1966), *Die Anfänge der Astronomie: Erwachende Wissenschaft*, vol. 2, (The Netherlands: Groningen). Published in English as *Science Awakening*, vol. 2 *The Birth of Astronomy*, (Leiden and New York, 1974).

Weidner, E. F. (1941–4; 1954–6; 1968–9), 'Die astrologische Serie Enûma Anu Enlil', *Archiv für Orientforschung*, vol. 14, pp. 172–95 and 308–18; vol. 17, pp. 71–89; vol. 22, pp. 65–75.

II

GREEK ASTROLOGY

Thomas Pattie

Commentary

'PROROGATIONS' OR 'INTERROGATIONS'

Horary Astrology

Horary astrology is a form of 'interrogation' used from very early times and still in use. The questioner (or querent) puts his question to the astrologer, who sets up a horoscope for the moment of asking. The horoscope must satisfy certain requirements before it is regarded as radical and therefore fit to be judged.

The matter asked about is the 'quesited' and the planet ruling the appropriate House will be its significator; the ruler of the ascendant will signify the querent, with the moon as co-significator.

The crucial difference between natal and horary is that a horary map is dynamic at the birth moment of the question. This is because the recent and potential movements of the moon, when she applies to, makes, or separates from aspects of planets, may be interpreted so long as she remains in the same sign. If the moon is 'void of course', that is, makes no major aspects before leaving her sign, then the map is not fit to be judged.

The selection of significators appropriate to the subject of the question is very important and depends upon a knowledge of all the planetary rulerships and associations between Houses and the matter in hand. There are also aphorisms to be considered, such as those of Guido Bonatus.

Electional Questions

The category 'prorogations' or 'interrogations' seems to include what we call 'elections'. Both electional and horary questions are questions put to the astrologer, but they may be distinguished by the method used to answer them. Mr Pattie mentions two questions which are clearly electional (on page 19): 'Is it a good time for one who wishes to flee . . . ?'; and 'when is it best to build a building?'. In both of these the astrologer is asked to find the most auspicious moment – of various possible moments – for the client to act. In the material on elections on page 172ff, there is discussion of the techniques; there is also a survey of many applications, particularly in seventeenth-century England; and on page 201 Derek Appleby demonstrates traditional electional methods applied to an historic moment. It will be found that there is a remarkable continuity of electional ideas. This applies both to the subjects of questions and the techniques for finding the most auspicious moment: emphasis on the moon waxing, the well-placed benefics, Venus and Jupiter, and weakly placed Mars and Saturn, which are the malefics.

The medical questions may be related to the medical canons in Nicholas of Lynn's *Kalendarium* (see page 179); and questions about theft – an extremely popular subject down the ages – are dealt with in very similar terms by William Lilly in seventeenth-century England (see page 237).

Astrology and Occupations

Mr Pattie refers to the 267 occupations mentioned by Firmicus Maternus. This early form of vocational advice was usually well regarded by the authorities down the ages. John Aubrey, who wrote interestingly on education in the seventeenth century, regarded this analysis of the natal horoscope in order to find the most suitable occupation for the native as one of the most valuable services astrology could render.

The Astrologer's Behaviour

The quotation from Firmicus on the astrologer's code of conduct is compared with that of William Lilly on page 25.

Note: For an explanation of the techniques of horary astrology according to traditional principles by a practising astrologer, see Derek Appleby, *Horary Astrology*, 1985.

A. L. K.

My interest in astrology is that of a classicist and historian. In the period in which I am interested astrology was central to the intellectual debates of the day – in a word it was respectable. It fitted in with the increasing tendency towards monotheism, for the complex and eternally recurring patterns of the heavenly bodies were self-evidently the work of a creator with a complex plan. As the old city religion decayed the idea that the planets exert an influence on human affairs became acceptable.

The notion that man is a microcosm and that the microcosm

corresponds in certain ways to the universe or macrocosm was a central tenet in the dominant philosophy of the time. The notion is familiar to us – we would say that the laws of physics are valid throughout the universe. Let me quote Firmicus Maternus, who lived in the fourth century AD and wrote a textbook called *Mathesis*:

> God the Creator, copying nature, has made man in the image of the universe, a mixture of four elements – fire, water, air and earth – so that a well-proportioned combination might produce the living being as a divine imitation. With his divine skill he so composed man that the whole force and essence of the elements is collected in that small body. In this way he prepared a lodging for the divine spirit which descends from the heavenly Soul to maintain the mortal body. This spirit, though fragile, is nevertheless a likeness of the spirit of the universe.
>
> Thus man, like a tiny universe, is sustained by the everlasting fiery movements of the five planets and the Sun and Moon.

Ptolemy, too, believed this, for he says in the first book of the *Tetrabiblos*:

> A very few considerations would make it apparent to all that a certain power emanating from the eternal ethereal substance is dispersed through and permeates the whole region about the earth, which throughout is subject to change, since the primary sublunar elements, fire and air, are encompassed and changed by the motions in the ether, and in turn encompass and change all else, earth and water and the plants and animals therein. For the sun, together with the ambient, is always in some way affecting everything on the earth, not only by the changes that accompany the seasons of the year to bring about the generation of animals and productiveness of plants, the flowing of waters and the changes of bodies, but also by its daily revolutions furnishing heat, moisture, dryness and cold in regular order and in correspondence with its positions relating to the zenith. The Moon too, as the heavenly body nearest to the earth, bestows her effluence most abundantly upon mundane things, for most of them, animate or inanimate, are sympathetic to her and change in company with her; the rivers

> increase and diminish their streams with her light, the seas turn their own tides with her rising and setting, and plants and animals in whole or in some part wax and wane with her. Moreover the passages of the fixed stars and the planets through the sky often signify hot windy and snowy conditions of the air, and mundane things are affected accordingly . . .

And so on. This kind of thing was widely believed and said in intellectual circles, and something similar was said by Cicero, Philo the Jew, Cleomedes and Manilius. It was Cicero, whose loyalty to the constitution earned him the reward of being murdered by the thugs of Antony on 7 December 43 BC, who said, 'Anyone who denies reason to the stars must himself be devoid of reason'.

I wondered which of the 267 occupations mentioned in Firmicus Maternus best fitted my own. I am not a dagger maker, dancer or dice player, nor an executioner, exorcist or provider of exotic pleasures and delights. I am not an innkeeper or a javelin thrower, but I might be a student of obscure languages, or a student of languages, skilled in difficult writings. For, we learn, Mercury in the second House in a morning rising makes the native of humble class, of criminal disposition, illiterate and destitute of all means of livelihood. But if Mercury is an evening star and in a nocturnal chart, he will make money lenders or managers of others' money. In a diurnal chart (now we come to me) he makes students of language, skilled in difficult writings, unwilling to compare their own nature with that of other men. For they are fond of all things that have not been handed down by tradition. They are wretched in life and always wear themselves out with various troubles. That seems to indicate that scholars are poor and intellectually arrogant – at least they keep asking awkward questions. But perhaps after all, I should count myself as something else, such as a keeper or manager of public records.

There is another reason, besides the history of ideas, for studying ancient astrology. It opens a door on what people were worried about – money, marriage, children, sickness, death. We are accustomed to thinking that no age was so sex-ridden as our own, but a cursory glance through one of the ancient textbooks shows that the ancients were just as preoccupied with sex as we are. The fifth book of Dorotheus of Sidon's *Astrological Poem* – the original Greek, written in the first century of our era, perhaps contemporary with Nero, was in verse, but it only survives in an Arabic prose translation – discusses 'prorogations', which I take it are answers to specific questions put by worried clients.

The questions include: Is it a good time for one who wishes to flee from the government (that is because he can't pay his taxes) or from his land, or for a slave to run away from his master? When is it best to build a building? (Answer: when the moon is increasing in computation and in light and when it is in the middle of the zone which is the equator, ascending towards the north while Jupiter or Venus is with the moon or aspects the moon from a strong place, but not when Saturn or Mars is with the moon or aspects it from a strong place – then Saturn will cause delay and Mars will cause a fire). Examples of other questions are: When is it best to demolish a building? (Answer: when the moon is leaving its elevation, descending towards its low point); What price will I buy or sell this thing at?; What sort of slave will this be which I am thinking of buying? If you want to hire something or let out for rent some cultivated land or trees or vineyards or houses, the ascendant indicates the condition in which you will hire these things or take them for rent, the seventh sign indicates the owner, and the tenth sign indicates the rent and the price.

There are questions on the buying of animals; and answers involve the quadruped signs, Aries, Taurus and Sagittarius. Other questions concern freeing slaves and asking a ruler for a gift. Writing or teaching a man a science involves Mercury with the moon and unafflicted, not under the sun's rays or retrograde, and the moon unafflicted.

QUESTIONS ABOUT SURGERY AND ILLNESS

A caesarian operation should be performed when the moon is waning and descending from the zone towards the south, while Mars and Venus aspect from quartile or trine the ascendant and the moon. This is best if the ascendant and the moon are in an effeminate sign and the ascendant and the moon are in signs straight in rising.

> If a querist asks about a sick person at a time when the Moon is flowing from the benefics, then it indicates [his] recovery from his illness. But if he asks when the Moon is flowing from Mars, then it indicates that his illness is from a fever which will exhaust him, or that one of [his] limbs will be cut from his body with an iron [knife], or that in cutting or

phlebotomy he will be bled from his veins with a knife. If the Moon is increasing in light, then it will be more hideous and worse for this illness.

But if the Moon is flowing from Saturn, then it indicates a fever that shakes him and a hidden malaise in his diet . . . or his spleen will swell and sometimes it will bring down a miserable disease on him, and a wound and difficult sore will reach him so that his limbs will be wounded or will be dislocated, and sometimes his black bile will be stirred up in him until his intestines are cramped and burn, and it is an indicator that every illness which reaches him will stay in him a long time.

Note: It is interesting to compare this passage with Nicholas of Lynn's medical canons in his *Kalendarium* and with Chaucer's description of the death of Arcite in 'The Knight's Tale'. A. L. K.

QUESTIONS ABOUT THEFT

Will the stolen article be recovered? What is its nature and what does the thief look like? The thief's indicator is the star or stars in the sign opposite the ascendant. Failing that there are some alternatives: if the thief's indicator is Jupiter he will be pale, fat, with big eyes, and the whites will be disproportionately small. His beard will be small and curly, and he will be good-natured.

If his significator is Saturn he will be repulsive, black, downward looking, his eyes shifty and small. He is pale, hairy limbed and his eyebrows meet. He is a liar, sickly, secretive and tricky. He is profound, contemplative and full of ideas.

If his indicator is Mars, then he will be red in colour, with reddish, lanky hair, sharp eyed, fat cheeked, gay, joking, capricious and spiteful.

A thief indicated by Venus will be fat, handsome, with plentiful hair, white in his extremity but mixed white and red; he has pleasant manners and is amenable to commands.

If the indicator is Mercury, the thief is slim, emaciated, powerful, bald, with good bones, pale and devious.

Lastly, to a question on when a will should be made the answer is when the ascendant or moon is in a tropical sign as it indicates that the will anc' the legacy will be changed.

Note: This device is mentioned by William Ramesey in his *Astrologia Restaurata* (1653; see page 194). A. L. K.

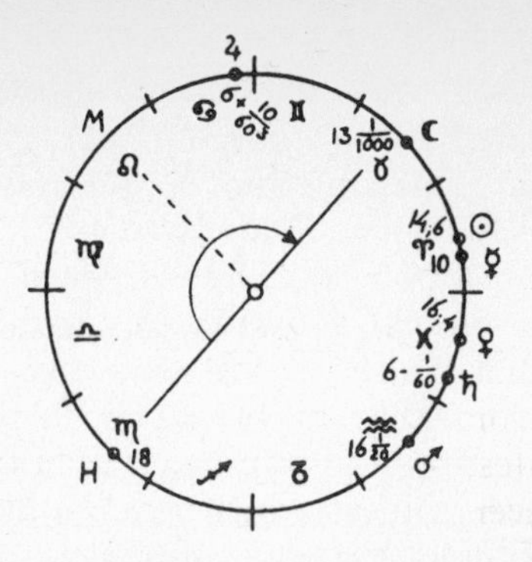

Figure 1 · Horoscope for Papyrus 130
H = ascendant; M = mid-heaven

TWO PAPYRI IN THE BRITISH LIBRARY

Two papyri in the British Library are much fuller than the usual chart, Papyrus 98, cast probably for 13 April AD 95, and Papyrus 130, cast for 1 April AD 81. Since this second one refers to the 'divine Titus', it must have been erected after the emperor Titus' death and deification in September of 81.

To take the earlier of the two first, it begins with a prefatory letter and introduction. If this was common, it is the only one that has survived. Titus Pitenius says in the prefatory letter to Hermon:

> The ancient Egyptians, who studied the heavenly bodies and perceived that the motion of the seven gods [i.e. sun, moon and planets] includes and directs all things, have generously left us their knowledge by means of perpetual tables; from them I have accurately calculated each god and have arranged them by degree and fraction, by aspect and phase, etc. In this way the method of astrological prediction is made correct and unambiguous, i.e. consistent. Farewell, dear Hermon.

The horoscope itself begins with the date: 'Time of the [equinoctial] tropic of the third year of the divine Titus, 6th of the month Pharmouthi (=1 April), at the third hour of the night; on the Kalends of April, Roman style; ancient Egyptian style, first to second day of the month of Pachon.' The ancient Egyptian style ignored leap years. Each year therefore contained 365 days.

The positions are then given for the sun, moon, Saturn, Jupiter, Mars, Mercury, then the Horoscopos (the rising point of the ecliptic) and one or two other points of astrological importance. The longitude of Jupiter is given as 'Cancer six degrees and ten sixtieths of the third order, or one twenty one thousand six hundredth part of a degree', that is, calculated from the perpetual tables to the third sexagesimal place, 96 degrees, 0 minutes, 0 seconds, 10 thirds. The moon's position is given thus:

> The divine and light-giving moon, waxing in crescent, was running in Taurus 13 degrees and a thousandth part of a degree; in the sign of Venus; in its own exaltation; in the terms of Mercury; in a female and solid sign; like gold; mounting the Back of Taurus; in the second Decan called Aroth; its dodekatemorion was shining about the same place in Scorpio.

The tables would express 'a thousandth part of a degree' as $0° 0' 3'' 36'''$. The decans, with their Egyptian names, each covered 10 degrees or one-third of a sign; Aroth extended from Taurus 10 degrees to Taurus 20 degrees. The 'dodekatemorion' of a planet was a point twelve times as distant from the planet as the planet was from the

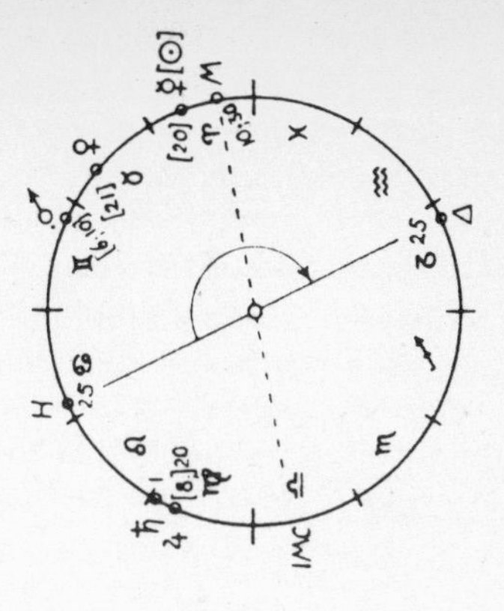

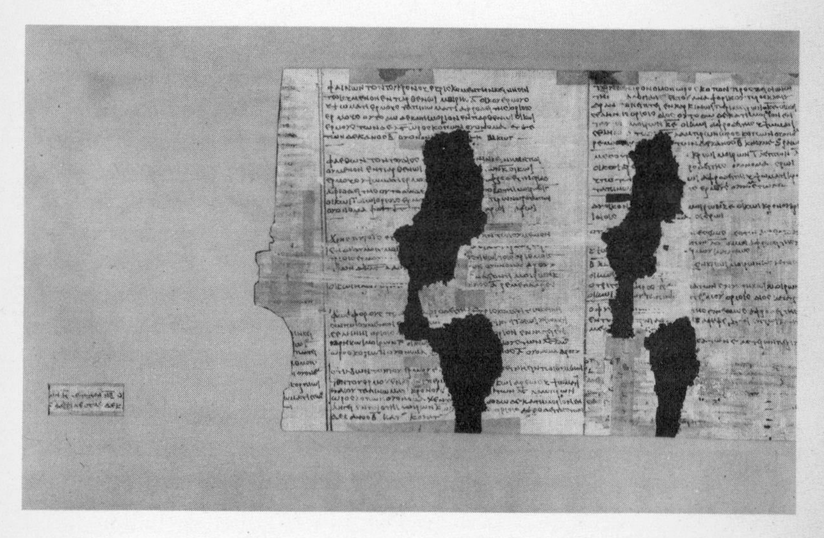

Figure 2 Horoscope for Papyrus 98
H = ascendant; M = mid-heaven

beginning of the sign it was in. The moon was in Taurus 13 degrees; its dodekatemorion should have been 156 degrees further advanced in the zodiac, that is Libra 19 degrees, apparently a whole sign wrong. The 'terms' are groups of degrees in the signs which are sub-ruled by planets. Thus in the sign Taurus 1 degree – 8 degrees are the terms of Venus, 9 degrees – 14 degrees those of Mercury, 15 degrees – 22 degrees those of Jupiter, 23 degrees – 27 degrees those of Saturn and 28 degrees – 30 degrees those of Mars. It is unusual to associate the moon with gold; usually it is associated with silver.

Another papyrus, Papyrus 98, is famous as the 'Old Coptic' horoscope. It has on its verso the Funeral Oration of Hyperides. The papyrus itself was purchased in Egypt in the winter of 1853/4 and formerly belonged to the collection of the Reverend Henry Stobart. On the recto of the papyrus is an elaborate Greek horoscope cast for 13 April AD 95 – at least the date fits the astronomical data best. The introduction which must have included the date is lost, and the surviving part of the papyrus begins with the positions and astrological characterizations of the planets. The horoscope proper is followed by a discussion of the periods of life, first in Greek, then in Coptic with Greek paragraph headings. Coptic, it should be explained, was the last phase of the Egyptian language, written in Greek characters with some Egyptian signs. It is an unusually detailed horoscope, followed by long excursuses in Greek and Coptic on astrological doctrine. There are so many differences from the orthodox doctrine that we may have to assume that the astrological doctrine of this date was different from the doctrine expounded by Ptolemy and other later experts. The treatise is badly damaged and the Coptic is very obscure but we give an extract:

> Third period: Jupiter decides from year 25, month 2, day 25 until year 34, month 5, day 24 [this is in Greek; the rest is in very obscure Coptic]. If Jupiter was a hostile star on the day of the native's birth, he may neglect his wife; or else he may quarrel with her; or else his children may . . . ; or it may be that he will lose some merchandise. If there was an evil star (on the day of his birth), . . . shall suffer; he shall get no children. Time and again, evil shall follow after him.

In the next period Mars is the ruler and part of the prediction is:

> If an evil star was in the Anaphora and in a malefic aspect, a woman shall cause him shame; or else he shall be a fugitive from the age of forty-two. He shall take a wife and remain married until the age of ninety-four. He shall witness his wife's death; or else he shall be separated from her . . . '

THE ASTROLOGER'S BEHAVIOUR

I should like to finish with the high standards of behaviour that Firmicus demands of an astrologer:

> Shape yourself in the image and likeness of divinity, so that you may always be a model of excellence. He who daily speaks about the gods or with the gods must shape his mind to approach the likeness of divinity. Be modest, upright, sober, eat little, be content with few goods, so that the shameful love of money may not defile the glory of this divine science. Outdo the training and principles of worthy priests. For the acolyte of the Sun and Moon and the other gods, through whom all earthly things are governed, must educate his mind to be proved worthy in the sight of all mankind. See that you give your responses publicly in a clear voice, so that nothing illegal may be asked of you. Do not give a response about the condition of the Republic or the life of the Emperor – that is illegal. Have a wife, a home, friends; be constantly available to the public; keep out of quarrels; do not undertake any harmful business; do not be tempted by the offer of more money; keep away from all passion of cruelty; never take pleasure in others' quarrels or capital sentences or fatal enmities. Avoid plots and riots and behave peacefully and moderately with everyone. Be generous, honest and truthful. Never ask interest on money. Never be present at nocturnal sacrifices, public or private. Be reticent about people's vices. Keep away from the enticements of the shows, for the priest of the gods must be above base pleasures. Do not give away the secrets of this religion to wicked men, for the astrologer must be pure and chaste.

Note on 'The Astrologer's Behaviour'

It is interesting to see how very close William Lilly, writing in 1647, kept to the advice of Firmicus to the astrologer. The following comes from Lilly's address 'To the Student in Astrology'.

> As thou daily conversest with the heavens, so instruct and form thy mind according to the image of divinity; learn all the ornaments of vertue, be sufficiently instructed therein; be humane, curteous, familiar to all . . . Covet not an estate,

give freely to the poor . . . let no worldly wealth procure an erroneous judgment from thee, or such as may dishonour the Art, or this divine Science . . . Be sparing in delivering Judgment against the Commonwealth thou livest in. Give not judgment of the death of thy Prince . . . Marry a wife of thy own, rejoice in the number of thy friends . . .

Christian Astrology, 3rd edn, facsimile (Regulus, 1985).

A. L. K.

Bibliography

Bram, Jean Rhys (trans.) (1975), *Ancient Astrology Theory and Practice: The Mathesis of Firmicus Maternus*.

Neugebauer, O. and van Hoesen, H. B. (1959), *Greek Horoscopes* (Memoirs of the American Philosophical Society), (Philadelphia).

Pattie, T. S. (1980), *Astrology*, (London: The British Library).

Pingree, D. (ed.) (1976), *Dorothei Sidonii Carmen Astrologicum* (Leipzig: Teubner).

Robbins, F. E. (ed. and trans.) (1944), *Ptolemy, Tetrabiblos (with Manetho)* (London: Heinemann, and Cambridge, Mass., US).

III

CELESTIAL AND TERRESTRIAL ORIENTATION

The Origins of House Division in Ancient Cosmology

Prudence Jones

Commentary

Prudence Jones, who read philosophy at Girton College, Cambridge, has researched into the foundations of logic and mathematics. This led to a continuing interest in the mystery cults which co-existed with the growth of rational thought in ancient times, and she has written and lectured extensively on ancient cosmology and astrology.

Following upon Christopher Walker's discussion of the zodiac in Mesopotamia, Prudence Jones deals with another fundamental astrological concept, the Houses. She investigates the derivation of House systems from ancient times, questioning the origins of Manilius' system. As she says, she returns to 'the roots of astrology in applied astronomy', and to what lay behind the first setting up of a House system.

The 'normal' cosmology of the ancient world, based on the divisions of the plane of the horizon rather than that of the prime vertical, is considered in various cultures, with special reference to northern latitudes, and to time telling.

The writer argues that what she calls 'normal' cosmology was still current in Roman culture about thirty years after Manilius was writing, and so probably influenced him. (It is generally accepted that Manilius was somewhat inaccurate and sometimes misunderstood his (unknown) sources.)

A. L. K.

The mundane Houses and the methods of their construction are one of the most under-investigated areas in astrology today. There is no clear agreement as to what they represent, astronomically; naively one would assume, in Cyril Fagan's words (1973, p. 161), that they form 'the invisible envelope, or aura, that is supposed to surround the earth and which revolves *pari passu* with the rotation of the earth on its own axis', that is a set of fixed spatial co-ordinates. However, if the Houses are to be computed from the rising degree of the zodiac, as most systems are, they are in no way fixed, but change continuously relative to the horizon and the meridian. Furthermore, the earliest descriptions of the rational zodiac, based on the solstices and equinoxes, go back to the fifth century BC, but the earliest description of a House system is that of Manilius, written around the year 10 of the Christian era.

It is easy then to assume that the Houses were derived from the signs in a straightforward way, with each House having a similar significance to its 'related' sign, and the same planetary ruler.[1] But in medieval and Renaissance astrology this was not so, nor is it so in Manilius' text. Furthermore, one of the earliest astrological predictions we have, dating from c. 2400 BC, identifies the moon according to the local circle of the observer, at what we should call the mid-heaven: 'you shall look to the South and observe the eclipse. To the King of Universal Dominion an omen is given: desolation of Ur, and destruction of its walls' (Holden, 1977, p. 44). The fixed circle of the observer, with its four cardinal directions, existed independently of the zodiac, and was referred to from earliest times.

Here I return to the roots of astrology in applied astronomy. I describe a conceptual and practical scheme governing local – and celestial – space, which was widespread, if not universal, in ancient times. This scheme, or world view, was part and parcel of the early astrologers' lives, and must be taken into account when considering what it was that prompted them to set up the circle of the Houses in the first place.

ASCENDANT VARIABILITY

It is important to understand the fallacy behind the idea of a fixed framework of Houses based on the ascendant. Anyone living in the northern hemisphere who looks at the night sky when facing south, towards the position of the mid-heaven, will see the constellations rising somewhere in the eastern quarter to their left (the distinction between tropical and sidereal zodiacs here is irrelevant), culminating high in the southern sky in front of them, and descending somewhere in the west to their right, at a point 180 degrees opposite the ascending point. The arc of the zodiac cannot be seen below and behind us, passing through the *imum coelum*, but it is shown on the horoscope wheel as the lower semi-circle. Hence, the horoscope is a diagram of local space, showing the plane of the ecliptic as it intersects with the meridian and horizon of a given location.

These points of intersection, however, are not constant through time. The ecliptic always intersects the meridian due south and due north, at the mid-heaven and *imum coelum* (vice versa in the southern hemisphere), but only with the first degrees of Aries and Libra does it cut the horizon due east. For the rest of the time, the ascendant and descendant wander back and forth across the eastern and western quarters of the visible horizon, with 0 degrees Cancer (the summer solstice point) rising and setting furthest north, 0 degrees Capricorn (the winter solstice point) furthest south for that latitude. Although astrologers know these facts in theory, the impact of these patterns is often lost on us. We do not notice the daily shift of the rising constellations along the horizon, but only, if at all, the movement of sunrise and sunset along the local skyline throughout the year, a pattern recorded also by the megalithic circle builders, who marked the azimuths of summer and winter solstice sunrise as seen from the centre of their circles, and thus mapped out the limits of the circle of Houses for their locality, defining not only the range of sunrise and sunset for each year, but implicitly that of the ecliptic generally for each day.

Displayed on the horoscope form in two dimensions, without perspective, the variable angle between the ecliptic and the equator results in the uneven size of the four quadrants in most horoscopes.

At the latitudes of Alexandria (31 degrees north), Baghdad (33 degrees north), and even Athens (40 degrees north), this variability is minimal. It is these latitudes which are the homeland of astrology. Towards the equator, there are problems as the summer signs culminate in the northern sky, the winter signs in the southern sky, a variation generally ignored in drawing up charts. But towards the poles, the problem will not go away, since in the Arctic circle the first degree of Cancer rises and sets due north, at the IC, and the first degree of Capricorn due south, at the MC, thus producing horoscopes which are not quartered but halved. In addition, the zodiac can rise very rapidly: one minute's difference of time at Reykjavik (64 degrees north), for example, produces 10 degrees difference in an Aries or Libra ascendant. No House system, including Equal House, based on the ascendant as fixed point is anything more than ephemeral at these latitudes.

In one sense, we realise this and pride ourselves on it; astrology

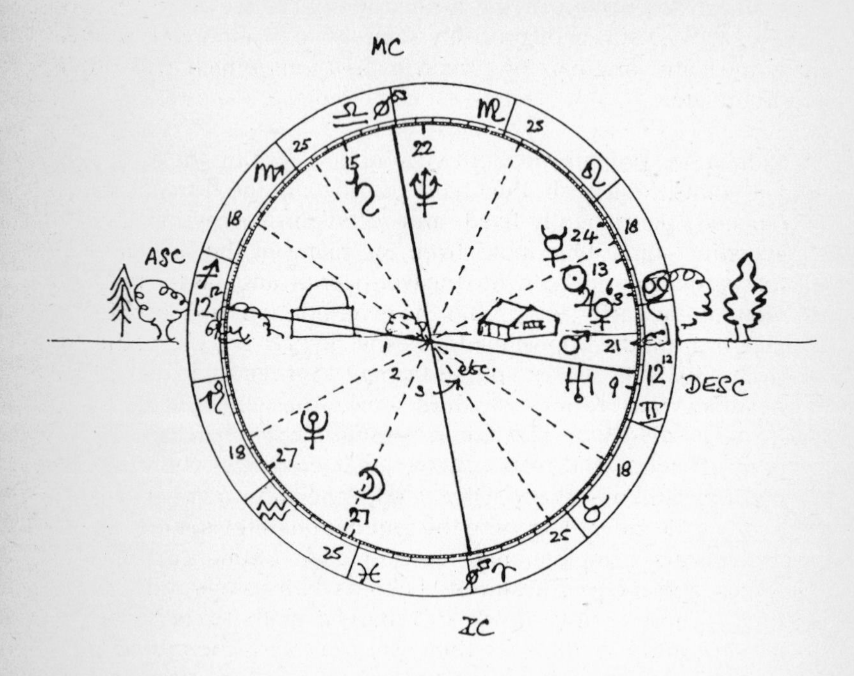

Figure 3 *Uneven size of quadrants in horoscope diagram represent three-dimensional coordinates of local space.*

captures the fleeting intersection of heaven (the ecliptic) and earth (the horizon, meridian etc.) at a given instant of time. It is an arcane and subtle science, far removed from the crude meteorology of farmers and fishermen. But to understand the mundane sphere as any sort of constant framework, we need a more abstract concept than the observation of one instant of time. The mundane circle based on the ascendant is the set of all possible intersections of horizon, meridian and ecliptic at a given latitude and longitude. It is a range of points, with the ecliptic moving continuously like a snake within it. Time-based systems of domification embrace this definition wholeheartedly, whereas the most puritanical approach of M-House and Morinus is to abandon the ascendant as a reference point altogether, thus avoiding the problems of its variability. But still the desire for 'an envelope which revolves with the earth' persists.

WORLD VIEW OF MANILIUS

The earliest description of the mundane sphere we have, that of Manilius (c. AD 10), is of precisely such a fixed framework. I have given the Latin originals of certain expressions which will prove important later.

> Come now, prepare an attentive mind for learning the cardinal points: four in all, they have positions in the firmament (*mundus*) permanently fixed, and receive in succession the speeding signs. One looks from the rising of the heavens (*caelum*) as they are born into the world (*orbis*) and has the first view of the Earth (*terra*) from the level horizon; the second faces it from the opposite edge of the sky (*aether*), the point from which the starry sphere (*mundus*) retires and hurtles headlong into Tartarus; a third marks the zenith of high heaven (*excelsum caelum*), where wearied Phoebus halts with panting steeds and rests the day and determines the midpoint of shadows; the fourth occupies the nadir (*imus orbis*), and has the glory of forming the foundation of the sphere; in it the stars complete their descent and commence their return, and at equal distances it beholds their risings and settings. These points (*loca*) are charged with exceptional powers, and the influence they exert on fate is the greatest known to our science, because the celestial circle (*orbis*) is totally held in position by them as by eternal supports; did they not receive the circle, sign after sign in succession, flying in its perpetual revolution, and clamp it with fetters at the two sides and the lowest and highest extremities of its compass (*imum summumque cacumen templi*), heaven (*mundus*) would fly apart and its fabric disintegrate and perish.[2]

Initially, it is unclear whether Manilius is describing the ecliptic or the prime vertical. From the astrologer's point of view, 'zenith' and 'nadir' are misleading translations: 'MC' and 'IC' would be more accurate. These, with the ascending and descending points also mentioned, are the four intersections of the zodiac (*orbis caeli*, lines 4–5) with the horizon and the meridian, the local great circles which move with the observer, described in I, 631–65. Astrologers also usually translate Manilius' *cardines* as 'angles', saving the term 'cardinal points' for 0 degrees of the cardinal signs and for the four fixed orientations of the horizon. (But see below, p. 38, for the way in which the angles do become true cardinal points once a day – this ambiguity may be deliberate on Manilius' part.)

The angles are *not* fixed relative to the firmament: Manilius himself describes the obliquity of the ecliptic (I, 257, 673) and the consequent variability in the zodiac's speed and angle of rising (III, 301 ff.). But although III, 340–6, seem to describe the variable azimuth of the zodiac's rising and setting (see above pp. 28–30) when Manilius states (lines 13–15 above) that the meridian bisects the arc from ascendant to descendant, he has confused the arc of the zodiac at any one instant with the diurnal path of the sun – which *is* bisected by the meridian, though not usually so as to form a foursquare 'temple'. Over one hundred years later, Ptolemy likewise defined the MC as being at right angles to the ascendant. We cannot fairly say that either of these authors is proposing an Equal House system, because both fail to distinguish between the MC and what we should call the cusp of the tenth House.

Note also that Manilius is concerned with the whole 'temple' (line 23) of the zodiac's path through local space, rather than with the ascendant in particular. We usually assume that the construction of the mundane Houses began because of interest in the rising sign, but Manilius shows no special regard for this; on the contrary he asserts, without emphasis, as does Ptolemy after him, that it is (not the ascendant but) the mid-heaven which has the greatest influence on the horoscope.

In fact it appears that Manilius, oblivious of or deliberately obscuring the difference between the sun's diurnal path, the arc of the ecliptic at any one time, and the prime vertical, the great circle bisecting both horizon and meridian, specifically intends to describe this third circle which moves with the observer, and thus to construct an idealised, foursquare 'temple' in local space, defined by the meridian, prime vertical, and horizon: the same mundane sphere which Campanus was to delineate 1,200 years later. Each quadrant of the sphere, traced out obliquely by the sun's path, is described as ruling a different stage of life, as the sun has four phases in its diurnal progress. These stages run in the opposite direction to our modern numbering of the Houses.

Next, Manilius goes on to describe the twelve 'divisions of the firmament' (*partes mundi*), which we call the Houses, and he makes it quite clear that they are fixed divisions of space:

> Each of the signs, as it revolves, receives the influences of heaven (*caelum*) and to heaven imparts its own. The nature of

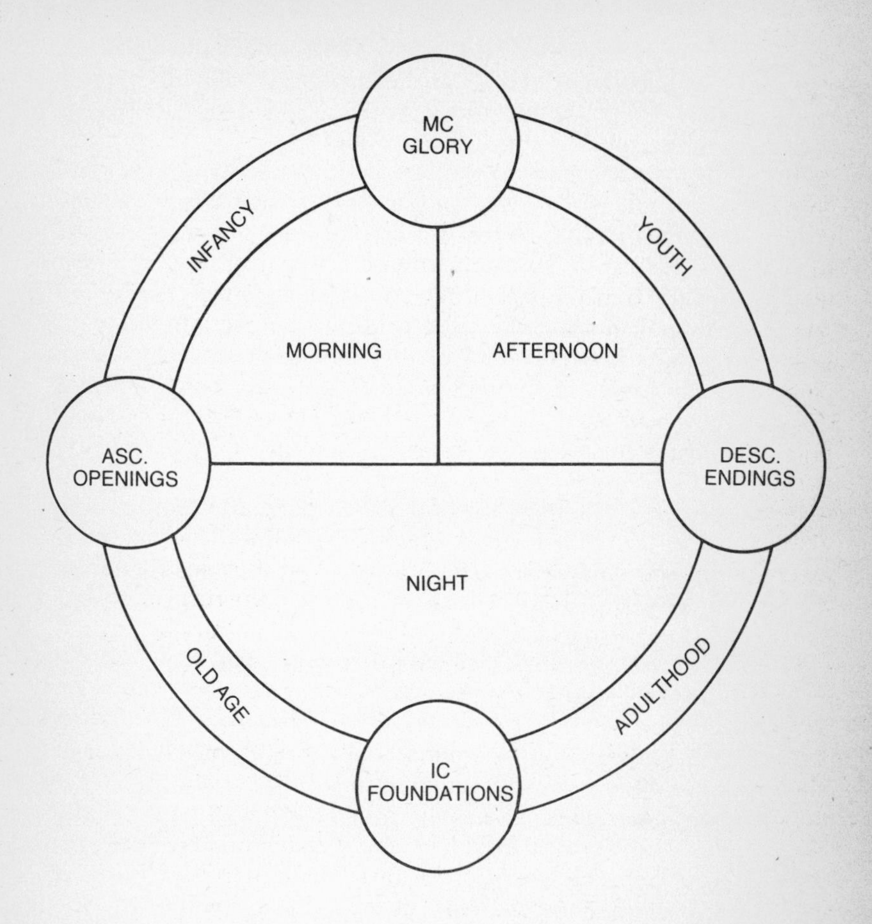

Figure 4 The mundane circle (microcosmic). After Manilius (AD 109).

> the position (*locus*) prevails, exercises jurisdiction within its province (*propriae fines*), and subjects to its own character the signs as they pass by, which now are enriched with distinction of every kind and now bear the penalty of a barren abode (*sedes*).[3]

He does not number the Houses (which are twelve), but his interpretation of the significance of each one derives from the clockwise (sunwise) motion of the ecliptic around this fixed circle. For example, what we would call the twelfth House is one that is doomed to climb; the fifth House aspires to become the foundation of the sphere (that is, fourth House), the tenth House can make no more movement except for ill, being the summit of heaven, etc. We are following the sun's extraverted encounter with the world, from dawn to noon to dusk and back again; whereas the modern anticlockwise numbering of the Houses, fully established by the time of Firmicus Maternus, 400 years later, lists the order of the signs as they rise, for example, the third House is the area of space now occupied by the third sign, archetypally Gemini, that will rise after the event in question.

Manilius also assigns ruling deities to his 'parts of the firmament'. Some of these are also planets, but others, for example Typhon, are not, nor does every House have a ruler. Suitably supplemented, however, this list of rulerships is the basis of that used in Renaissance astrology, before the modern equation of the Houses with the signs and their rulers. These earlier rulerships appear to stem from cosmology, the ordering and interpretation of the parts of the universe, rather than from the study of the zodiac proper. Not only is Manilius' system of Houses a gigantic clock face, a measuring device for time, but it is also a cosmological diagram. Whereas the gnomon of a sundial throws its shadow onto the plane of the horizon, whose divisions measure the time, Manilius asks us to watch the sun in its diurnal arc, measuring the time directly. But each of his twelve divisions of time, based on the four quarters of the sky, has its own nature, and usually its own presiding deity, as does each quarter of the earth in a normal cosmological diagram.[4]

ORIENTATION: THE FOUR CORNERS OF THE EARTH

The 'normal' cosmology of the ancient world, based on divisions of the plane of the horizon rather than that of the prime vertical, is shown symbolically in, for example, the Hindus' mythical island of Jambu-dvipa, whose four temples on the outside mark the cardinal directions, with Mount Meru, the 'pillar of heaven', in the centre.[5] It is symbolised likewise by the 'teaching wand' of the Ojibway Indians, consisting of two crossed wands representing the cardinal directions, pierced by a vertical wand showing the sky and the underworld. Each of these six directions is presided over by the spirits of the ancestors; their crossing point is the heart of the worshipper (Newbery, 1979, pp. 171–7). For the ancient Chinese, the 28 mansions of the Moon were assigned to the four cardinal direc-

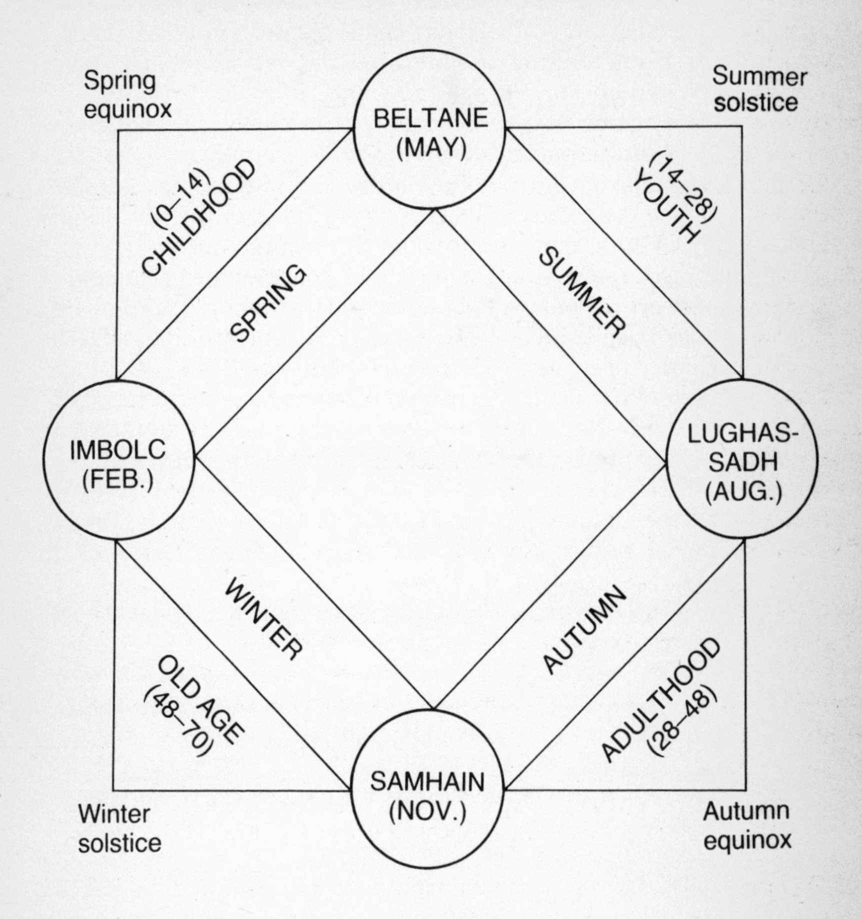

Figure 5 The plane of the mundus *(macrocosmic). After Byrhtferth (AD 1011).*

tions, each of which had a totem animal and was ruled by a planet, with Saturn ruling the centre point (Eitel, 1979, pp. 14–15). The ancient Irish had the four kingdoms of Leinster, Ulster, Connaught and Munster, with the central fortress of Tara in Meath ruling them all.

There is a certain ambiguity in horizon-based cosmologies, an unclarity about whether the centre of the local landscape merely represents the centre of the earth or actually is it. There is no such unclarity, however, when the viewpoint of the local observer is related to the plane of the cliptic. A diagram based on the work of the monk Byrhtferth, dated 1011 (Dames, 1979, p. 15), shows the yearly version of Manilius' diurnal circuit, the solar cycle running through the cardinal points of the solstices and equinoxes, forming with them the eightfold year of the agricultural festivals.

This solar–sidereal plane of the ecliptic, unchanging during any one lifetime, but slowly dissolving and re-forming in folk memory as the equinoxes precess and the cardinal points move backwards against the constellations, is the 'flat earth' mocked at by the heirs of Galileo and, uncomprehendingly, by Manilius himself. But it is not the *terra* or *tellus* (I, 228) which is flat; rather it is the four corners of the plane of the ecliptic, the *mundus* or firmament to which Manilius refers consistently throughout his poem as the celestial mechanism or framework. In Book I, the poet actually describes the pole of the heavens, with its great circles of the equinoxes and solstices, called *colures*, which cut the plane of the ecliptic and equator. This is a gigantic armillary sphere, the whole fabric of the firmament (*machina mundi*, cf. II, 807), which has been the basis of cosmology in all ages.[6]

The *mundus* is the 'world', both heaven and earth, defined in space and in time by the earth's relationship to the sun and to the galaxy. It 'ends' periodically, when the solstice and equinox constellations, and their associated North Star, have shifted enough to throw the calendar out of joint and to confuse people's celestial orientation, which is not only a means of navigation, but which once underlay the positioning of buildings and, as we shall see, even the conduct of day-to-day affairs. A physical reorientation as well as a psychological one had to take place as the universe changed and each new age began, or else the 'world' would indeed fly apart and its fabric disintegrate and perish.

The three levels of the 'world' – that above the tropic of Cancer, that between Cancer and Capricorn, and that below Capricorn – to astrologers are reminiscent of the three ways of Enlil, Anu and Ea used by the Babylonians, c. 1300–700 BC, to locate celestial activity.[7] They will be less familiar as Gwynvyd, the Celtic upperworld, Abred, the human plane, with its four *caerau* which guard the sacred treasures, and Annwn, the underworld. Likewise they are the Norsemen's Asgard, the home of the gods, 'which we call Troy' (Sturluson, 1966, p. 37), that is, the turning-point of the heavens,[8] Midgard, with its four dwarfs, the gatekeepers of the four corners, and Niflheim, 'abode of mists', the underworld. The north American

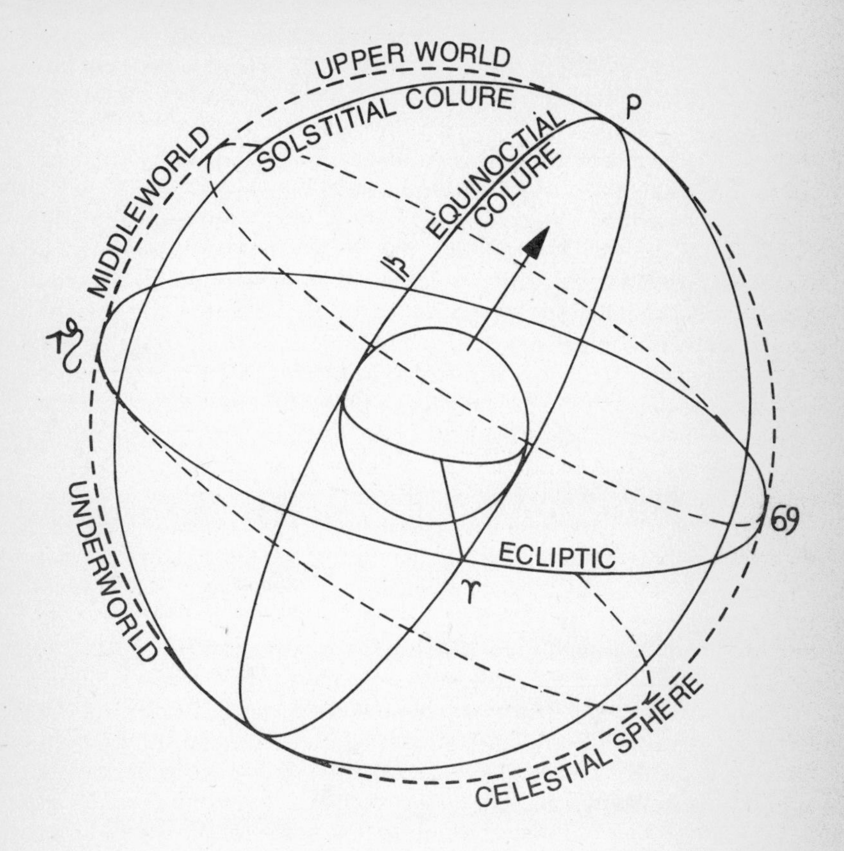

Figure 6 The mundus *– the celestial mundane sphere, divided into three along the polar axis by the two tropics, and quartered across the plane of the ecliptic by the solstice and equinox points. The plane of the ecliptic, thus quartered and hence visibly defined, is the* planus mundus, *the 'flat earth' referred to by the ancients.*

Ojibway medicine wheel too elaborated the middle plane symbolised by the crossed sticks of the teaching wand, as a circle having four quarters, each with animal, colour, seasonal and life-phase attributions, with the voice of the drum in the centre, linking the heartbeat of earth with the thunder of the sky.

The axis of this three-tiered world was Mount Meru to the Hindus, Irminsul, the 'pillar of heaven', to the Saxons, and Yggdrasil, the world tree, to the Norsemen. Anglo-Saxons called it the World Nail, and around it they saw circling the two Waggons or, in Ptolemy's words, 'they have the Bears above them' (II, 2, 56). The sevenfold ziggurats of Ur showed the world pillar, here defined as the axis of the ecliptic rather than that of the earth's rotation, emerging from the seven planetary cycles.

From any point on earth, when looking out at night to the great plane of the ecliptic, an observer is always at the centre of the cardinal paths leading to Aries, Cancer, Libra and Capricorn. Furthermore, once a day, when the cusp of Aries rises, these celestial cardinal points line up with the cardinal directions, the compass points of that locality; the four corners of the horizon, conversely, lead to the four ends of the (flat) earth. Hence any earthly location whatever is at the centre of the world, of the firmament or *mundus*.

THE LINKAGE OF TIME AND SPACE

In Mediterranean lands, where half of the sun's path is invisible below the earth, observation of the sun's diurnal path or, in practice, of the shadow cast by a sundial, had to be supplemented at night by observation of the rising of the constellations, as Cyril Fagan tirelessly pointed out throughout his work. Time telling in northern latitudes, however, was easier, as the plane of the ecliptic comes closer to that of the horizon, and so both the sun and the constellations of the upper heavens could be located, in their season, by their position above the four quarters of the earth. Our detailed knowledge of this system of time telling makes the interpretation of Manilius' system of Houses as a cosmological diagram seem less gratuitous than it might otherwise appear.[9]

The earthly horizon was divided according to the four cardinal directions and their intermediate points, the centres of the eight *ættir*, as they were called in Old Norse, or 'airts', in Lowland Scots.[10] Because of the variable azimuth of sunrise in these latitudes, east and west were not observed directly, but derived from the primary north–south axis, and do not have strong mythological connotations. These eight major orientations were marked on the horizon by prominent landmarks or, where these were lacking, by an artificial pillar or cairn, and the time was told by the sun's passage in summer over these arcs, in winter by the passage of certain stars and constellations over the same areas.

The north was the sacred orientation. Celestial north was the seat of the gods, Asgard, and many churches in Britain and Scandinavia have their north doors walled up as a means of preventing their erstwhile pagan congregations from gathering there to salute the old gods. North on the horizon was the road to the underworld, the abode of the dead. In secular life, law courts were oriented north to south, with the judge in the north and the plaintiff in the south, and so were moot hills like Tynwald on the Isle of Man (later re-oriented to the east, presumably with the introduction of Christianity). East was generally an ill-favoured region, being the home of the wolf Fenrir, who was to slay the gods at Ragnarok, but 'sun in east', a relatively constant timing in northern latitudes during the summer months, was a time marker in frequent use. At the time of the sagas, west was also a direction of ill omen, where the mistletoe grew that slew Baldur, but earlier tradition makes west the home of the Vanir, the fertility gods who preceded the Æsir of the sagas. This is reminiscent of Celtic legend, where west is the land of faerie, home of Gwynn ap Nydd, king of plenty and of the Wild Hunt.

Quarter guardians, inhabitants of the corner 'temples', persist even to our day. The children's rhyme, 'Matthew, Mark, Luke and John', is an invocation of such, suitably disguised in esoteric Christian symbolism via the astrology of the fixed signs, which appear also in the description of the 'land wights' of Iceland, the dragon, the giant, the ox and the huge bird, equally recognisable as Leo, Aquarius, Taurus and Scorpio, or as the four faces of the Jewish cherubs, part of the *lingua franca* of medieval iconography, but possibly based on native originals.

For accurate chronometry, a fixed observation point was needed, which was the centre of the settlement, marked by a pillar, a pole, or what we now know as a buttercross. The central point was a place of sanctuary, not totally superseded even in Christian times by the church altar, for, even when marked by a temporary pole with a gauntlet on top at the middle of a fairground, it was still held to represent the 'King's peace' (cf. Drake–Carnell, 1938, p. 63, and Reuter, 1934, p. 41). More practically, each outlying farmstead had a 'hearthstone', so-called, *outside* the house, which was used for observation of the tides of day.

Our colloquial four tides, morning, noon, evening and night, are a remnant of the eight *stunds* or watches, called *eyktir* in Old Norse and defined by the sun's travel through the airts. We read in the *Lawbook of Iceland* (c. 1117–18) that the night *stund* was to be defined, during the summer months, as the time of the sun's passage through the northern airt (Dennis *et al.*, 1980, K 18, p. 50). In northern Iceland at midsummer, the sun would be visible for the whole of this *stund*, and even further south its light would still be seen as a glow on the northern horizon. The Old English names of the eight *stunds* can be translated thus: sun from NNW to NNE is midnight; NNE to ENE, cockcrow; ENE to ESE, morning; ESE to SSE, daytime or forenoon; SSE to SSW, noon or midday; SSW to WSW, afternoon; WSW to WNW, evening; and WNW to NNW, night-time (Haigh, 1896, pp. 169 ff.). The length of the *stunds* originally varied according to the season and the latitude, although by the nineteenth century, in places such as Norway and the Faroes which kept to the old reckoning, the solar orientations were used to refer to precise three-hour periods, for example, ENE, *halvga eystur* in Faroese, simply meant 0430 hours. Several sundials divided into eight or sixteen remain in eastern England from Saxon times. Eightfold time telling remains to this day in the eight shipboard watches.

Astrologers at one time assumed that Manilius described not twelve but eight Houses, following three verses apparently interpolated at the end of Book II, but not borne out by the twelve *partes mundi* described by the poet beforehand. Four hundred years later, Firmicus Maternus likewise reported the existence of a system of eight Houses, that is the first eight of the modern, anticlockwise-numbered, system, but he does not integrate them into the latter. It is possible that an eightfold division of solar time did exist in ancient Rome, since it existed elsewhere in the Far East, and not only around the North Sea in later times. Roman soldiers divided the hours of darkness into four *vigilia*, or watches. Parts of Hindustan, Bengal and Burma used an eightfold system, although generally the Vedic tenfold system prevailed; and the famous wind tower at Athens, c. 100 BC, had eight sides. The Chaldeans, as we know, generally trisected their four quadrants, producing the twelvefold division of astrology and of circular measure generally. Haigh (1896, p. 166), however, reports an eighth-century BC proclamation by King Sargon: 'Before and behind, in all the sides opposite to the eight winds, I opened eight great gates.' It could be then that both Firmicus and the interpolator of Manilius are recalling an earlier system of reckoning which had not totally died out although the twelvefold system was current.

To return to the north of Europe, however, there the quarters of earth and the quarters of heaven were actively related as one vast chronometer. Now the Romans, as far as we know, like the Chaldeans, measured their twenty-four hours by sundials and by water clocks. No record has come down to us of their dividing the heavens into regions, each with its own nature, as the Norsemen did, but we do know that they divided the plane of the horizon in precisely such a way. They took this eightfold system from the Etruscans, their predecessors in Tuscany, experts in augury and divination.[11] The Etruscans would mark the centre of any new settlement with an offering pit, which later became an underground temple. From this ran four major roads in the four cardinal directions, each marked by a gate in the city wall, the north–south roads being collectively known as the *cardo*, the hinge which separated day from night, and the east–west roads as the *decumanus*, a word usually thought to be derived from the name of the Roman 'decuman' or tenth legion, which was stationed by the western gate. The site on which the augur stood, under which the offering pit was dug, was interestingly enough called by the Romans the *mundus*.

The Romanised Etruscan system exists in England, for example, in the street plan and history of Colchester, the county town of Essex, built by the Romans thirty-three years after Manilius was writing. The modern city follows the original foursquare plan, and in the west the Balkerne Gate still stands, with the Roman cemetery beyond it. Since the western gate in a Roman camp was the site of punishment, at which offenders were executed, following its Etruscan symbolism as the abode of the Fates, this survival may be due more to popular superstition – fear of the ill-omened quarter – than to conscious antiquarianism. North–west of the town is the site of the British settlement, home of the native gods who would appear to the Romans as the 'underworld spirits' who naturally inhabited the north–west in Etruscan cosmology. The north-east belonged to the weather-god, the Roman Jupiter and, true to form, in Colchester this is the site of the temples of Claudius, the deified emperor whose cult had replaced that of Jupiter. The eastern gate, associated with light and victory in the Etruscan system, was that through which the legions always marched on their way to war, even if the war lay to the west of the city. The south-eastern quarter, abode of 'human activity' for the Etruscans, was the red light district of Roman Colchester, and in medieval times it was the site of the July fair, granted by Richard I, outside the city walls at Magdalen Green, by the church of St Mary Magdalene on the way to the harbour.

No serious attempt has been made to look for an underground shrine at the crossing of the two main streets, although the present town hall and the medieval St Rædwald's Church at this site mark it as being of continuing central importance. On a spire at the top of the town hall is a statue of St Helena who, according to local legend, was the daughter of King Coel, after whom the city is reputedly named, and who is more generally thought to have been the mother of the Emperor Constantine and the finder of the four pieces of the True Cross, which in the Colchester statue she holds in her hand. These four pieces are said to have been distributed by her to Rome, Alexandria, Constantinople and Jerusalem – cities which by no means form an exact cardinal cross on modern maps, but whose connecting lines happen to cross in Turkey, traditional centre of the earth in classical cosmology. In addition, four villages outside the city, each about one mile from its centre, are known as the 'Four Liberties of Colchester': villages which were subject to the jurisdiction of the city and not to that of the county of Essex. The cross formed by the churches of these villages, centring on the churchyard of St Mary-by-the-Walls, just south of the Balkerne Gate, lies 2½ degrees east of north, 3½ degrees south of east, again approximating to the cardinal points of the horizon.

Whatever this curious medieval survival of classical fourfold patterning might mean, we see clearly that the 'normal' practice of cosmology, the orientation of the local horizon in alignment with the four cardinal points, for sacred as well as secular purposes, was still being carried on by the Romans even after the time of Manilius. His description of the fixed circle of the observer, then, with its twelve 'divisions of the firmament' which are the temples of various deities, must be seen against this background.

CONCLUSIONS

The earliest system of domification which remains to us, that of Manilius, divides up the fixed sphere of the observer, defined by the horizon, meridian and prime vertical, which is constant for any location. In following this pattern, Manilius follows the earliest Babylonian omens, which likewise refer to local space – 'you shall look to the south and observe the eclipse' – and to the four corners of the *mundus* or firmament – defining the three Ways of Enlil, Anu and Ea. Manilius' method of division is fundamentally that of Campanus. In northern latitudes, the same fixed sphere of the observer was indeed used for telling the time, though calculated by division not of the prime vertical but of the horizon. If used to form the cusps of a horoscope, the indigenous north European system would be a version of the zenith method, beginning, however, from the midheaven rather than from the ascendant. The division of local space, then, existed independently of astrology, and seems to have been adapted by Manilius or his predecessors to the uses of the latter.

It would appear that in Book II Manilius was attempting to construct a *local* mundane sphere based on three great circles corresponding to those of the *celestial* mundane sphere described in Book I, whose plane, the 'flat earth', corresponded to the local horizon, whose polar circles, the solstitial and equinoctial *colures*, corresponded to the local meridian and prime vertical respectively, and whose yearly solar path, the ecliptic, was mirrored each day in the diurnal path of the sun. In doing so, Manilius was entirely in accord with ancient tradition; it is we, following his successors who based their calculations primarily upon the shifting azimuth of the ascendant, who have forgotten that the circle of the Houses is indeed a fixed 'temple' in space, a halfway station between the utter subjectivity of the birth or event in question, and the vast, impartial objectivity of the wheeling of the heavens through their seasonal and precessional cycles.

Notes

1 For example Holden, 1977, pp. 35 ff., Nevin, 1982, pp. 75 ff.; and for planetary rulers, Greene, 1977, p. 28.
2 Manilius, 1977, II, 788 ff. Reprinted by permission of the publishers and the Loeb Classical Library from *Manilius, Astronomica*, trans. G. P. Gould (Cambridge, Mass.: Harvard University Press, 1977).
3 Manilius, 1977, II, 858 ff.
4 Manilius invites us to consider the progress of any one sign through his 'parts of the firmament' in the following order (modern House numbers in brackets): (1) Concerned with the fortunes of children, ruled by the Glittering One (Mercury); (12) a place of ill omen, hostile to future activity, doomed to climb, ruled by the Evil Daemon; (11) a place ambitious and triumphant, more secure than the zenith, the abode of happy fortune, ruled by Jupiter; (10) Fortune (Venus) rules, governing wedlock and the bridal chamber, but as it is the consummation of aspiration, unable to make any movement except for ill; (9) nourished by the sun's splendour, concerned with physical well being, ruled by the sun; (8) facing down onto the western horizon, afraid to fall into the latter's clutches, abode of Typhon; (7) portal of Pluto, governing the end of life, but also good faith and constancy of heart; (6) a place of ill omen, doomed to fall, like the opposite House, the abode of evil fortune; (5) wearied after active service, aspiring to become the foundation (fourth

House), the sport of chance and hidden enemies; (4) concerned for the fortunes of fathers and those cast down from power, ruled by Saturn; (3) the first to rise from the depths, bringing back the sky, ruled by the moon and ruling brothers; (2) looking upwards to the orient, afraid to be dropped back into the depths, abode of Typhon.

These descriptions, although clearly derived from the path of the signs around the sky, are also, tantalisingly, compatible with the modern anticlockwise order. There is, for example, no clear reason why (our) House three should rule brothers in Manilius' system. It is thus possible that as Holden (1977, p. 49) implies, Manilius was offering a new, and to him more logical, explanation of the 'parts of the firmament' than that based on the rising sign, which may already have existed. However, the observation of local (and celestial) space according to the four cardinal directions has already been shown to have been accepted practice long before Manilius.

5 Mookherjee, 1977, pp. 70–1. Also see Bharati, 1965, p. 79 n. on the Jambu tree on Mount Meru – another version of the World Tree.

6 Santillana and Dechend, esp. ch. 4a, 'Intermezzo'.

7 In fact the way of Enlil is said to have lain 17 degrees north of the equator, that of Ea as far south, defining the way of Anu between them, whereas the tropics proper are 23½ degrees north and south of the equator. However, the common epithet of the god Ea, 'the antelope of the subterranean ocean', recalls not only the horned icon of Capricorn, but also the watery abyss which was a common classical epithet for the heavens below the celestial equator.

8 Turf mazes in England, Germany and Scandinavia are commonly called 'Troytowns', a usage whose etymology is obscure but which more likely derives from a description of their turning paths than by reference to geography. (Irish *cuairtean*, derived from *cuairt*, to turn, means a turf maze – or a water-eddy, interestingly, since an alternative Old Norse name for the celestial pole is *idavöll*, 'eddy-plain', and the Welsh *caerdroia*, 'turning castle', likewise derives from the verb meaning 'to turn', *troi*.) However, Snorri himself, in the *Gylfaginning*, gives the origin of the Æsir as Troy in Asia Minor (modern Turkey). This might seem to be an uncomprehending rationalization of ancient legend, were it not that in classical geography the earthly Troy is actually portrayed as the centre of the world (*terra*), with

Europe and Asia to the north of it, and Africa to the south. Christian geography replaced Troy, simply enough, by Jerusalem, and thus Snorri's origin myth refers to the home of his celestial gods as being at the centre of the earth plane of the pagan world. The earthly Troy is a static centre; but celestial Troy is the centre of rotation of the visible universe.

9 Most of the information in the following section is based on the researches of O. S. Reuter (see Bibliography) and further reference to his primary sources.

10 Curiously, *ætt* means 'house' in the sense of race or lineage, whereas astrological Houses in the modern sense are known to Manilius as *loca*, 'places'. In the sense of the sign of a planet's rulership, a house is *sedes* or *domicilius*, 'abode', and so we must conclude that the Icelandic usage is a strange coincidence.

11 The Etruscans attributed significance to the eight airts as follows: that straddling the northern point was of night; north-east, of weather; east, of fire, light, victory; south-east, of human activity; south, of sun; south-west, of nature deities; west, of fate, punishment; north-west, of underworld spirits.

Bibliography

Bharati, A. (1965), *The Tantric Tradition* (London: Rider).

Dames, M. (1977), *The Avebury Cycle* (London: Thames and Hudson).

Dennis, A., Foote, P. and Perkins, R. (1980), *Grágás, the Law Book of Iceland* (University of Manitoba Press).

Drake-Carnell, F. J. (1938), *Old English Customs and Ceremonies* (London: Batsford).

Eitel, E. J. (1979), *Feng-Shui*, 3rd edn (Bristol: Pentacle).

Fagan, C. (1973), *Astrological Origins* (St Paul, Minn.: Llewellyn).

Greene, L. (1977), *Relating* (London: Coventure).

Haigh, Rev. D. H. (1896), 'Yorkshire dials', *Yorkshire Archaeological Journal*, 1896, pp. 134–222.

Holden, R. W. (1977), *The Elements of House Division* (Romford: Fowler).

Jones, P. H. (1982), *Sundial and Compass Rose* (Cambridge: Fenris-Wolf).

Keller, W. (1975), *The Etruscans*, trans. A. and E. Henderson (London: Cape).

Manilius, M. (1977), *Astronomica*, trans. G. P. Gould (London: Heinemann).

Maternus, J. Firmicus (1975), *Ancient Astrology, Theory and Practice*, trans. J. W. Bram (New Jersey: Park Ridge).
Mookherjee, A. and Khanna, M. (1977), *The Tantric Way* (London: Thames and Hudson).
Nevin, B. (1982), *Astrology inside out* (Rockport, Mass.: Para Research).
Newbery, J. E. (1979), 'The universe at prayer', in E. H. Waugh and K. D. Prithipaul (eds), *Native Religious Traditions* (Waterloo, Ontario: Laurier University Press).
Pennick, N. (1987), *The Cosmic Axis* (Cambridge: Runestaff).
Ptolemy, C. (1940), *Tetrabiblos*, trans. F. E. Robbins (London: Heinemann).
Reuter, O. S. (1921), *Das Rätsel der Edda* (Munich: Lehmann).
Reuter, O. S. (1934), *Germanische Himmelskunde* (Munich: Lehmann).
Santillana, G. de, and Dechend, H. von (1969), *Hamlet's Mill* (London: Macmillan).
Sturluson, S. (1966), *The Prose Edda*, trans. J. I. Young (Cambridge: Cambridge University Press).

IV

THE STAR TEMPLES OF HARRAN

Nick Kollerstrom

Commentary

There have been some fairly recent archaeological excavations of interest in relation to Nick Kollerstrom's work on the planetary temples of Harran.

This immensely ancient city, which has suffered so many vicissitudes, will fascinate astrologers as much as it does historians and archaeologists. The höyük in the centre is known to have been continuously inhabited from the third millennium BC to the thirteenth century AD. According to Al Biruni (who died in 440/1048), Harran was first dedicated to the moon because it resembled the moon in shape.

In 675 BC Esarhaddon visited the site and saw on the outskirts of the (then) city, a temple of cedar wood. In it the moon god Sin was leaning upon a staff with two crowns.[1] There was also a female moon deity: An-Nadim reported in AD 987 that in April the Sabian priests offered a bullock to their moon goddess.

It has been suggested[2] that in regions where, as sometimes happens, various names of the moon deity appear, these may be derived from aspects of the lunar cycle or other attributes, perhaps Mansions of the moon? (see the sections Elections by Lunar Phase and The Mansions of the Moon in Elections in 'Some Varieties of Electional Astrology' on pp. 174 and 176 of this book). Various moon-shaped emblems are carried by figures represented on steles which have been excavated. There is a description of figures with planetary emblems (Sun, Moon and Venus).[3] Monuments of the reign of Nabonidus (the last Chaldean king, who was a devotee of the moon god Sin at Harran 'whose cult he had favoured and restored')[4] have been found at or near Harran and are thought to belong to Sin's temple.

Excavations were made in 1952 and 1956 by David Storm Rice, but when he died in 1962 these studies lapsed. They were resumed by Dr Nurettin Yardunci, who reported on the work in 1983; he said the modern population was dense, new concrete buildings were being constructed while buildings made of mud-brick were being destroyed. There was a report that the excavations near the city centre at the end of 1985 convinced the archaeologists that they were near the temple of the moon god Sin in the höyük.[5] Finds from under the first Islamic level included a piece of brick cuneiform inscription. The name 'Sin' occurred in an inscription which mentions the construction of the E-Hul-Hul temple: 'We therefore regard these finds as proof positive that we are near the temple of the god Sin.' Photographs of the ruins of Harran may be seen in *Anatolian Studies*, vol. I (1951), p. 77.

The tower of the city was supposed to contain two copper jinns, which were talismans against snakes. It is interesting to note that in seventeenth century England Elias Ashmole used Venus talismans (also made of copper, Venus's metal) but for rather different purposes (see the section on Elections for the Casting of Talismans in 'Some Varieties of Electional Astrology' on p. 187 of this book).

The descriptions of the planetary temples here given mention planetary attributes which have come down to modern times in Western astrology. An interesting example of the temple idea in Western literature may be found in the article in this book on 'Chaucer's Astrology' where temples of Mars and Venus are discussed by Chaucer.

The common features in these descriptions are the pictures on the temple walls, the appropriate metals, colours and other attributes. For example, the Harran temple of Venus is described as containing musical instruments – a well-known association with that planet, mentioned in Chaucer; musicians are ruled by Venus as a profession, as William Lilly mentions when assigning all the planetary attributes and rulerships in *Christian Astrology* (1647), p. 74.

Nick Kollerstrom introduces his account of the Harranian planetary metals with a brief excursus on Isaac Newton's tabulation of the seventeenth-century seven metals and their correspondences.

A. L. K.

Notes

1 *Anatolian Studies* (1958), vol. 8, pp. 36–45.
2 *Encyclopaedia Britannica*, vol. 1, p. 1, 058.
3 See C. J. Gadd's note to 'Harran inscriptions of Mabonidus' in *Anatolian Studies*, op. cit.
4 Campbell, Joseph, *Occidental Mythology*, p. 216.
5 See Dr Nurettin Yardunci in *Anatolian Studies* (1986), vol. 36, p. 194.

NEWTON AND THE SEVEN METALS

In the mid-seventeenth century, the number of different metals was recognised as being seven, and, like the seven strings of Apollo's lyre, each of these was invested with a distinct character and identity. Drawing on a widespread literature on alchemy then available, Isaac Newton summarised these correspondences as follows:

			Planetae septem			
Noah	Ham	Chus	Assur	Thoth	Pathros	
Kiun	Hammon	Hercules	Astarte	Anubis	Orus	Bubash
Saturn	Jupiter	Mars	Venus	Merc.	Apollo	Diana
Plumb.	Stannum	Ferrum	Cuprum	Argenvive	Aurum	Argent.

This was composed in the 1680s, for his (unpublished) opus, 'Theologiae Gentilis Origines Philosophicae.' The list contains – a recent biographer of Newton explains – a metal, a planetary glyph, Egyptian and Roman deities and 'a member of Noah's family'.[1]

So, did Newton believe it? The question is not readily answerable. He wrote reams on alchemy, but published none of it. A recent publication on Newton's alchemical works[2] has been criticised for too readily supposing that Newton *believed* what he might in fact have been merely *transcribing*.[3] He was strongly opposed to astrology,[4] contrary to what is alleged with no valid basis, in most astrology textbooks, but on the other hand he was a keen believer in the mystic significance of the number seven!

The French have never swallowed Newton's story that there were seven colours in the rainbow and count merely six! Newton inserted a seventh, indigo, which no one could see, to bolster his unusual theory that the colours of the spectrum were related to the musical scale,[5] a theory curiously omitted by his biographers. His *Optics* had seven sections, his description of the diffraction rings seen around lenses was sevenfold, his view of the design of Solomon's temple was sevenfold, and so forth.[6]

One can say that the language of alchemy was a matter of urgent importance for the creative decades of Newton's life but that it faded out after his nervous breakdown of 1693, when he became a public figure as running the Mint and the Royal Society simultaneously in London. All his alchemic/chemical records are dotted with planetary glyphs, signifying the seven metals, which is perhaps where astrologers got the notion that he believed in their art.

THE SABIANS OF HARRAN

From the notebooks of a Cambridge mathematics lecturer we now move somewhat unexpectedly back seven centuries in time and east by 45 degrees of longitude to a city on the banks of the Euphrates where the seven metals were used to construct temples for invoking cosmic powers: Harran, where dwelt 'the Sabians'. As well as a centre of trade for metals, Harran was also the repository for the philosophy of the ancient Chaldeans when it had been obliterated elsewhere. 'From Harran, Alchemy spread to Egypt.'[7] The inhabitants of this city were thus a pagan sect which survived under Islam, which had elsewhere eradicated old astral religions in its expansion.

An archaeological article of 1951 about Harran commences with the observation that,

> So many references to Harran, either under its own name or in the classical guise of Carrhae, occur throughout the length of Mesopotamian, Roman and mediaeval Arab literature, that it has acquired a strong historical personality, almost without reference to its material remains, and referred to 'the several religious shrines for which the city was famous during nearly three millenia.'[8]

In AD 833 the Harranians were ordered to become Muslims. They adopted the Qu'ranic race name Sabians so that they could claim to be such. The last temple to their old religion left standing was a moon temple, destroyed in AD 1032 by the Tartars. The sect itself disappeared during Mongol invasions of the thirteenth century, when its water supply was diverted to a neighbouring town, thus ignominiously terminating its long and illustrious history.

Unfortunately the only substantial account of the star temples of

Harran comes from a Muslim who was opposed to the Hermetic basis of their beliefs, Al Dimishqui of c. AD 1300 – a tertiary source! There is no record of any original manuscripts by the Sabians concerning their beliefs, and the town of Harran is now but a series of mounds; yet, 'Owing to the fame acquired by various professional men and writers belonging to this community, they attracted the attention of Muslim authors', to quote from the *Encyclopaedia of Religion and Ethics*. Some of these comments survive in Arabic.

This *Encyclopaedia* quotes a nineteenth-century Russian source, Chwolsohn, as inferring

> that the Harranians were, as the Christians called them, pagans, *viz.* a community who had retained a mixture of Babylonian and Hellenic religion, over which there had been superimposed a coating of Neo-Platonic philosophy (chiefly among the educated) . . .

Originally the Sabians were scattered throughout the north of Mesopotamia and Harran was their principal centre. As this town had seen diverse empires rise and fall it accreted an unusual blend of beliefs. It 'continued till the 10th century AD to be the last outpost of Sumerian, Hittite and Babylonian civilisations' according to H. E. Stapleton.[9]

We turn now to the sole extensive account of the beliefs and rites of the Sabian people, in the *Memoirs of the Assyrian Society of Bengal* (1927), translated into English from the Russian Chwolsohn's German account *Die Ssabier und der Ssabismus*, translated from the Arabic writer Al Dimishqui (1265–1327). The first paragraph of this account states, 'but verily in this they lie', and 'But in these statements also they lie', and calls them idolaters. The 'lie', we gather, was the belief of the Sabians that their doctrines had been received from Hermes, and another prophet called Agathodemon. These are both persons whom they cited as authors of alchemic treatises.

Al Dimishqui gives a Pythonesque account of the Sabian's Hermetic philosophy, whereby a different type of person was sacrificed on each day of the week. On Monday, the moon day, a 'moon-faced man' is to be found, shot and his blood sprinkled over the pure silver temple idol, mounted on three steps. On Tuesday, Mars' day, a 'red-haired man' was immersed in an acid bath to 'dissolve skin and flesh' and the head severed, and 'the head was supposed to prophesy for 7 days what was supposed to happen for the next year'. The iron idol of the Mars temple, coloured red, was given this dismembered head to hold in one hand, while it brandished a sword in the other. Wednesday, Mercury's day, required 'a brown youth who was a good scribe', who had to be quartered and burnt, and the ashes thrown onto the image. Need I continue?

Such calumny surely testifies to the vigour of the Harranian belief system and the efforts made to suppress it. The sober pages of *Ambix*, the journal of the history of early chemistry, recount these sacrifices without suggesting that they may be calumny; and yet both of the accounts in the *Encyclopaedia of Religion and Ethics* and the *Shorter Encyclopaedia of Islam* dismiss the notion, equally because no such sect would have been tolerated under centuries of Muslim rule and because of the generally high esteem in which the sect was held. 'Undoubtedly [it] is not to be maintained', to quote the latter source.

The Sabians linked the days of the week to their astral planetary deities as follows:

Helios	(Sun)	Sunday
Sin	(Moon)	Monday
Ares	(Mars)	Tuesday
Nabuq	(Mercury)	Wednesday
Bal	(Jupiter)	Thursday
Balthi	(Venus)	Friday
Kronos	(Saturn)	Saturday

the names showing the mixture of Greek and Near-Eastern mythology in their religion. On the other hand, the number of steps on each temple, leading up to the metallic image in the centre, showed the Ptolemaic ordering:

Image of planet	*Associated metal*	*Associated colour*	*Number of steps in pediment*
Saturn	Lead	black	9
Jupiter	Tin	green	8
Mars	Iron	red	7
Sun	Gold	yellow	6
Venus	Copper	blue	5
Mercury	Mercury	brown	4
Moon	Silver	white	3

One notes that the Harranian ordering of the seven metals in this list is that given by their physical properties, and their chemical valence number: the lowest 'step score' is for silver, which is monovalent, and the valences increase in order to lead, which has a valence of 4+2. The valences (that is chemical combining ratios) are in order from silver to lead: 1, 1 or 2, 1 or 2, 1 or 3, 2 or 3, 2 or 4, 2 or 4. Thermal and electrical conductivity follow the reverse order, going from silver down to lead, the slowest conductor. Lustre follows this same ordering but not exactly, from silver, the most lustrous, down to lead, the dullest, but tin is more lustrous than iron, so this ordering is not exact. This scale would also have given a rough guide to the notion of chemical activity, in that the top three metals (belonging to 'above the sun' planets) are quite reactive and will liberate hydrogen from an acid, whereas the bottom three (or 'below the sun' planets) are less reactive and will not liberate hydrogen from an acid. This is a modern formulation, while the Sabian metallurgists and alchemists would have experienced chemical activity in terms of such things as the readiness with which a metal could be separated from its ore. Thus a metallic significance did exist in the reported sequence of the seven–metal temples of Harran; and it echoes the ordering of the planets according to their simplest observable property, namely the rate at which they are seen to move across the sky, from Saturn, the slowest moving, to the moon as the fastest.

Concerning the metallurgical techniques of the area, Stapleton comments:

> Harran must be regarded as the great centre of communication and trade in the ancient East, and specialising, above all, in the metals produced in the mines of Asia Minor, Kurdistan and Persia. It may be visualised, with comparative certainty, as one of the chief markets from which successive Mesopotamian dynasties satisfied their needs for gold, silver, copper and tin, as well as mineral substances, such as the arsenic sulphides, borax and sulphur. Iron too must have been bought and sold by the Harranians after 1200 B.C. when the Hittite monopoly in this metal came to an end: while – at some early date (certainly before 1500 B.C.) – lead was added to the list.

Such a vista indicates a tradition in metallurgy stretching back to the very dawn of the Age of Iron: for the above date of 1200 BC seems as good as any to mark its beginning, before which the Martial Hittite race guarded jealously their fire secret of extracting iron from its ore, and traded iron for several times its weight in gold with the Egyptians. One could add that mercury would have become an article of trade around the first or second century AD, as its extraction procedure from cinnabar became established.

Stapleton suggests that these distinct series of steps leading up to the altar trace back to the Babylonian ziggurat motif, showing 'The intimate connection between the Harranian worship and that of the ancient Babylonians'. Various details of religious custom are given, such as a law of purity; a table of unlawful meats forbade the flesh of swine, dogs, birds with talons and camels, whereas the Muslim law permitted the eating of camel. Divorce was allowed only by decree of a judge and bigamy was forbidden. There were various calendar days for fasting. The source for this is the Arab writer Al–Shahrastani of the tenth century AD (summarised by the *Encyclopaedia of Islam*).

Later on, 'In Mas'udi's time only one temple remained – that of *μεγάληθά*, 'the great goddess', which, however, the Muslims supposed to be dedicated to Abraham's father, called in the Qur'an 'Azar',[10] suggesting a politically rather delicate situation. (There was a tradition that Abraham was born in Harran.) In AD 985 the architect Muquaddasi from Jerusalem wrote, 'Harran has a stone citadel. The masonry resembles that of Jerusalem in beauty.'[11] It seems that this 'citadel' was one of the Moon temples there.

THE TEMPLES

The first temple of the Harranians, which Al-Dimishqui, writing in the early fourteenth century, describes is a 'Temple of the First Cause' with a circular dome and forty-eight windows, so that the sun shone in through different windows through the course of the year. Next there is a 'Temple of The First Reason', similar to the first in shape but without the windows. Was the First Reason obscure, perhaps? He then describes how

> The Sabians had seven others dedicated to the Seven Planets, which they considered as intermediaries employed in their relation to God. They said that the Planets lead to the Angels, who are the Directors of the Planets in the Spheres and that the angels will bring them into relation with God. To the Seven Metals were attached the properties of the Seven Planets, and hence the images of the Planets were made of these metals.

Al–Dimishqui describes the temple of Saturn as hexagonal, made of black stone with pictures of old men on the walls, and with an image of lead or black stone on a pediment of nine steps. That of Jupiter was triangular at the base, built of green stone and with an image of tin or some ore thereof. Mars' temple was 'oblong' with weapons hung on the walls. The sun temple was square and golden in colour, while the Venus temple was triangular, cornflower blue in colour and held musical instruments played continually. The temple of Mercury was hexagonal, with pictures of youths holding scrolls on the walls and with an idol made of 'all the metals and of *khar sini* [porcelain] and it is made hollow. In the hollow much quicksilver was poured.' The moon temple was pentagonal with three steps to its throne, of colours golden and white and with its idol made of silver.

According to E. O. von Lippman, in *Hermes and Hermetica*, 'the Arabs had received from the Sabians of Harran the writings of Hermes as the "greatest old Greek philosopher"'. Here one seems to be looking at the very crucible in which the 'Hermetic corpus' of literature came into being, or rather at the obliterated remains thereof. It was written in Greek, and the Sabian alchemists tended to take the names of revered Greeks of old as authors for their texts, as Stapleton indicates:

> An even more likely repository of Harranian science are the alchemical writings that pass under the revered names of Socrates, Plato and Aristotle . . . the best way of avoiding inconvenient questioning, or too much interference by the local authorities in their alchemical researches, would be to associate their beliefs with the names of one or more of the leading Sages of their Greek overlords.[12]

He adds that as well as Hermes and Adhimun (Agathademon) as their two chief philosopher–prophets, identified with Seth and Idris respectively, Orpheus was also one of their prophets.

An extensive astrological literature burgeoned from Harran and Muhammad al-Musabbi'hi wrote a book of 6,000 pages on the subject in the early eleventh century; however, no mention of Harran is to be found in *A History of Western Astrology* (1987) by J. Tester, which seems odd. The temples were designed to attune to the powers attached to the celestial spheres, as intermediaries between the First Cause and man. 'The days on which the planets reached their culminating points were celebrated as festivals', according to Partington's account,[13] and one wonders what was here meant by 'culminating point'. It is said that the greatest Arab astrology school run by Jews existed in Harran.

'The great men who have rendered this sect illustrious', to quote from *The Encyclopaedia of Islam*, were

> Thabit ben Kurra, the eminent geometrician, original astronomer, translator and philosopher; Sinan ben Thabit, physician and meteorologist; other physicians and astronomers of the same family; Thabit ben Sinan and Hilal ben al-Muhassin, historians; Abu Ishak ben Hilal, vizier, and other members of his family; al-Battani (Albategnus), the celebrated astronomer; Abu Dja'far al-Khazin, mathematician. Ibn al-Wahshiya, the author of the *K. al-Filaha al-Nabatiya*, although professing to be a Muslim, in every way belonged to the Sabaean school.

The first-mentioned Thabit ben Kurra (AD 826–900) was their most eminent man of science and translated various Greek scientific works into Syriac and Arabic. 'Equally distinguished', to quote from Hastings, 'as a secretary of state was Ibrahim ben Hilal (925–994) many of whose letters and poems are preserved. We learn from his biography . . . that the family profession was medicine, as was the case with other Sabi'ans of note.' Histories of Harran and Harranians are known to have existed in medieval times but have been lost: for example, that by Hammad ben Hibatallah, who made a history of the town and biographies of its scholars, poets and persons of distinction; or that by Abu Abdallah Muh, the famous Egyptian historian whose family originated from Harran.

AL-BATTANI

The most distinguished astronomer of the Middle Ages was Al-Battani (died 929), if Tycho Brahe's armillary sphere is a guide; on it Brahe had inscribed pictures of Ptolemy, Al-Battani, Copernicus and himself. Al-Battani was born in Harran and lived and worked in a neighbouring town, Racca. He ascertained the obliquity of the ecliptic to be 23 degrees 35 minutes, as did other astronomers of his time, a value less by 16 minutes than Ptolemy's (23 degrees 31 minutes is the modern value).[14] A date of AD 891 is given for this determination by Flamsteed, writing c. 1705. Less successful was Al-Battani's estimate of the value for precession, where he obtained a value of 1 degree every sixty-six years, compared with Ptolemy's value of 1 degree per hundred years. Al-Battani's error in this (as Flamsteed later explained)[15] was due to his taking Ptolemy's star positons which were mostly out by 1 degree, owing to Ptolemy's having adjusted Hipparchus' data with his own inaccurate value for precession. Al-Battani is credited with having discovered the motion of the solar apsides, by determining the longitude of the sun's apogee and comparing it with Ptolemy's value.[16]

'Above the Moon', wrote Al-Battani, 'is the Alacir, the fifth essence, which is devoid of lightness and heaviness, and is not perceptible to the human senses; of this substance the spheres and planets are formed.'[17] The greatest distance of the moon from the earth (that is, at its apogee) he gave as 64 1/6 semi-diameters of earth, while it is actually 63.8 – an error of a mere 0.6 per cent. His works, including his tables of planetary motion, were translated as *De Scientia Stellarum* and published in Italy in 1537.

Closing his account of the people of Harran, Hastings comments, 'Until some discovery is made of genuine works belonging to the sect, their origin and tenets must remain obscure', which is indisputable. In preparing this tentative account, where the author should in no way be regarded as an expert on the subject, one has been peering through several opaque layers at something which vanished long ago, remembered only in the histories of its opponents. This writer has functioned as a mere quaternary source. Many of the basic Harranian texts would have been stored in the great library of Baghdad, which went up in flames in the thirteenth century. If it is the case that the Sabians of Harran experienced a unity in their religion, science and philosophy not well achieved by later peoples, then it would seem to be a subject worthy of further study. Their system involved an experience of metal–planet concordances in a manner that was culturally of a creative and long-enduring quality.

'SEVEN STEPS TO HEAVEN'

The earliest tradition of 'seven metals' as linked to the spheres of the planets occurs in the religious system of Mithraism as described by Celsus, writing in Rome about AD 180. Again the sole text describing this belief is by an opponent as Celsus' text has been lost and only a polemic of c. AD 248 by Origen, *Contra Celsum*, remains. To quote from this,

> These things are hinted at in the accounts of the Persians and especially the mysteries of Mithras which are celebrated amongst them . . . There is a ladder (or stair) with seven gates and above that an eighth gate. The first gate is of lead,

> the second tin, the third of bronze (or copper), the fourth of iron, the fifth of mixed metal, the sixth of silver, and the seventh of gold. The first gate they assign to Kronos, indicating by lead the slowness of this star . . .[18]

A rather mixed-up list of correspondences ensues, such as 'the fourth to Hermes, since both Hermes and iron are fit to endure all things and are money making and laborious', a doubtful sounding analogy not found in other lists by alchemists of the time and possibly inserted to derogate the whole philosophy. The Greek phrase for 'mixed metal' may, it is thought, have referred to electrum, a gold–silver alloy used for coinage. The eighth gate corresponds, it has been supposed, to the sphere of the fixed stars. The steps of a ladder of Mithras would not have been constructed of the actual metals, Partington explained, as gold and silver would have been too expensive, but were painted to represent them. The quote by Origen continues,

> He [Celsus] next proceeds to examine the reason for the stars being arranged in this order, which is symbolised by the different kinds of matter; musical reasons, moreover, are added or quoted by the Persian theology, and to these again he tries to add a second explanation, also connected with musical considerations.

And that is all! One surmises that 'to examine the reason for the stars being arranged in this order' would indeed have been difficult, because the order given was not astronomical, but alchemical: a scale of perfection from lead, the 'basest' metal, up to incorruptible gold. Later alchemists would put copper above iron in this list, but as iron was then a relatively new metal, presumably it was regarded as more valuable than copper. With that slight adjustment, and with the insertion of quicksilver in place of 'mixed metal', this list remained for the best part of two millenia the standard ordering used by alchemists as their 'scale of perfection', as part of their alluring notion that the baser metals could be transformed into gold. It lasted up into the eighteenth century when new metals such as zinc – isolated at last from the brassmaking technology – and platinum from the New World broke up the sevenfold scheme. Returning to the *Contra Celsum* text, the planetary order given by Origen for Celsus' seven steps (SA, VE, JU, ME, MA, MO, and SU) was unlikely to make sense in any terms, but then that may have been the aim of the exercise.

Notes

Acknowledgements: I am grateful to Michael Baigeant for advice over sources for Harran.

1 R. S. Westfall, *Never at Rest, a Biography of Isaac Newton* (Cambridge: CUP, 1980).
2 B. J. Dobbs, *The Foundations of Newton's Alchemy* (Cambridge: CUP, 1975).
3 D. T. Whiteside, 'From his claw the Greene Lyon . . . ', book review in *Isis*, vol. 68 (1977), pp. 16–121.
4 S. Schaffer, 'Newton's comets and the transformation of astrology', in P. Curry (ed.) *Astrology, Science and Society* (Boydell, 1987), p. 242.
5 J. Lohne, 'Newton's "proof" of the sine law and his mathematical principles of colours', in *Archive for History of Exact Sciences*, vol. 1 (1960), p. 399.
6 D. Castillejo, *The Expanding Force in Newton's Cosmos*, (Madrid, 1986), p. 97. For Newton's comments on the seven strings of Apollo's lyre, see J. E. McGuire and P. M. Rattansi, 'Newton and the Pipes of Pan' in *Notes and Records of the Royal Society of London*, 1966, pp. 108–43.
7 H. E. Stapleton, 'The antiquity of alchemy', *Journal for the Study of Alchemy and Early Chemistry*, vol. 3 (1953), p. 38.
8 S. Lloyd and W. Brice, 'Harran', *Anatolian Studies*, vol. 1 (1951), p. 77.
9 H. E. Stapleton, op. cit., p. 23.
10 J. Hastings (ed.), *Encyclopaedia of Religion and Ethics* (1913) (Edinburgh: T. & T. Clark), p. 520.
11 D. S. Rice, 'Mediaeval Harran', *Anatolian Studies*, vol. 2 (1952), p. 42.
12 Stapleton, op. cit., p. 32.
13 J. R. Partington, *A History of Chemistry*, vol. 1, p. 336, (London: Macmillan, n.d.).
14 J. Flamsteed, *Historia Coelestis Britannica* (1725), Preface (ed. A. Chapman and A. D. Johnson), p. 49, (London: Greenwich Maritime Monograph, 1983).
15 Ibid., p. 51.
16 J. L. E. Dreyer, *A History of Astronomy from Thales to Kepler*, p. 251, (Dover Pubns, 1953).
17 Ibid., p. 257.
18 J. R. Partington, op. cit., p. 299.

Bibliography

Chwolsohn, D. (1856), *Die Ssabier und der Ssabismus*, 2 vols (St Petersburg).
Gibb and Kramers (eds) (1961), *Shorter Encyclopaedia of Islam*.
Hastings, James (ed.) (1913), *Encyclopaedia of Religion and Ethics*, (Edinburgh: T. & T. Clark).
Mehren, A. F. (ed.) (1866), *Cosmographie*. Chapter 1 has a translation in French of Al Dimishqui's account. Excerpts translated into English are given in Stapleton, H. E. (1927), 'Chemistry in Iraq and Persia' in *Memoirs of the Assyrian Society of Bengal*, vol. 8, section on 'The Religious Beliefs of the Sabians (Harranians or Chaldaeans) and the Bearing of those Beliefs on the Ideas of Ar-Razi'. The most comprehensive study of the Sabians there has been.
Partington, J. R., 'The Harranians (Sabians)', in *History of Chemistry*, vol. 1, ch. 19, pp. 330–43.

CHAUCER'S ASTROLOGY

Some Aspects of its Influence

Annabella Kitson

Commentary

Nicholas Kollerstrom has shown how early the astrological system of correspondences between planets, metals, colours and so on developed in Harran; for example, in Al Dimishqui's account which he quotes and where the sequence is traced 'Tuesday – Mars – red – severed head (Mars rules the sign Aries, which also rules the head) – sword – iron'. This links very interestingly with the temple of Mars described in detail by Chaucer in 'The Knight's Tale' and discussed in the following paper.

While many attributes remain constant, the planets have varying reputations according to the way they are represented in art and literature and in the practice of astrology. Sometimes one aspect of their ancestry as gods, sometimes another, is emphasized. Chaucer delineates Mars, Venus and Saturn a number of times and because his poetry is memorable these delineations have been influential.

The multitude of his detailed astrological references has reached a

Saturn. Aquarius, the water bearer, is shown in the sky and Capricorn, the goat, on the left. Saturn is about to devour one of his children. The scythe of Time is by his foot. The setting is rocky and remote. See the introduction to the article on 'Kepler's Belief in Astrology' (p. 153), and the section on Saturn in 'Chaucer's Astrology' (p. 74). (Engraving, 'Seven Planets' series, the Master 'I.B.' of Nuremburg, 1529.)

This engraving, 'Luna' on page 173, and 'Urania and Clio' on the cover, are reproduced by courtesy of the Trustees of the Victoria and Albert Museum, London.

vast audience over the centuries. His *Treatise on the Astrolabe* explained clearly how that instrument was used in the practice of astrology; it was much valued by his successors. Today we can enter a whole world of astrology through his poetry.

I read English language and literature at Girton College, Cambridge, and write and lecture on this and other arts subjects. I have a special interest in the history of ideas which involve symbolism. Astrology fascinates me as a symbolic language of great richness and subtlety which has engaged many fine minds over the centuries.

Note: Apart from glossaries in editions of Chaucer's collected works by F. N. Robinson and John H. Fisher, the 'Middle English Vocabulary' by J. R. R. Tolkien in *Fourteenth Century Verse and Prose*, 1978, edited by Kenneth Sisam, is helpful.

It is a commonplace that Chaucer's continuing influence upon English language and literature has been immense. But he has also mediated ideas which he inherited from many sources and to which he responded in ways which give him an exceptional place in the history of those ideas. Take the notion of pilgrimage: throughout the Western world today that idea is made vivid by the *Canterbury Tales* and the atmosphere that surrounds them. Chaucer has made this concept not merely picturesque, but immediate and real; separate but not remote from our experience.

So there are certain ideas which Chaucer stitched into the fabric of the language, giving them a durability and appeal they might never have retained but for him. This powerfully affects how we receive them. Yet looking beyond our own interests, there may be ideas lying dormant in his writing, awaiting the different perceptions of a later time, when they may become as engaging as are now, for example, his presentation of marriage and its variants.

It is my contention that Chaucer had an important effect on the history of astrological ideas – and that this effect is by no means played out. Because of the range of material at his disposal he was eclectic; but he preserved and disseminated much that might otherwise have dropped from view. It was a quirk of history that sent Caxton so soon to supplement the manuscripts with printed copies for a growing public, but it was Chaucer's genius that kept the editions flowing from that day to this.

As a preliminary I should like to characterize some of the ways he handled astrological themes and to note in passing that he does not merely make glancing, decorative allusions as do some of his contemporaries for whom astrological time references were a conventional rhetorical device. Chaucer uses these themes for dramatic and poetic effect; in the creation of mood and atmosphere; and in characterization, comic and otherwise. Sometimes they emphasize man's place in the cosmos, or in some spiritual hierarchy, and so touch on philosophical questions.

In a very distinctive way Chaucer also used these themes as a means of encoding a level of meaning which it might have been politically indiscreet or artistically undesirable to present unambiguously. Lastly, and significantly, astrological concepts and techniques are presented in considerable detail – not only in the *Treatise on the Astrolabe* but throughout the poetry – and in ways which capture the attention and stimulate curiosity.

I suggest that it is by the encoding of secret meanings and the detailed technicalities – so often in departures from his source material – that we are led to what is peculiar and intense in Chaucer's relationship with astrology. It is never extraneous, it always illuminates and interacts with character, theme and plot.

Chauncy Wood (in *Chaucer and the Country of the Stars*) has well argued that it is pointless to try to define Chaucer's 'attitude' to astrology – and indeed that of medieval people generally. Chaucer certainly gave it a great deal of space, beyond what his sources dictated. In both earlier and later times views among clerics and laity fluctuated more than is always realised. For example, in 1186, as Professor Southern has pointed out,[1] the Archbishop of Canterbury ordered a three-day fast when ominous planetary conjunctions were approaching, so as to avert the disasters which might follow. Robert Grosseteste calculated times of conjunctions for the same reason. As late as the beginning of Charles I's reign – as John Aubrey tells us in his 'Converse with Angels and Spirits' – Archbishop Laud 'affirms the power of prayer to be so great That though there be a Conjunction or Opposition of Saturn or Mars (as there was one of them then) it will overcome the malignity of it'.[2]

It is important to remember that much of Chaucer's astrological material is put into the mouths of characters and tellers of tales. The attitudes often reflect the character of the speaker – as with the Man of Law and the Franklin – and should not necessarily be attributed to Chaucer, though they often have been. What does reflect his intentions at a time when it was normal to use source material is the choice of source and the deliberate insertion of astrological ideas not present in that source.

THE 'COMPLAINT OF MARS'

This poem is exceptionally interesting for our purposes. For one thing it juxtaposes gods and goddesses and their characteristics in mythology with planets and their astrological attributes, reminding us how the one coloured the other from time to time. The tendency of a good story to stay in the mind may well have given planetary beings a fresh infusion of mythological qualities in the reader's memory.

The *Complaint* is also an important example of how Chaucer's astrology interacts with the plot – indeed, *is* the plot at one level. It raises the question of encoding because of the strong possibility that the characters stand for real contemporary people. It displays astronomical realities in ordinary life; the sun must rise, and threatens the lovers with discovery in the Proem; and, passing relentlessly through the zodiac, he chases them from their adultery. Day must come, years must pass.

Evidently there was a significant change in views of Mars and Venus as planets in relation to one another during the Renaissance when Neoplatonists emphasized their good qualities.[3] This was not the view in relation to planetary conjunction, or their adultery in myth, in the Middle Ages. On the contrary, the theme in this poem is ridicule of bad behaviour – guilty infatuation, not true love.

Homer's version of the story in Book VIII of the *Odyssey* shows Ares (Mars) and Aphrodite (Venus) being discovered by Apollo (the sun). The sun tells tales to Hephaestus (Vulcan), Aphrodite's husband. He makes a snare around their bed and catches them *in flagrante delicto*, calling the other gods to mock their embarrassment. In Ovid's version (*Metamorphoses* IV) Mars and Venus are discovered by the sun and are also trapped by Vulcan.

Unless we understand how strongly – vehemently even – the negative side of various planets was projected in the Middle Ages we shall not appreciate the significance of later variations.

While modern astrologers may recognize the side of Venus which is said to figure often in the horoscopes of generals, on the whole the attributes of that planet as viewed by Ptolemy tend to be forgotten. On predicting marriage for women he says that Venus with Mars makes women 'ardent, impetuous and adulterous'.[4]

Considering synastry he writes: 'Venus with Mars produces merely amorous dispositions, but if Mercury is present, notoriety too.' The remark about Mercury is interesting in relation to this

poem, where both he and notoriety are certainly involved, at least by implication.

Chaucer's version shows Mars and Venus as planets in aspect, coming to a conjunction (*copulare* is the Latin term) in Taurus, the sign of Venus' dignity and Mars' fall. The Sun is behind them in the zodiac, about to catch up with Mars, but not with Venus who is – in both senses – fast; despite her vows of love she moves into Gemini and into the arms of Mercury, who is in his masculine dignity there.

The astrological technicalities interact with the story in a way which is amusing to explore; and this demonstrates Chaucer's complete mastery of technique and symbolism. His audience was attuned to accept comedy at the expense of both characters, with overtones of sadness at the folly of excess; and they would appreciate the technical virtuosity.

The behaviour of Mars in Taurus, his fall, is amusingly in keeping with astrological tradition; the notion of Mars–Venus configurations producing excess and wantonness is borne out. Venus deserts Mars and moves into Gemini where she loses the power she had in Taurus and is dominated by Mercury. Mars is left in Taurus, lamenting at great length. Readers of William Lilly's *Christian Astrology* (1647) will pick up points not dwelt on by students of literature. Venus, entering Gemini, is in 'Cilenios' Tour', that is, Mercury's stronghold. He not only rules Gemini, he has degrees 1 to 7 of the sign as his 'terms', which give him additional strength. Meanwhile Venus has neither terms nor dignity. Perhaps another historical figure lurks behind this well-placed Mercury?

To sustain the human aspect of his characters Chaucer intermingles non-astrological words which may be interpreted in their technical sense. Sometimes this is not obvious. This quotation gives an interesting clue to the history of a technique and hints at an implication perhaps not yet noticed. The following lines have been frequently glossed:

> Now fleeth Venus unto Cilenios Tour
> With voide cours
> [making no aspect before leaving the sign]
> for fere of Phebus lyght
> [for fear of discovery, being combust the sun, which destroys].

Venus finds no one to help her and, as we know, is weakly placed, so she decides to hide:

> Within the gate she fledde into a cave
> Derk was this cave, and smokyng as the helle;
> not but two pas within the yate hit stod.
>
> *Complaint of Mars*, lines 113–14; 119–21

Here the 'gate' ('yate') stands for the beginning of the sign. The 'cave' was long ago identified by Skeat (*Works*, I, p. 499) as the second degree of Gemini, taking 'cave' as a translation of the Latin *puteus* (a pit or well), referring to a 'dark or pitted' degree. Such degrees can be studied in Lilly's *Christian Astrology* where there is a table giving the special qualities of certain degrees.[5] He explains these categories and how they may be used. His third column has 'light, darke, smoakie and voyd' degrees. These may be considered in nativities and horary questions. If the ascending degree falls in one of them they relate to the appearance of the native or querent. If the ascendant or moon is in a 'smoakie' degree the querent or native will be of medium complexion, stature or condition. However, if the moon, ascendant or lord of the ascendant is in a deep or 'pitted' degree (like Venus' cave) 'it shows the man at a stand in the question he asks, not knowing which way to turn himself and that he had need of help to bring him into a better condition . . . ' (p. 118).

Lilly, writing in the seventeenth century, mentions rather limited uses for these categories of degree – now only applied in practice by the most devout Lillyists, I suspect. Chaucer, by placing Venus in one of them, *en passant* as it were, hints at a wider use, applied to the condition of a planet (or person–planet) in such a degree. Certainly the description of a pitted degree fits admirably with Venus' predicament. Given Chaucer's expertise this may suggest how they were used at a time when they could be seen depicted in architectural terms, as a 'hell-mouth', in illuminated Books of Hours.

> Derk was this cave, and smokying as the helle.

There are comparatively few 'smoakie' degrees: one each in Cancer, Leo, Virgo, Scorpio, Sagittarius and Aquarius. Lilly says they give a mediocre appearance and a condition 'neither very judicious or a very Asse'. To Chaucer's knowing contemporaries this might be a sly description of the historical Venus–person.

This brings us to the much debated question of whether Mars and Venus stood in this poem for real people, and also to the dating of the configurations described. There is a consensus that Tuckerman's Tables show that the astronomical requirements are best – though not exactly – satisfied in 1385. J. C. Eade in *The Forgotten Sky* (1984) points out that Mercury was in Taurus not Aries at the critical time.[6] Professor Howard, in *Chaucer and the Medieval World*, agrees with Chauncy Wood that, allowing for differences in the tables used, 1385 was probably intended.

John Shirley wrote on the Trinity College manuscript of this poem a comment purporting to identify the people in it:

> Thus endethe here this complaint whiche some men sayne was made by my lady of york doughter to the kyng of Spaygne [John of Gaunt] and my lord of huntyngdon [John Holland] some tyme duc of Excestre . . .

There is evidence of a scandal involving John Holland and John of Gaunt's sister-in-law, Isabella, Duchess of York.[7] Shirley also says the poem was written at the 'comandement' of John of Gaunt. There is no evidence to link John Holland with Gaunt's sister-in-law, Isabella, but he is known to have seduced and later married Gaunt's daughter, Elizabeth. 'No evidence' now does not necessarily preclude the possibility of two scandals, which might have confused Shirley, a bookseller writing in the fifteenth century. It was suggested that John of Gaunt was Mars and Katharine Swynford (Chaucer's sister-in-law) Venus, the sun as common gossip. But since Katharine was Gaunt's mistress for many years before he was free to marry her this does not fit very well.

Perhaps one may conclude that scandals at court abounded, that gossip was often contradictory and inhibited by the danger of retaliation by powerful protagonists. But we must note that the Holland scandal was in 1385–6, which gives the best fit astronomically. Despite the uncertainties it is hard to resist the impression that real people are behind these characters; or that in the creative process several real personages and situations may be portrayed. Katharine (if she was involved) was close to Chaucer; is there a secret delineation of the Venus–person within the meaning of a 'smoakie' degree?

One point emerges very clearly from all the complicated debate: the encoding of a real-life story in astrological terms was an acceptable notion. There is an amusing parallel between enskying a recent scandal and the translation of mythological persons into constellations; this is very much in keeping with Chaucer's sense of the absurd. At the same time, to elevate people from terrestrial reality was to protect the poet. The device emphasizes the cruel lack of privacy in court life where, as with Chaucer, husbands and wives were seldom free to enjoy tranquil domesticity. It may also mock the exaggerated grandeur of court figures.

An interesting point about the use of a well-known myth in a poem where the protagonists can be identified with real people is that readers are free to accept more of the myth than the poet chooses to mention explicitly. This is a way of encoding dangerous material. For example, Chaucer's readers might know that Aphrodite–Venus eventually had a very brief affair with Hermes–Mercury, who figures only marginally in the poem. They might also know that the myth involved a row over Venus' marriage portion, which might, in real life, have been at issue too. One remembers that the supposed real-life Mars seduced the real-life Venus before marriage, which might have upset his father-in-law, John of Gaunt.

We see that the language of astrology is finely adapted to making covert communications, sometimes topical or personal, but not necessarily always so. Recent work on numerology in poetry reveals other secret devices. Helena Shire in *A Preface to Spenser* notes that 'the central line of the central Book in Chaucer's "Troilus and Criseyde"' identifies Criseyde with Fortune. This was a device Spenser and other admirers of Chaucer used.

The theme of secrecy recurs. Meanwhile, I emphasize that Chaucer added to his source material the striking astrological element, linking gods and a goddess to actual planetary movements at an identifiable time. He originated this particular interweaving of astrological, mythological, and (probably) biographical strands. Would astrological Mars and Venus emerge untinged by such interweaving?

MARS

It is very desirable that literary critics should emphasize the poetic effects of Chaucer's astrology; they should not allow the glossing of technicalities (sometimes viewed as 'vexatious astrological detail') to take over. Surely it is just as important that historians of astrology should be sensitive to these poetic effects if their influence upon generations of his readers is to be at all understood? For it is when the imagination is enhanced and stimulated by poetry that ideas may enter and take up residence in the reader's mind and memory. What is encountered may be rejection, acceptance, or reassessment – but the idea registers.

The poetic impact of the dense, terse passage describing the temple of Mars in 'The Knight's Tale' is very powerful (line 1995 ff.).

While it follows Boccaccio's 'Teseida', there are additions and variations by Chaucer; for example, 'The smyler with the knyf under the cloke' – a line which is echoed in Shakespeare's *Othello*, 'that a man may smile and smile and be a villain'. Perhaps we have some autobiographical input here, secretly slipped into this context? Living close to the centre of power Chaucer very likely experienced treachery to himself and, later, to friends of his who had supported Richard II and who were hanged or beheaded.

> Ther saugh I first the derke imagynyng
> Of Felonye, and al the compassyng [plotting];
> The cruel Ire, reed as any gleede [burning coal];
> The pykepurs, and eek the pale Dreede [extreme fear];
> The smylere with the knyf under the cloke;
> The shepne [ship] brennynge with the blake smoke . . .
> The sleere [slayer] of himself yet saugh I ther, –
> His herte-blood hath bathed al his heer . . .
>
> 'The Knight's Tale', lines 1,995–2,006

These 'derke imagynings' are pictures, painted on the walls of the temple of Mars, of all the devastation wrought by rage, fire and the sword. The temple itself is, appropriately, of burnished steel, its vast pillars of shining iron, its door of adamant. All the astrological associations are there, down to the barber, butcher and smith – people of Mars becuse they live by the knife. But there is no hint of military glory – all is hateful destruction. Whereas in the *Complaint of Mars* the god's amorousness was ridiculed, here only the cruel side of Mars' energies is depicted.

At the end of the description of the temple we see the statue of the gods, looking 'grym as he were wood' (mad, raging); a red-eyed wolf lies at his feet, eating a man. The anti-chivalric portrayal of Mars is a curious commentary on the tale told by the Knight. His persona as narrator is not consistently maintained, but we do see him as a real person with experience, like Chaucer, of the realities of battle, and telling a tale with a knightly atmosphere. Chaucer's selection of material from his sources and his chosen emphases cannot but make the contrast between this chivalric story and the dark, inglorious images in the temple curiously striking.

The planetary temples which are described in such detail in this Tale are set up as part of the arrangements for the single combat of Palamon and Arcite, prisoners of Theseus, who allows them to fight for the hand of his sister-in-law, Emelye.[8] Arcite, a devotee of Mars, wins the contest; but in his moment of victory Venus and Saturn intervene. Arcite is thrown from his horse and killed because Pluto, at Saturn's request, caused the earth to move.[9] His opponent, Palamon, for whom Venus intervened, marries Emelye after long mourning for Arcite who was his dearest friend. So we see that Mars gives Arcite victory and death, while Venus gives Palamon his beloved, but also the loss of his friend; for she cannot prevail against Saturn, she can only modify Mars.

Saturn's part in this contention will be considered later.

Both Saturn and Mars are painted in dark colours. Where is righteous energy symbolized, one might ask? Intellectual energy is Mercurial, together with other less attractive attributes such as trickery. Jupiter's energy is that of the ruler, but in 'The Knight's Tale' he cannot settle the dispute between Venus and Mars when they find they have granted contradictory wishes to Palamon and Arcite.

THE TWO VENUSES

Having considered Mars and Venus as planetary personages in the *Complaint of Mars*, there are two kinds of example I would like to focus upon next: Venus in relation to character and the attributes of Venus as an entity.

The self-description of the Wife of Bath gives a partial view of her horoscope in terms of Taurus rising with Mars in the ascendant.[10] She says that Venus ruling her ascendant gives her her lecherousness while Mars provides her 'sturdy hardynesse'. She characterizes herself, too, by the fatalism of her view.

She also says she has the 'seel' or birthmark of Mars on her body.[11] It is interesting that Lilly retained this tradition and attached great importance to it.[12] She explains the antagonism between women and 'clerkes' by pointing out that Mercury (ruling writers and philosophy), and Venus (signifying women and physical pleasure here), each has its Exaltation in the other's Fall; a succinct expression of her view that women always had a bad press. In the *Legend of Good Women*, Chaucer introduces a passage not in his source material, into the ninth legend of Hypermnestra; her horoscope is related to her character.[13] It is very different from the Wife of Bath example.

Venus gives her beauty, and is configured with Jupiter so she is sensitive, serious, wise and 'trewe as stel'. As Mars in her horoscope is weak, and 'tempered' by the power of Venus and by House position, 'his venim is adoun'. Her father, Egistes, marries her to his nephew, whom he fears, and tells her on her wedding day to kill her husband that night – threatening death if she disobeys. Her weak Mars makes her unable to use the knife he gives her, and the qualities of her Venus–Jupiter aspect lead her to warn her husband to escape. However, bad Saturn aspects cause her to die imprisoned by her father; her weak Mars, which makes her reject the (Martian) knife, also prevents her from escaping with her husband. This is all expressed in a very deterministic way.

I have taken the Wife of Bath, Hypermnestra, and the Venus–person–planet of the *Complaint of Mars* as examples of Chaucer's presentation of Venus in relation to women seen as real. With Hypermnestra, good comes of Venus being configured with Jupiter – only so, it seems, can Venus *be* 'good'. The other two women stand, with more or less charm, for excessive sexuality – lecherousness, as the Wife of Bath says.

THE BACKGROUND OF THE TWO VENUSES

At this point we have to consider the two Venuses of Greek mythology. (In Roman mythology she had a modest place, symbolizing spring and fruitfulness.) The elder Venus was Aphrodite, daughter of Uranus. She was born from the foam when Cronus (known later as Kronos, and later still as Saturnus) castrated his father, Uranus, and threw his genitals into the sea. Thus she had no mother – no female taint – and was known as 'Heavenly Aphrodite'. It is this aspect of Venus as a heavenly goddess to whom Troilus prays that is invoked in *Troilus and Criseyde*.

The second, 'common', Venus–Aphrodite was the daughter of Zeus and Dione, who herself was the daughter of either Oceanus and Tethys, the sea-nymph, or of Air and Earth. Her mother's air and earth origins are commemorated astrologically by Venus' dignities in Libra (air) and Taurus (earth). Her Exaltation in Pisces relates well to her foam-born nature, while her Detriment in Scorpio may be appropriate to her reputation for promiscuity. Doves and sparrows, which are among her attributes, were known for their lechery.

These two Aphrodites are discussed in Plato's *Symposium* with varying degrees of seriousness, the 'common' Aphrodite being identified with heterosexuality, and disparaged for that reason. Heavenly Aphrodite was seen as belonging to the love of men for other men, and for lofty abstract concepts and aspirations.

Chaucer's emphasis is upon the very 'earthy' side of common Venus, and upon her deceptiveness which leads to sorrows. He deals also with the airy, celestial side of heavenly Venus (though he calls her the daughter of Jove). For example, in *Troilus and Criseyde* the goddess is invoked and praised: nothing in the living world exists without her, she is the cause of harmony whether cosmic or between friends.[14] There are touches of another Venus, doubtfully benign, throughout the poem. We are told that she is not hostile in Troilus' horoscope; also that she was in Seventh House Libra at the moment when Criseyde, knowing he loves her, sees Troilus for the first time. So much for the deluding nature of Venus – here the faithlessness of Criseyde is a comment on the planet's dubious powers.

We see again that it is only when Venus relates to Jupiter that she is helpful, as in the horoscope of Hypermnestra, and when she intercedes for Aeneas. Even when she helps Palamon in 'The Knight's Tale', Saturn brings the death of their friend to sadden the lovers. In her temples we see her welcoming all and sundry who 'have the attribute of Priapus' to her bower, and her charms are seen in a context of sordid intrigue and prostitution. It is, of course, a question of emphasis, and of selection by a very selective writer.

The best that can be said is that Venus can 'temper' Mars, reducing his venom.

> And she hath take him in subjeccioun,
> And as a maistresse taught him his lessoun . . .
> For she forbad him jelosye at alle,
> And crueltee, and bost, and tyrannye . . .
> And thus she brydeleth him in hir manere,
> With no-thing but with scourgyng [chastening him]
> of hir chere [with a look].
>
> *Complaint of Mars*, lines 32–3, 36–7, 41–2

Even when the celestial Venus is praised (for example in Book III of *Troilus and Criseyde*), this plea is added:

> And this knowe I by hem that lovers be,
> That whoso stryveth with yow hath the werse.
> Now, Lady bryght, for thi benignite,
> At reverence of hem that serven the,
> Whose clerc I am, so techeth me devyse
> Som joye of that is felt in thi servyse.[15]

Writing about Chaucer's admirer and successor, Edmund Spenser, Professor Fowler refers to 'the ninety or so Venuses distinguished by the mythographers'.[16] Boccaccio, whose *Filostrato* Chaucer transformed and mingled with other sources in the *Troilus*, was also a learned mythographer. Chaucer knew his *Genealogia Deorum Gentilium* (*On the Genealogy of the Gentile Gods*), and knew too a range of sources from classical to contemporary, which his Italian, French and adequate Latin made available to him.

What Chaucer chose to do with this range of material about Venus was to acknowledge her charms but always to add a cautionary note. Even when he writes of celestial Venus we see that he adds:

> And this knowe I by hem [them] that lovers be,
> That who so stryveth with yow hath the werse.

This is something of the picture of Venus that Chaucer has presented to generations of hearers and readers. His poetry holds goddess and planet there, shimmering, shifting, merging, with outlines often blurred; and all the time there is a drifting of the goddess's qualities which cluster round the astrological notions. It is, of course, an age-old process, this interaction between the reputations of gods and planets.

THE TEMPLES OF VENUS AND HER ATTRIBUTES

There are three passages – two of them descriptions of her temples – which deal with the attributes of Venus in detail, and which exemplify a tendency to emphasize deception and the negative side of her influence.

The description of the temple of Venus in 'The Knight's Tale' is based on Boccaccio's *Teseida*, but with the source condensed and varied. Chaucer handles this theme elsewhere, in the *House of Fame* and in the *Parlement of Fowles*.

The first wall paintings in the temple described by the Knight show the sorrows of love, followed by:

> Pleasaunce and Hope, Desir, Foolhardynesse,
> Beautee and Youthe, Bauderie, Richesse,
> Charmes and Force, Lesynges [deceptions, losses]
> Flaterye,
> Despense Bisynesse [care, anxiety], and Jalousye . . .[17]

Venus is garlanded with yellow flowers – yellow stands for jealousy – and there is the ill-omened cuckoo on her hand. All the paraphernalia of love is shown, and Venus' garden with its porter, called Ydelnesse. There are references to the folly of Solomon, the enchantments of Medea and Circe: all 'thise folk so caught were in her las' (Venus' snare). The atmosphere is pervaded by sadness and deception. The delightful vision of Venus, garlanded and naked in the sea, with doves fluttering above her head, ends with a view of the sharp arrows of Cupid, her son.

The passage in the *Parlement of Fowles*[18] begins with an idyllic description of Venus' garden, where all is peace and harmony in a temperate climate, but again we see Cupid with his arrows, 'some for to sle [slay] and some to wounde and kerve [pierce]'. There is emphasis on go-betweens and bribery (Venus rules money, here in a negative way), on jealousy as the cause of sorrow, and on the god Priapus and the lasciviousness of Venus. There follows a list of those who have suffered through love.

In *The House of Fame*[19] the narrator in his dream finds himself in a temple of glass; its luxurious Venusian appointments are described at some length; elaborate decorations, paintings and golden images. A passage follows which is close to 'The Knight's Tale' description of Venus 'naked fletyng in the sea'. Next the dreamer sees (in lines summarised from early parts of Virgil's *Aeneid*) the fall of Troy, caused by the deception the Greeks practised with the Trojan horse.

It is interesting that there was a very general medieval belief that the fall of Troy – that event which dominated the imagination – was caused by Venusian excesses.

But the negative Venus traits are not emphasized here as they are in the other two temple descriptions, perhaps because Venus makes a divine intervention in her celestial guise, telling Aeneas to flee from Troy, and later persuading Jupiter to save the Trojan navy; thus she is seen in a merciful role. However, the poem continues with a gallery of men as deceivers,[20] and examples of unfaithful lovers, so the atmosphere of deception is there. The narrator, quite disoriented by all he has seen, longs to be delivered from 'fantomes and illusion'.

SATURN

As we have seen, there are memorable concentrations of planetary attributes in 'The Knight's Tale', in the descriptions of the temples of Venus and Mars. It is a poem of great astrological decorum where planetary hours are matched to appropriate deeds. The gods are presented both as people and as astrological beings, and we see them in contention.

Arcite has prayed to Mars and been promised victory in his combat with Palamon, who in turn has been promised by Venus the hand of Emelye for whose love they fight. Jupiter is unable to reconcile Mars and Venus, and Saturnus intervenes.

> 'My deere doghter Venus,' quod Saturne,
> My cours, that hath so wyde for to turne,
> Hath more power than woot any man.
> Myn is the drenching in the sea so wan;
> Myn is the prison in the derke cote;
> Myn is the stranglyng and hangyng by the throte,
> . . .
> Myn is the ruyne of the hye halles,
> The fallyng of the toures and of the walles
> Upon the mynour or the carpenter.
> . . .
> And myne be the maladyes colde,
> The dark treasons, and the castes [devices] old.
> 'The Knight's Tale', lines 2,453–8, 2,463–5, 2,467–8

Beginning with an untypical endearment to Venus, he says that as her aiel (grandfather) he will arrange that Arcite shall have the victory but Palamon shall have his love, Emilye. We find that this comes about when Theseus allows the marriage after a characteristically Saturnian delay.

Saturn's self description is a dark, horrific speech that must have coloured views of him indelibly in many minds. Arcite's fall from his frightened horse is in his moment of victory:

> His brest torbresten [shattered by] his saddle-bowe,
> As blak he lay as any cole or crowe,
> So was the blood yronnen on his face.
> 'The Knight's Tale', lines 2,691–3

Arcite's long-drawn-out death is grisly and Saturnian, even to the detail that his system cannot in any way expel the corruption within it, for bodily retention is Saturnian too.[21]

Saturn claims the deaths caused by constraint, strangling and hanging; Mars kills with knives but also those 'strangled with the wilde beres' and 'the cartere overryden with his carte', which seem outside his province.

Because of his vast orbit (*cours*) Saturn asserts his immense power, beyond the knowledge of Mars and Venus. Jupiter too seems ineffectual at this point. Saturn's would-be conciliatory 'My deere doghter Venus' masks his cruel, ironic device; he delegates to Pluto the subsidence that makes Arcite's horse fall, not a task for Saturn; whereas Pluto, Lord of the Underworld, was an appropriate agent.

In the Middle Ages generally Saturn is a very dark figure. Yet Chaucer knew Dante's 'paradiso', where the golden ladder which leads to the heights of spiritual contemplation is placed in the heaven of Saturn. This thread is picked up today by writers such as Isabel Hickey[22] who writes of the solitary mountain goat side of Saturn-ruled Capricorn who climbs to the spiritual heights, and who brings discipline. It was C. E. O. Carter who wrote that the 'virtues' of the malefics are 'practical and even severe. Fortitude, duty and self-control . . . '[23] Others have followed this trend. Edward Whitman links Saturn to business capacity, responsibility, patience, planning and hard work.[24]

This links up with Saturn in Roman mythology; some say he was an ancient agricultural divinity of Latin origin, a working god who sowed seeds and tended vines – activities to promote future benefit; this was before Hellenization identified him with Kronos. The Romans believed him to be a foreign god and his story fitted in with the flight of Kronos from Zeus.[25]

Kronos would account for the darkest side of Saturn. The youngest son of Heaven and Earth, he castrated his father, Uranus, and later swallowed all his male children except the youngest, Zeus. (This story is considered so bizarre that it may be pre-Hellenic.) To protect their son, Zeus, his wife wrapped a stone in swaddling clothes which Kronos swallowed, later vomiting up all his children, who overcame him.

The more agreeable attributes of Saturn descend from writers such as Jovianus Pontanus[26] quoted by Robert Burton (1577–1640) in his *Anatomy of Melancholy*,[27] where Saturn is said to be 'still delighting in husbandry, woods, orchards . . . thoughts turn on plans of buildings, planting trees, tilling fields . . . '

In that strange poem, *The House of Fame*, which describes a sort of vision or intellectual journey, Chaucer presents the nature of Saturn in a rather different guise. The poet sees the great writers of the past standing on pillars made of metals with planetary significance:

> Upon a piler stonde on high,
> That was of led [lead] and yren [iron] fyn,
> Hym of secte saturnyn,

The Ebrayk Josephus, the olde,
That of Jewes gestes [exploits] tolde;
And he bar [bore] on hys shuldres hye
The fame up of the Jewerye.

Saturn is associated with Josephus, writer of the *Historia Judaeorum*, because of the astrological doctrine that the Jewish religion, from which other religions descend, is represented by the father of the planets. Seven other (unspecified) worthies support him.

And for they writen of batayles,
As wel as other olde mervayles,
Therfor was, loo, thys piler
Of which that I yow telle her,
Of led and yren both, ywys,
For yren Martes metal ys,
Which that god is of bataylle;
And the led, withouten faille,
Is, loo, the metal of Saturne,
That hath a ful large whel to turne.
The House of Fame, Book III, lines 1,430–1,436, and 1,441–1,450

These points are made insistently. After the unusual twinning of Mars with Saturn in this context, Chaucer ends by referring to the grandeur of Saturn's orbit. Homer is set on an iron pillar, Virgil on one 'that was of tynned iron cler', which suggests Jupiter and Mars. This has been interpreted as a reference to Jupiter controlling Mars in Virgil's *Aeneid*. Venus' metal, copper, was an obvious choice for Ovid. Claudian, the late Roman poet who wrote of Pluto and Proserpina, has a pillar of sulphur (brimstone), alluding to the Underworld. (Chaucer seems here to have suggested a substance for the then undiscovered planet Pluto to rule.) But these other attributions are presented with little comment, as if the reader would find them obviously appropriate.

Chaucer is here extending the repertoire of planetary associations. Placing writers like planetary gods on metal plinths in *The House of Fame*, he prompts the reader to consider the planetary nature of their stories – in other words, to think astrologically.

Notes on the Background of Chaucer's Technical Knowledge of Astrology

Chaucer did not go to university where he would have studied astronomy in the Quadrivium, a course of studies consisting of arithmetic, geometry, astronomy and music. He went to a London grammar school, probably the Almonry School at St Paul's Cathedral. Professor D. R. Howard, in *Chaucer and the Medieval World*,[28] has an interesting chapter on his probable early studies. He was then educated as a courtier in the household of the Countess of Ulster, where he served as a page; later, as a young squire in the royal household, he was probably trained at the Inns of Court for his distinguished career as diplomat and important administrator.

If, as Professor Howard suggests, Chaucer did go to St Paul's and came under the influence of William Shenstone, an early humanist, he would have had access to a generous boys' school library. This included classical and literary books as well as Boethius, Euclid, Pythagoras and Ptolemy, which were less to Shenstone's taste.

As early as 1095 the first English astrolabe was in the possession of Walcher, Prior of Malvern. In about 1120 Adelard of Bath returned from his travels to Antioch bringing Arabic tables which he adapted to English latitudes and texts which he translated into Latin, working with other scientists in the Worcester–Hereford–Malvern area, which was a centre for such studies. Their work is described by R. W. Southern[29] in *Robert Grosseteste* and in *Adelard of Bath*, by Margaret Gibson.[30] They included Daniel of Morley and Alfred of Shareshill – men adventurous enough to give up conventional careers and seek fresh knowledge which had passed from Greek into Arabic translations.

There had been tremendous activity in Arabian astrology from the tenth to the twelfth century, when many earlier authors were compiled; this was followed by much translation of Arabic into Latin in the twelfth century. In the process it became unclear what had been originally written by whom, and when.

Chaucer had many astrological authorities available to him but he only mentions three: Ptolemy, Alcabitius and Alkindi. However, there are sometimes marginal notes on manuscripts of his poems; these supposedly identify the authorities he used, giving quotations from them. For example, in 'The Man of Law's Tale', where Chaucer introduces material not in his source, the Man of Law deplores the emperor's folly in not having the moment for his daughter's departure on her wedding journey astrologically elected.

Is no time bet than oother in swich cas?
Of viage is ther noon eleccioun . . . ?

lines 311–12

In the Ellesmere and Hengwrt MSS there are marginal notes[31] quoting the *Liber Electionum* of Zael, an early ninth century astronomer. Chaucer attracts the reader's sympathy for his heroine and rebukes her father's carelessness. This more than satisfies the narrative demands; but, as so often, Chaucer introduces astrological detail of his own. This has often been discussed: my point is that it raises – and satisfies – curiosity about astrological elections and their purpose.

THE 'TREATISE ON THE ASTROLABE'

The *Treatise on the Astrolabe* was written about 1391 for Little Lowis, a boy of 10 years who may have been Chaucer's own child or his friend Lowis Clifford's son. The boy died and this may have been why the *Treatise* was not completed. Only the Prologue, Part I and an incomplete Part II survive. The book is not mentioned in Chaucer's *Retractions* as something he repented of writing – quite a significant point since he withdrew all that he thought was contrary to religion.

The striking fact for the history of astrology is that this treatise was written in English: 'And preie God save the king that is lord of this language.' This choice was a considered act: was it only for the little boy who did not know much Latin? 'Now wol I preie mekely every discret persone that redith or herith this litel tretys . . . ' – Chaucer is speaking, over the head of the little boy to a larger audience, asking them to excuse the simple and repetitive style suitable for a child. Professor Howard remarks that the scholar John Trevisa observed 'that children in grammar schools now learned their lessons in English, not French' (by 1385). Like Little Lowis, grammar school boys would learn Latin but might find the Latin into which Arabic works were translated a hard struggle.[32]

It was a dramatic and democratic act to write the first treatise of its kind in the vernacular (it is comparable to the decision of John Dee to explain and introduce Euclid in English – but that was in the seventeenth century). The simplicity and straightforwardness of the style, with problems to work for practice, would be helpful to many readers besides children.

Twenty-five manuscripts survive. Some of these are illustrated with drawings; one has more than sixty fine ones. Illustrations are reproduced by R. C. Gunther.[33]

Chaucer writes in his prologue: 'I n'am but a lewd compilator of the labour of olde astrologiens.' His treatise is largely a translation, sometimes amplified, from Messahalla, the eighth-century Arab astronomer, with some explanations and definitions from other sources, including interpolations of purely astrological matter.

We have only the Prologue, Part I, and an incomplete Part II. Five parts are promised in the Prologue. Part I is very much a 'naming of parts' of what Chaucer emphasizes is a small, portative astrolabe; this would be convenient for travel and perhaps for the medical purposes mentioned in the canons of Nicholas of Lynn's *Kalendarium*, to which I shall return.

In fact Part I also deals briefly with the signs of the zodiac, saying (without disclaimer) that the sun and planets take on the properties of each sign as they enter it; and that when a hot planet enters a hot sign it becomes hotter, or less cold if it is a cold planet. This, he says, applies to all the signs, be they moist or dry, movable or fixed. Chaucer promises that correspondences between the signs and parts of the body, only mentioned in Part I, will be 'shewid more plleyn' in Part V.

Since we have no trace of Part V this is interesting, for the Brussels MS has a drawing showing the relation between signs and parts of the body.[34] One wonders if drawings were executed or commissioned before the writing was done, or if this example belongs with lost Part V material.

The Prologue says Part II will teach how to operate the astrolabe; there is also, in section four, a 'special declaracioun of the ascendent'. It is pointed out that the ascendant is something that 'astrologiens gretly observen' so that 'me semeth convenyent' to give it attention.[35]

Chaucer then defines the astrological requirements for a fortunate ascendant. The passage is not in Messahalla; Chaucer decided to interpolate it. Then comes a ritual disclaimer whose precise application is not absolutely clear:

> Natheles these ben observaunces of judicial matere and rytes of payens, in whiche my spirit hath no feith, ne knowing of her [their] *horoscopum*. For they seyn that every signe is departid [divided] in thre even parties by 10 degrees, and thilke porcioun they clepe [call] a face. And although that a planete have a latitude fro the ecliptik, yit sey somme folk, so

> [if] that the planete arise in the same signe with eny degre of the forseide face in which his longitude is rekned, that yit is the planete *in horoscopo*, be it in nativyte or in eleccion, etc.
> 'Treatise on the Astrolabe', Part II, section 4, line 57 ff., in F. N. Robinson (ed.) *Works*, (1974)

It is not clear if exception is taken to what has gone before (that is, the definition of when a planet is said to be in the ascendant according to 'statutes of astrologiens', and the other conditions for a fortunate ascendant, such as benign aspects), or if exception is taken particularly to those who use loose criteria in deciding when a planet is *in horoscopo*. This involved the three ten-degree 'faces', a usage he may have found 'payen'; he certainly seems to be distancing himself from it. The first face of a sign is ruled by that sign's planet; the second by the planetary ruler of the next sign in the same element fowards in the zodiac; and the third by the third. I suggest that 'somme folk' are distinguished from astrologers in general and that Chaucer is getting at something both illogical and dependent on a doctrine he disapproves of.

Part II includes House division with the practical instruction promised and warns the astrologer that a small instrument cannot be very accurate.

Chaucer writes that he will include in Part III a number of tables from unspecified sources: longitudes and latitudes of fixed stars; declinations of the sun; longitudes of cities and towns; and for the 'governaunce of a clokke as for to fynde the altitude meridian'. He adds finally: 'and many another notable conclusioun after the Kalenders of the reverent clerkes, Frere J. Somer and Frere N. [Nicholas] Lenne [Lynn]'.[36]

Nicholas was a Carmelite friar working in Oxford. In 1386 he composed a *Kalendarium* to begin in 1387 and continue to 1462. He says he writes at the request of John of Gaunt, Duke of Lancaster, with whom Chaucer, of course, had connections.

Four of the fifteen surviving manuscripts could have been seen by Chaucer; others, Professor Eisner writes, were probably copied after his death. One can only speculate on what other 'notable conclusiouns' from the *Kalendarium* Chaucer would have included in his third part. His treatise, with all he promised, would have been remarkably compendious if completed.

Nicholas includes the famous shadow scale so often referred to in Chaucer's poetry. It shows how, by the altitude of the sun and a shadow of a man one may know the hour and minute of the clock at any time of the artificial day. There is much detail on solar and lunar eclipses, fully illustrated with diagrams; how to find the cusps of Houses; dignities and strengths of planets in the signs; planetary hours; daily moon positions. All this material is explained in canons at the end including medical ones giving suitable conditions for bloodletting, purging and receiving medicine.

Chaucer's Part IV was to have included a theoretical explanation of the movements of the celestial bodies, with the causes. Also – surely very ambitious – he would show the motion of the moon for every hour in every day; very useful in astrology and perhaps particularly so for electional, horary and medical purposes. Lastly:

> The fifthe partie shal be an introductorie, after the statutes of our doctours, in which thou maist lerne a gret part of the generrall rewles of theorik in astrologie. In which fifthe partie shalt thou fynden tables of equaciouns of houses after the latitude of Oxenforde; and tables of dignitees of planetes, and other noteful thinges, yf God wol vouche sauf [permit] and his Moder the Maide [Mother the Virgin], moo than I behete [more than I promise].
>
> 'Treatise on the Astrolabe', Prologue, line 100 ff., in F. N. Robinson (ed.), *Works*

It may be that Chaucer would have used Nicholas' table of Planetary Hours (*Kalendarium*, unnumbered pages 176–7); in this fifth part, and also his table of dignities of planets in the signs, which included terms and faces. The columns for terms have the heading: '*Termini planetarum in signis secundum Egypcios et dicuntur esse hermetis*', which Eisner translates as: 'The terms of the planets in signs according to the Egyptians they are said to be from the desert [*hermetis*]' (*Kalendarium*, pp. 180–1). We are left to speculate on what 'more than he promised' Chaucer might have intended to include in this astrological part.

This brief look at what astrological material Chaucer included and said he intended to include in his treatise gives us a view of what the literate but unlearned reader had presented to him – and may have had presented to him if other parts were later lost – from 1392 onwards, and after the advent of printing.

It is interesting to compare the last quotation from Chaucer's

Prologue with the following, which considers the prose style of the 'Retractions' and this treatise:

> The only passage like [the 'Retractions'] is the opening of the 'Treatise on the Astrolabe', addressed to 'Little Louis my son', in which he appears – this once – in the role of a loving father teaching his child how to operate an instrument for navigation, the astrolabe, ancestor of the sextant.
> D. R. Howard, *Chaucer and the Medieval World* (1987), p. 499

It is not easy to see what 'rewles of theorik of astrology' had to do with navigation – mentioned to exorcize Chaucer's astrology.

Whatever else the historian of astrology can learn from the *Treatise on the Astrolabe*, he certainly receives some striking facts. First, Chaucer, an immensely busy man, chose to give time to the arduous task of translating Messahalla into clear, straightforward English, vastly increasing its availability; then he chose to insert astrological matter with the promise of more to come. Astrology was thus disseminated with the practical instructions for the operation of the instrument. It seemed to him 'convenyent' to give special attention to the astrological conditions for a fortunate ascendant – because, he says, those are *important to astrologers*. He also proposed to include material from Nicholas of Lynn – already available to the learned in the Latin he would translate. Lastly, if we take little Lewis seriously as his audience, Chaucer must have regarded his material as of the highest educational value.

On the basis of Chaucer's continuous popularity with a widening audience, and of the survival of twenty-five manuscripts, it is not wild speculation to conclude that this treatise enabled many potential astrologers to practise their art.

In considering how Chaucer disseminated a knowledge of astrology the *Treatise on the Astrolabe* must come first in importance, but it would appeal chiefly to those already interested in the subject. John Lydgate, writing about thirty years after Chaucer's death, attributes a treatise on astronomy and astrology to him: 'a tretis, full noble and of gret pris, upon thastrolabe'. A number of manuscripts confirm the attribution which is no longer disputed. A more sophisticated work from the scientific point of view is the *Equatorie of the Planetis*, which was discovered and edited by Dr Derek Price. The attribution of this to Chaucer remains in doubt.

An example of a more popular kind of publicity for astrology is found in the repeated references to the 'shadow scale' which recurs in the poetry, amongst a miscellany of other astrological references. When Chaucer wrote that the Host in *Canterbury Tales* knew that on 18 April shadows at 10 a.m. are just as long as the objects which cause them he could hardly have guessed that in the later twentieth century a professor would come to England to verify the fact:

> The Host is right here; his statement agrees with Nicholas's shadow scale. I also knew that the host is right because on one 27 April, our Gregorian equivalent to Chaucer's Julian 18 April, standing in the rare sunshine of Chaucer's island and latitude, I too measured a shadow . . .
>
> Sigmund Eisner, *Nicholas of Lynn's Kalendarium*, p. 30

CHAUCER'S SUCCESSIVE AUDIENCES

To consider Chaucer's effect on the history of astrological ideas one must look first at the salient fact that he wrote in English and in his uniquely memorable way. This greatly increased the availability of those ideas, presented sometimes very explicitly, sometimes ambivalently, sometimes, one might say, encoded.

With the courtly shorter poems and *Troilus and Criseyde* Chaucer is seen as addressing a more or less immediate courtly audience, which would have increasingly included women – who protested when they thought his poetry maligned them. To assess the atmosphere we should remember that European royal libraries contained beautifully illuminated books on astrology and the occult. (An example is the one which included a geomancy and was commissioned by Richard II.) We know that John of Gaunt (whose mistress was Chaucer's sister-in-law) was patron to Nicholas of Lynn, whose *Kalendarium* with its unique shadow scale Chaucer constantly publicized in the *Canterbury Tales*. All this suggests the interests current in a leisured circle, where certain hours were set aside for civilized discussion, and where Chaucer, a trained courtier, was welcome for his recitations. Whether he played the astrologer at court would always have been secret, but no one reading him closely can doubt his competence.

By 1386 the *Troilus* was complete and Chaucer turned his mind to the *Canterbury Tales*. He was living by then in Kent, further from a court which had become unsettled and dangerous. The people he presents stand for both town and country; they include business people (the Wyf of Bath owned a cloth-making concern), and the expanding administrative and merchant class. The poem itself is acutely audience-conscious. The teller defines himself in the telling of his tale; the interchanges – notably between the touchy Reeve and the drunken Miller – give audience responses to a tale which may prove too near the bone. Chaucer mediates this to his reading audience by pointing out that they may 'turne over the leef and chese another tale'; he promises plenty of 'moralitee and hoolynesse', all tastes catered for.

Probably Chaucer was thinking of a largely male readership – after all more men than women were literate. The reader can not only select, he can return frequently to certain passages, as his friends Gower and Hoccleve would, and as other readers curious about astrology might do. His readership would include men of the expanding merchant class who, like Chaucer himself, might move via the Inns of Court training into administration, by-passing the university and so missing its schooling in astronomy and advanced Latin. Such men had a wide range of contacts with other classes, as Chaucer did. (One should not forget his fluency in Italian, and diplomatic journeys to Genoa and Florence as sources of astrological ideas.) Our means of assessing the number of his readers is from the state of the manuscripts which shows that many private copies of the *Tales* were made.

To a solitary reader or to those listening in a group in his own day Chaucer's style is extremely inviting. He does not have an aggressively 'button-holing' manner, but his hand is often engagingly at the reader's elbow, suggesting parallels between the story and his own experience, prompting reflection, using the second person singular or plural to invoke sympathy and understanding, flattering the reader with the assumption that his judgement counts.

As in the poetry, so in the *Treatise on the Astrolabe*: the reader is nudged and cajoled into participation in the problems or 'conclusions' he must work out to practise his knowledge.

Various indications survive to show how Chaucer was received and valued in the early times after his death. An unknown writer in 1477 advised his son to read everything by Chaucer; his language was so 'fayr and pertinente'. About 1540 someone wrote that 'Chaucer wrote much to do us good'. A man who would not swear on the Bible said he would agree to swear 'on the book called Chaucer'. Caxton, who first printed the *Canterbury Tales* in 1478 wrote in 1483, 'He wryteth no voyde words'; this not only praised conciseness but perhaps advised close reading, when 'more is meant than meets the ear', as Milton was to write of Spenser's *Faerie Queene* with its complex astrological basis.

There are, as it were, branches to the dissemination and survival of ideas presented by Chaucer. By translating Boethius' *Consolations of Philosophy* into English he made widely available to literate but not learned readers a text with astrological content, known in Latin throughout the Middle Ages. We have seen the practical technical value of the *Treatise on the Astrolabe*. I have exemplified the poetic impact of certain astrological themes – a few among many – and suggested the intimate way they are woven into the texture of situation and character. When gods and planets inhabit the same story, a subtle interchange occurs.

Scholars, sometimes with distaste, have faced the need to understand Chaucer's astrology in order to understand his poetry. The multiplicity and variety of astrological allusions are valuable pointers to technical practice, needing close examination and informed interpretation. For the preservation of such material we have to thank the excellence of his writing and the respectability his name could confer – for we know his work was exempt from certain forms of censorship just because it was his.

Within the political and religious constraints of his day Chaucer had the great prerogative of creative writers: the power to choose. We see him exercise this in his choice of source material; his selection therefrom; his insertion of his own astrological material at key points; and we see him choose to be explicit where vagueness would have done in descriptions of astrological techniques.

Another significant 'branch' of Chaucer's influence has been on later writers. Astrological ideas pervade the poetry of Edmund Spenser, Chaucer's admirer and successor, as John Heath-Stubbs shows in a later chapter of this book.

During its long history Chaucer's writing has served as a reservoir of astrological ideas. This has continued to be accessible when other sources dried up or fell into disrepute. The extent of its influence is obvious in such poetry as Edmund Spenser's. It can only be guessed at in that unrecorded world of practice which, of its nature, will always remain obscure, especially in years when astrology went deeply underground.

No one can detach astrology from Chaucer, so long as his text itself is closely and candidly read. If we are to understand something of the mental furnishings of Chaucer's contemporaries and successors, from his day to ours, we cannot ignore these ideas. As I have suggested in discussing the changing reputations of the planets, the poet influence and still influences his readers' views of the celestial, forever prompting reflection and reappraisal.

Notes

1. R. Southern, *Robert Grosseteste* (1988).
2. John Buchanan-Brown (ed.), *Three Prose Works of John Aubrey*, ch. 16, (Centaur, 1972), p. 103.
3. Frances Yates, *Giordano Bruno and the Hermetic Tradition*, chs 2 and 4 (London: Routledge, 1964); for Ficino on Mars and Venus, see Ernst Gombrich, *Symbolic Images* (1972), pp. 66–9.
4. Claudius Ptolemy (1940), *Tetrabiblos* (Loeb, 1985), p. 397.
5. William Lilly, *Christian Astrology* (Regulus Pub. Co., 1647), pp. 116–18.
6. J. C. Eade, *The Forgotten Sky* (Oxford: OUP, 1984), p. 110.
7. D. R. Howard, *Chaucer and the Medieval World* (1987), p. 268 and note.
8. For the description of the temple of Venus see 'The Knight's Tale', line 1,918; and for the temple of Mars, see line 1,967. It is compared with the temple of Mars in Thrace. See also the paper in this book by Nicholas Kollerstrom, 'The Star Temples of Harran', for interesting comparisons.
9. G. Chaucer, 'The Knight's Tale', line 2,684.
10. G. Chaucer, 'The Wyf of Bath's Prologue', lines 609–20.
11. Ibid., line 604.
12. William Lilly, op. cit., pp. 148–9.
13. 'The Legend of Hypermnestra', *The Legend of Good Women*, IX lines 2, 580–99.
14. *Troilus and Criseyde*, Book 3, lines 1–49.
15. Ibid., lines 37–42.
16. Alastair Fowler, *Spenser and the Numbers of Time* (1964), p. 163.
17. 'The Knight's Tale', line 1925, ff.
18. *The Parlement of Fowles*, line 183.
19. *The House of Fame*, lines 119–39.
20. Ibid., lines 269–85.
21. See canon 12 in Nicholas of Lynn's *Kalendarium*.
22. Isabel Hickey, *A Cosmic Science* (1970).
23. C. E. Carter, *The Zodiac of the Soul* (US: Gordon, 1987).
24. Edward Whitman, *The Influence of the Planets* (Fowler, 1970).
25. *Larousse Encyclopaedia of Mythology*, p. 205, *Oxford Classical Dictionary* (1970).
26. Jovianus Pontanus, 'De Rebus Coelestibus', lib. 10, cap. 13.
27. Robert Burton, *The Anatomy of Melancholy* (1628), edited by Holbrook Jackson (Random House, 1977). The quotation is on pages 397–8 of Part 1, section 3, where a number of authorities

are cited for various attributes of Saturn.

28 D. R. Howard, *Chaucer and the Medieval World* (1987), p. 408.

29 Robert Southern, *Robert Grosseteste* (1988).

30 Margaret Gibson, 'Adelard of Bath', in Kraye, J. and Ryan, W. F. (eds), *Adelard of Bath*, ch. 14, p. 15 (Warburg Institute Surveys and Texts, 1987).

31 See F. N. Robinson (ed.) *Works* (1974), Explanatory Notes, p. 693, note to line 312.

32 D. R. Howard, op. cit., p. 25.

33 R. C. Gunther, 'Chaucer and Messahalla on the Astrolabe', *Early Science at Oxford*, vol. 5 (1929).

34 F. N. Robinson, op. cit., textual notes, p. 921, column 2, paragraph 3.

35 Ibid., p. 551, column 1.

36 Sigmund Eisner, *The Kalendarium of Nicholas of Lynn* (1980), p. 29, (Scolar). Professor Eisner points out here that none of the tables Chaucer mentions appears in the work of the Nicholas referred to, though he has material on the sun, the clock and the meridian, which was to be found elsewhere.

V

ASTROLOGICAL HISTORIOGRAPHY IN THE RENAISSANCE

The Work of Jean Bodin and Louis Le Roy

Nicholas Campion

Commentary

MUNDANE ASTROLOGY

> The Greeks have designated the world by a word that means 'ornament', and we have given it the name of mundus, because of its perfect finish and grace'
>
> Pliny, *De Natura Rerum*, Book 2, 111, 8

Mundane astrology is that branch of astrology that deals with society, or with the world as a whole. The original astrology of the Babylonians from c. 2000 to 500 BC was mundane in that it was concerned solely with the success and survival of the community. Predictions were made in relation to political events such as the prospects for peace or war, or climatic factors such as the imminence of drought or flood.

Genetheliacal astrology, in which horoscopes were cast for individuals, evolved during the fifth century, the first example dating from 410 BC, and after this time mundane astrology was gradually distinguished as a sub-division of astrology with its own rules.

The *Tetrabiblos*, written during the second century by the Alexandrian astrologer Claudius Ptolemy, included sections on the astrological rulership of nations that were accepted almost without question in medieval Europe and were finally discarded as late as the seventeenth century. Even now they continue in use amongst some astrologers.

To the Islamic astrologers of the early medieval period, mundane astrology was known as the study of 'Revolutions', their concern being mainly with the great revolutions of the planets, primarily Jupiter and

Saturn, and the grand cycles of history which these were said to rule. A number of standard texts were produced during this time, of which the great work by Abu Ma'shar, known to Europeans as Albumazar, became one of the foundations of European historiography until the seventeenth century.

A mundane astrologer had two tasks, to analyse short-term political trends and to shed light on the nature of long-term historical cycles. The latter were interpreted and measured with reference primarily to the Jupiter–Saturn cycles, but also to a host of minor cycles created partly by the relationship of other planets to these two, partly by reference to Pythagorean and other mystical numerology. Historical epochs were also divided according to general symbolic, cosmological principles quite aside from the astronomical motions of the planets.

Both short- and long-term trends were studied via the casting of horoscopes for precise astronomical moments such as, for example, a significant Jupiter–Saturn conjunction. Horoscopes were cast for the solar ingress (entry) into the four cardinal signs, Aries, Cancer, Libra and Capricorn, of which the most important was always the Aries ingress, this being the spring equinox and hence the beginning of the astrological year. Horoscopes for new and full moons offered detailed information for the coming month and the new moon of the year; the annual new moon in Aries was said to reveal the character of the year as a whole. Important political events such as the succession and coronation of monarchs or the beginnings of battles were made the subject of horoscopes and, where possible, timed in advance. The mundane astrologer in the service of a political patron would also be required to apply the rules of interrogations (horary astrology), use nativities to study the lives of his patron's family, friends and rivals, and refer to the rules of elections when advising on auspicious moments.

Mundane astrology was widely used as a result of its natural appeal to political leaders, whether spiritual or secular, for it promised a glimpse into the political future. The holder of this knowledge thus possessed a natural advantage in any conflict. It also held the power to destabilise shaky regimes, witness the frequent attempts to suppress almanacs and the other mass-produced astrological predictions which flooded the market after the invention of printing. In spite of its general acceptance mundane astrology also remained one of the most controversial branches of astrology, for its claim to predict the rise and fall of religions put it on a collision course with the church. That friction between the two was rare is a testimony to the discretion of the astrologers, but also to astrology's indispensable role as a means of political and historical analysis in Europe from the twelfth to seventeenth centuries.

N.C.

HISTORIOGRAPHY

Historiography, simply defined as 'the writing of history', is a word which distances one somewhat from those who write the history concerned, whether recent or ancient. In studying historiography one is taking a view of the views of others about the past, and considering those views from a different perspective.

Plutarch established the principle that history is not just a matter of dry abstractions, but that the will and feeling of individuals enter into it. He was even-handed in his presentation of Greek and Roman people in his biographies, and this 'illustrates the readiness with which Hellenistic historians perceived the significance of the Roman conquests and influenced Roman culture and historical writing. Greek authors were the first to realize the problem and importance for world history of the Roman Empire, and through them the Romans became conscious of the mission they were called on to fulfil'. (See the *Oxford Classical Dictionary*, 1970, article on Greek historiography, paragraph 7, p. 522.)

This is an impressive example of an influence seen to work benignly – the writing of history affecting history. But, as Nicholas Campion shows, such effects are not always benign.

The system of *astrological* historiography, in which epochs are defined in relation to planetary cycles, is part of Nicholas Campion's subject.

Nicholas Campion read history at Queens' College, Cambridge; he took postgraduate studies at London University, reading history and politics at the School of Oriental and African Studies and international relations at the London School of Economics. His books include *An Introduction to the History of Astrology*, *Mundane Astrology* and *The Book of World Horoscopes*.

He is a former president of the Astrological Lodge of London.

A. L. K.

TRADITION AND REVISION IN RENAISSANCE STUDIES

From the twelfth to the seventeenth century, astrology occupied an honoured role in European thought as a means of historical analysis. It could hardly be otherwise in a culture whose learning found its authority in the works of Plato and Aristotle as much as in the scriptures. Yet although the importance of astrological beliefs in European culture as a whole has been thoroughly documented by Lynn Thorndyke in his classic *History of Magic and Experimental*

Science,[1] historians have been noticeably slow to acknowledge its role in shaping historical beliefs, let alone to admit that astrology itself, as a study intimately concerned with the nature of time, served as a comprehensive philosophy of history.

Such disregard for the principle of free enquiry which is held to be a characteristic of modern historical method has led to various distortions in our understanding of the development of historical theory. For example, R. G. Collingwood writing in 1947, ascribed the division of history into epochs to early Christian historians, in complete defiance of the weight of evidence detailing the same practice in Babylonian, Assyrian, Persian, Greek and Roman historiography.[2] For Collingwood to do otherwise would have been to confront the role of astrology, and of related cosmological mythology, in shaping European concepts of historical change. Only within the last two decades have historians been generally prepared to acknowledge astrology's function as a philosophy of history or its role in shaping certain models of historical analysis which persist to this day. These historians, who are reassessing the general view of astrology's role in history, may be defined as revisionists in relation to those traditionalists for whom classical, medieval or Renaissance belief in astrology amounts to no more than irrelevant superstition.

Foremost among the revisionists is Eugenio Garin of the Istituto Nazionale di Studi sul Rinascimento in Florence. Garin has written that, during the Renaissance, astrology constituted a 'precise philosophy of history based on a conception of the universe and characterised by a consistent naturalism and a rigid determinism'.[3] Garin's judgement has been reinforced by Keith Thomas at Oxford, who argued that 'During the Italian Renaissance astrological doctrines about the recurrence of planetary conjunctions and their influence upon the course of affairs had helped to form the concept of a historical period'.[4] That historians are able to acknowledge the role of astrology in historical thought is welcome, yet these revisionists share traditionalist tendencies in a number of forms and have consequently repeated certain errors. Frequently, historical mistakes may be traced to a fundamental lack of familiarity with the nature and practices of astrology in the past. It is, for example, astonishing that Garin could claim that astrology was imbued with a rigid determinism when a substantial part of popular astrological practice, the diagnosis of disease and the treatment of the sick by the administration of medicinal remedies or the creation of talismans, was designed to change the future. The application of electional astrology by royal and ecclesiastical patrons to divine the most auspicious moment for the commencement of enterprises as significant as battles or royal reigns was clearly intended to shape the future to the individual will, a far cry from the passive acceptance of fate which most historians ascribe to astrology's medieval and Renaissance devotees. Similarly, Thomas's view that astrological notions gave rise to the idea of the historical period as late as the Renaissance is as erroneous as Collingwood's opinion that the same idea was conceived by the early Christians. The error is not deliberate, but a result of the lack of attention paid by past scholars to the history of astrology.

Those revisionists, including Garin, Thomas and Frank E. Manuel,[5] who have drawn attention to astrology's role in historical thought, nevertheless find agreement with the proposal put forward by Collingwood and others that modern models of historical development owe a profound debt to certain Renaissance historians, particularly Jean Bodin and Louis Le Roy, who are described as notable proponents of sixteenth-century humanism. The assessment of the nature of the debt, though, differs from historian to historian. Traditionalists such as Collingwood and Julian Franklin argue that the work of the sixteenth- and seventeenth-century French historians, including Melchior Cano and François Baudouin, represented a substantial move towards the modern critical approach to history.[6] In his work on political theory, economics, history and the law, Bodin is generally presented as a founder of modern thought. Collingwood enthusiastically described Bodin as a principal figure in the Renaissance humanist revolution, whose 'positive fruits . . . were found first of all in a great clearing away of what had been fanciful and ill-founded medieval historiography'.[7] Bodin's great attack on fashionable protestant German historiography in chapter 7 of the *Methodus* is said to mark him out as the father of modern critical thought; his dismissal of the traditional idea of the degeneration of man through successive epochs is said to be responsible for the idea of progress. Unreason was replaced by reason, irrationality by rationality.

These may indeed have been the consequences of Bodin's or Le Roy's work, and I do not at this stage wish to dispute their influence on the subsequent development of historiography. It is time, however, to challenge the generally accepted view regarding their intellectual allegiances and motivations. To what extent did their work genuinely result from what has been called a rational, critical, humanist outlook, in contrast to the supposedly 'fanciful and ill-founded' nature of medieval historiography? I shall argue that both Bodin and Le Roy, far from reacting against medieval tradition, were deeply influenced by it, and that their subsequent influence on European thought can only be understood in this context. Arbitrarily to exclude those sections of their work which most clearly reveal medieval influences can lead only to a distorted understanding of their role and importance.

That Jean Bodin's views on historical periodisation are located deeply in medieval thought, in astrology, numerology and Pythagorean mysticism is perhaps not surprising to the modern scholar. It is now some years since Frances Yates and others first argued that the belief that the Renaissance represented a rational rebirth after the dark years of medieval superstition is a highly misleading generalisation, and it is now becoming acceptable to argue that during the sixteenth century the irrational held as deep a grip over men's minds as ever. Medieval superstitions had, if anything, been reinforced by the revival of Neoplatonic and Hermetic mysticism, itself resting on deep pagan foundations.[8] However, the general historical position has rested on the belief that when Renaissance culture is studied astrology may be treated as anachronistic and therefore safely ignored. If the work of an otherwise admired figure is studied, it is considered indiscreet or merely irrelevant to mention any interest in astrology. Hence political scientists have fallen into the trap of considering one part of Bodin's work in isolation from another, sometimes dismissing his astrological passages with a contemptuous aside. For example, Allen remarks that in the *Republic* Bodin 'interlards the discussion with lengthy disquisitions on astrology and the magic that is hidden in numbers',[9] taking this as evidence of deep confusion. Harmon substituted abuse for argument, commenting that Bodin's theory of climatic and geographic influences 'is of course absurd: but it does not require much perception to see in it the ancestor thought of some much more modern asininities'.[10] Even Tooley, who admitted that Bodin's political theory could not be understood in isolation from his cosmology, excluded the astrological chapter from his edition of the *Republic*, only one of five out of forty-three chapters to be so honoured. Marwick merely appeared completely ignorant of both the astrological dimension of Bodin's work and his intellectual ancestry:

> The great theorist of historical study was Jean Bodin who declared the subject to be both of intellectual interest and pragmatic value for morals and politics: if studied carefully,

> he maintained, history did manifest certain orderly principles.[11]

In Marwick's world such characteristics were marks of Bodin's innovative modernism, yet an examination of classical and medieval historiography reveals that Bodin was merely repeating principles which had long been universally accepted.

A reassessment of Bodin's and Le Roy's historical reputation must begin with a critique of the modern treatment both of their work and of the history of astrology. In particular I wish to illustrate the weaknesses of the traditionalist view and amplify the implications and conclusions of the revisionist perspective.

The latter view, which accepts the importance of astrology in the Renaissance must, I believe, open the way to an understanding of the role of the irrational in the work of Bodin, Le Roy and their fellows, presenting them as an intellectual bridge between the medieval and modern worlds.[12] On the one hand their work can be shown to have inherited many assumptions from the astrological theories of such ninth- to twelfth-century Moslem historians as Al-Biruni and Abu M'ashar, combined in Bodin's case with the medieval millenarianism epitomised by Joachim of Fiore. On the other hand, its legacy in the post-Renaissance tradition of apocalyptic or epochal historiography can be shown to extend from the *New Science* of Giambattista Vico through to the German idealism of Lessing, Schiller, Fichte and Hegel, the materialistic millenarianism of Marx and the universal history of Spengler and Toynbee.[13]

BODIN'S LIFE

Jean Bodin was described by Pierre Bayle in 1697 as 'one of the most learned men that were in France in the XVIth century'.[14] He was born at Angers in the county of Anjou in 1529 or 1530, the son of prosperous bourgeois parents. He arrived in Paris to be educated at the house of the Carmelite Order, a home of traditional Aristotelian learning, but he was reputedly more attracted to the Collège des Quatre Langues, later renamed the Collège de France, where Aristotle's master, Plato, was held in higher esteem. Tooley speculates that around this time, in 1547, he may have been called before the *parlement* of Paris for having 'too freely debated matters of faith' and suggests that a possible visit to Geneva in 1552 may have been on account of Calvinist influence, both examples of an unfettered quest for the truth.

Between 1550 and 1561 he studied law in Toulouse, his studies coming to an end when he was called to the bar in Paris. In 1571 he entered the world of high politics, becoming secretary of commands in the household of François, Duc d'Alençon, youngest son of the late King Henry II and his formidable widow, Catherine de Medici, and younger brother of the reigning monarch, Charles IX. In this capacity he accompanied Alençon to England during the latter's courtship of Queen Elizabeth, finding time to visit Cambridge, where he was honoured by a public reading of the *Republic*. In the turbulent politics of the time Bodin was at first actively identified with the politiques who believed that the function of the state was to maintain order, not to impose the one true religion, a party represented in France by Alençon himself and in England by Elizabeth. The monarch rather than the Church was thus endowed with the absolute power to regulate religious affairs and resistance to the monarch on religious grounds was thus forbidden. He subsequently changed his allegiances for, as Frances Yates noted,[15] he later seems to have veered in the direction of the Catholic League and Mary, Queen of Scots, accepting the state's right to dictate matters of individual belief. This move may, however, have been undertaken for purely pragmatic reasons, and some biographers speculate that at the time of his death in 1596 he had converted to Judaism.

Bodin found the chance to argue for toleration as a member of the Estates General at Blois in 1576, where he made a number of recommendations, including a passionate plea for negotiation to end the wars of religion which had torn the country apart since 1562. As a result he lost the favour of Henry III, aspiring leader of the Catholic League. Following the death of Alençon in 1583 he was deprived of royal protection and found it expedient to retire from Paris, taking up the office of Procurateur au Presidial de Laon, a post inherited from his brother-in-law in 1578.

Life seemed secure until 1588 when the assassination of the Duc de Guise, leader of the Catholic League, initiated a reign of terror against Protestants and dissenters. It was only then that Bodin joined the Catholic League, for reasons which appear to have been purely cynical. Unfortunately, when the politiques triumphed with the accession of Henry IV in 1594, his membership of the League cost him any chance of renewed royal favour. Throughout his life Bodin argued for public toleration of individual conscience, yet in his own life he trod a path of prudence, becoming a nominal member of the winning side when necessary, yet retaining such discretion in matters of personal belief that we will never know the truth of rumours that he was at different times a Calvinist and a convert to Judaism. He was, perhaps, not so different from a long series of medieval scholars who had dabbled in occult wisdom, or in what were in strict terms heretical beliefs, while pragmatically maintaining a respectable Catholic persona. Much of Bodin's work arises out of the issues facing people such as he who wished to follow the dictates of their conscience without necessarily confronting the state. He demanded little more of the state than that it allow both him and other dissenters the right to adhere to their individual beliefs. He projected his own opinions on to the state only in that he believed that the stable and peaceful state would be one which paid due attention to astrology and numerology.

In 1566 Bodin published his first major work, the *Methodus ad Facilem Historiarum Cognitionem*, a volume whose purpose is made clear in English translation: 'The Method for the Easy Comprehension of History'. He followed this in 1568 with a contribution to economic debate, the *Réponse aux paradoxes de M. de Malestroicht, touchant le fait des monnaies et l'encherissement de toutes choses*. In 1576 he published his great work on political theory, *The Six Books of the Commonwealth*, commonly known as the *Republic*, and his last major work, the highly influential denunciation of neoplatonic and hermetic magic and witchcraft, *De la Démonomanie des Sorciers*, appeared in 1580. In 1594 he published an attempt to describe the universal system of nature, the *Novum Theatrum Naturae*. The unpublished 'Heptaplomeres' was a search for the principles of universal religion. One theme, then, runs through Bodin's work: the quest for universal truth in both belief and the organisation of society, a vision we may compare with the Stoic universalism of the age of Alexander.

As someone who was both employed at court and possessed of strong political views, Bodin clearly intended his work to have definite practical value. The *Methodus* was to be a manual for the thinking statesman and he declared that his intention was to concentrate long and hard upon 'human activities and the rulers governing them',[16] an ambition appropriate enough for any humanist. In doing this he would discover and illustrate the laws of historical change, enabling people to live in harmony with them. Yet, having established this worldly aim, he quickly prepared the ground for an astrological perspective. In the *Republic* he wrote that 'A true king is one who observes the laws of nature'.[17] To do this it was essential to understand the patterns of nature in both their terrestrial and celestial guises. From such an understanding would flow the ability to make predictions by projecting these laws into the future. According to Manuel's succinct assessment, 'Armed with astrological and numerological foreknowledge Bodin's statesman might mitigate the influence of the stars or devise ways of assuaging their painful effects upon the body politic'.[18] In spite of his doubts, which we shall come to later, as to the astrological element of such a programme, Bodin was nothing short of convinced that his analysis of the astrological and numerological laws governing the rise and fall of states could be projected into the future to aid in the prediction of, and therefore the preparation for, political crises.[19] A more practical purpose could not be imagined.

MEDIEVAL INFLUENCES ON BODIN

Although Bodin's move to the Collège des Quatre Langues signified a move away from Aristotelianism to Platonism, and in spite of Tooley's assertion that he more often treated Aristotle as an antagonist to be refuted than a master to be followed,[20] Bodin's work clearly shows the influences of both Greek philosophers. From Plato, Bodin derived both his concern with universal history and his opinions as to its nature. Fully in line with philosophical Platonic idealism, Bodin believed that 'the best part of universal law lies hidden, and what is of great weight and importance for the best appraisal of legislation – the custom of the peoples, and the beginnings of growth, conditions, changes, and decline of all states, are obtained from it'.[21] The *Methodus* was also heavily influenced by Aristotelian naturalism, a tendency which Copplestone considered to be 'remarkable', though why it should be so in view of Aristotle's long dominance in European thought is not explained. Perhaps Copplestone too was influenced by the myth of the Renaissance as a rational reaction to medieval learning, and his view is typical of those who would present Bodin as an innovator and a precursor of modern scientific history. After quoting Bodin's intention to 'explain the nature of peoples who dwell to the north and to the south, then of those who live to the east and the west', Copplestone points out that the same notion, that geographical effects must be considered in historical causation, appears in the writings of philosophers like Montesquieu.[22] Bodin is thus made to appear as a progressive thinker in Copplestone's scheme, in complete contrast with Harmon who, with equally little argument, regarded the same climatic theory as absurd and asinine. Neither judgement is sound for neither is based on a comprehensive reading of Bodin's work in its sixteenth-century context.

Far from innovating, Bodin was repeating the fundamental model of historical change outlined by the second-century Alexandrian Aristotelian astrologer, Claudius Ptolemy, in his *Tetrabiblos*. Copplestone's reasoning suggests no more that Bodin was an innovator by virtue of his influence on Montesquieu than that Montesquieu was a reactionary by virtue of his debt to Ptolemy. If, on the other hand, Bodin's theory was absurd and asinine then so was the mass of medieval science and philosophy which shared his assumptions.

Ptolemy's scheme of historical change had been current in Europe since the translation of the *Tetrabiblos* into Latin in 1138 by Plato of Tivoli. His approach was universal, and founded on the hypothesis that all events on earth owe their origins to a hierarchy of causative factors with superior causes having a greater importance than inferior ones. The highest cause was represented by the motions of the stars and planets, whose influence then descended through climate and topography down to human biology and physiology, human culture and, ultimately, to the individual. In Ptolemaic astrology it is, therefore, quite possible to make absolute predictions about human destiny using the stars alone, but a genuinely complete view necessitates an understanding of all five levels of existence.[23] For example, in the diagnosis and treatment of disease a physician would obviously have to consider the position of the stars but would also be obliged to analyse the patient's physiology and cultural background together with a complete range of environmental factors.

Extended to historical studies, such an approach required an analysis in which geographical causes, which appear rational to the modern mind, coexisted, indeed were inextricably linked, with astrological causes which appear equally irrational. Such causes should be understood less in terms of cause and effect through time than as a descending series of correspondences from the celestial macrocosm to the terrestrial microcosm. The scheme was adapted into Christian culture by the addition of the Aristotelian dogma that God was the first cause, his influence being mediated via the planets, themselves then functioning as secondary causes. Bodin's sole innovation was to insert numerology as a mediating factor between God and the stars.

Frank E. Manuel, foremost among those revisionist historians who have acknowledged the place of astrology in Renaissance thought, is in no doubt that the *Tetrabiblos* was a profound influence on Renaissance historiography and that Bodin himself was a firm believer in astrological cycles:

GOD
↓
NUMEROLOGY
(The mathematical laws regulating the universe)
↓
ASTROLOGY
(The cycles and conjunctions of the planets)
↓
CLIMATE
(The physical environment, geographical and meteorological factors)
↓
THE COMMONWEALE
(The community of citizens united in the state)
↓
THE INDIVIDUAL

Figure 7 Historical causation in Bodin's Republic *and* Methodus.
I have defined climate as the physical environment alone. In some usages climate may include astrological and numerological factors, these being part of the greater natural environment.

> Jean Bodin and Louis Le Roy were . . . heirs to a great astrological tradition and contemporary witnesses of an astronomical revolution and the proliferation of a host of numerological theories. They were therefore understandably curious about the relationship between the cycle of the nations and more measurable and objective scientific cycles in nature.[24]

Manuel agrees that Bodin's adoption of the biological conception that the purpose of each being, and hence each state, was to fulfil its own nature through a cycle of growth and decay, was thoroughly Aristotelian. In other words, Bodin was imposing classical *a priori* assumptions of the nature of political society and change on his work. Yet Manuel conforms to the traditional view that Bodin set about his task empirically, determined to correlate historical chronology with astronomical cycles and so discover a pattern with precise rules, or at least uncover certain orderly principles, rejecting the overt unquestioning symbolism of astrological periodisation. While Bodin did encourage attention to chronology, Manuel's opinion of his cultural position requires as much clarification as does Collingwood's far less informed conclusion. Manuel's confusion raises two questions: first, to what extent was Bodin's work empirical and, secondly, how far was it innovatory?

It is true that Bodin made serious criticisms of central aspects of astrological practice, and these have contributed to his reputation as an anti-medievalist. Yet the vacuum created by his argument with classical authorities such as Claudius Ptolemy and modern scholars such as Jerome Cardan was filled both by his own version of astrology and dependence on Pythagorean numerology. In the *Methodus* he argued that God has united all things by number, which by itself does not act as a cause of historical events, but as a measure of the rise and decline of the human polity. The use of number as a measure rather than as a cause is brought forward by the traditionalists as evidence that Bodin's work was modern in spirit, yet this practice may also be seen as both thoroughly Platonic and completely medieval in spirit. In fact, in his correlation of events with a preconceived system, Bodin was adhering to a procedure whose origins may be traced to Assyrian beliefs, were introduced to classical culture by Pythagoras and Plato and conveyed to medieval Europe via Islamic historiography. Once again we find that the only way to paint Bodin as a progressive is by censoring reference to his methodological ancestry.

In Book 4, chapter 2, of the *Republic* Bodin discussed numerology in relation to the changes of empires, claiming that his was the first serious investigation. He found that the most important numbers were 7 and 9, and the most fatal 63 (that is 7×9). He noted that St Augustine congratulated himself on passing his sixty-third year and that Aristotle, Boccaccio, St Bernard, Erasmus, Luther, Melanchton and others had all died aged 63. Extending his conclusions from the individual to the collective, he found that 496 (that is 7×70 plus a perfect number, 6) was the number which measured the rise and fall of states: 'All cities in the revolution of five hundred years do suffer either some great chaunge or else some utter ruine.' The fact that he produced as evidence the erroneous claims that the ascent of Augustus to supreme power at the Battle of Actium was separated from the abdication of Romulus Augustulus, the last Western Roman emperor, by 496 years, and that the same span of time separated this event from the coronation of Charlemagne may be taken as a testimony to the inadequacies of the available historical records. Taking the three dates as 31 BC, AD 476 and AD 800, the real figures were 507 and 324 years respectively. A more realistic conclusion might be that, far from adhering to chronology in anything resembling a rigorous manner, Bodin was imposing his Pythagorean,

Platonic, Qabalistic chronology on history in complete contradiction of the available evidence.

BODIN'S CRITICISM OF ASTROLOGY

Bodin freely admitted that his system of historical analysis was imperfect, for only God can know everything, but he insisted that at least it had more to recommend it than the astrological conjectures of Jerome Cardan, who, he said, believed that the fate of all great empires depended on the tail of the Great Bear. He rejected Cardan's belief that this constellation had been overhead at the foundation of Rome and that it was responsible for the rise of the empire. He also attacked the common practice of casting a horoscope for the creation of the world.

Bodin devoted his greatest effort to refuting the geographical correlations with the zodiac formulated by Ptolemy in which particular areas of the world were allotted to various of the twelve signs. He was obviously pleased with his attack on this system in chapter 5 of the *Methodus* for he repeated it, almost verbatim, in Book 4, chapter 2, of the *Republic*. He brought forward various reasons to support his argument. On the one hand it was absurd to divide the globe neatly into four quadrants and have each ruled by one of the triplicities, or groups of three signs. In Ptolemy's scheme, outlined in Book 2, chapter 3, of the *Tetrabiblos*, Aries, Leo and Sagittarius ruled all of Europe except the Balkans, Cancer, Scorpio and Pisces ruled north Africa, Gemini, Libra and Aquarius ruled western and central Asia and Taurus, Virgo and Capricorn ruled Mesopotamia, Persia and India. Bodin regarded these attributions as both completely arbitrary and in contradiction of the available evidence:

> Moreover he [Ptolemy] called the Jews, the Syrians and the Idumaeans bold and impious, because they were subservient to Aries, Scorpion [*sic*] and Mars. By unanimous agreement of all historians the Syrians are tractable to the point of servility; the Jews were born for religion. Nothing can be more pliant than the Idumaeans.[25]

Such was Bodin's contempt for this scheme that he doubted whether a man as great as Ptolemy could have written the *Tetrabiblos*.

Other points of disagreement with the conventions of astrological historiography were philosophical. Neither music nor astrology, Bodin believed, could be a perfect guide to history, as both were relatively imperfect, being governed by number and therefore lesser factors in the hierarchy of causation. Astrology was thus inherently uncertain as well as technically weak. Only number, which was closest to God, offered a totally accurate analysis of historical change.

Bodin's major technical complaint against astrology was derived from astronomical considerations. He picked up from previous critics, such as the thirteenth-century astrologer Guido Bonatti, the fact that due to the precession of the equinoxes the stellar groups recognised as the constellations no longer occupied the same regions of the heavens as the signs of the zodiac which shared the same names. He anticipated that precession since Augustus' time had resulted in a shift of the constellations of 17 degrees relative to the signs of the zodiac. Ptolemy's error, he continued, was compounded by the fact that he had underestimated the rate of precession, showing himself to be a weak astronomer as well as a poor astrologer. In fact it was Bodin who was wrong, apparently assuming a rate of precession of approximately 1 degree every ninety-four years as against the true rate, measured by Ptolemy, of 1 degree every seventy-two years.[26]

He also dismissed Cardan's attempt to save Ptolemy's outmoded astrological-geographical rulerships by adapting them to precession. For example, according to Bodin, Cardan claimed that the Spaniards, Britons and Normans, formerly ruled by Sagittarius, were now ruled by Scorpio. They had, therefore, lost their true and loyal Sagittarian virtues and, like the Scorpion, had become rapacious and cunning. Apart from the fact that Ptolemy had attributed rulership of the Britons to Aries and not Sagittarius, a point on which Bodin did not comment, he found no more relevance in Cardan's version than in the Greek original.

Bodin also maintained that references to the orbits of the superior planets, Jupiter and Saturn, whose cycle was the conventional focus of astrological historiography, also revealed alleged errors in Ptolemy's scheme. For example, the Jupiter–Saturn conjunction in Scorpio coincided with the civil war prior to the founding of the Roman Empire, but the change of government took place in Europe, which was ruled by the fiery triplicity (Italy was ruled by Leo), rather than in a Scorpionic region such as north Africa.

Bodin thus rejected one important facet of Ptolemy's scheme of historical causation, the strict zodiacal rulership of precise regions of the globe, while retaining the concept of climatic influences such as topography and weather. This alone should not allow us to prevent him as a modernist, for he also rejected Copernicanism, for once finding common cause with Ptolemy. In fact, he regarded heliocentric theory as absurd and adhered loyally to Ptolemaic geocentrism. Consequently he also dismissed Copernicus' belief that historical change depended on the eccentric motion of the Earth. Bodin's conservative attitude to Copernicanism compares with the progressive line taken by some of his contemporaries such as John Dee, the celebrated magician–astrologer, and Giordano Bruno, the cosmological mystic, both of whom were enthusiastic supporters of the sun-centred solar system.

Bodin was highly critical of almost anyone's theories but his own and his attack on medieval astrological beliefs did not prevent him from promoting his own versions. For example, he proposed his own theory of the astrological rulership of peoples, retaining the generality while rejecting only the particulars of Ptolemy's original scheme. Furthermore, in his own correlations of historical events with astrological cycles it is difficult to see that he held any real disagreement of principle with Cardan. Indeed, what disagreement there was seems to have been more a matter of personal competition than of scholarship.

Bodin's interest in the planets was based primarily on the numerologically significant fact that there were seven of them rather than on account of any astrological influence they might exert. He believed that, understood mathematically, the cycles of the planets were the orderly agencies of God, providing the grid against which history might be measured. Even when considering the role of astrology, God lay at the centre, being the first and original cause. Such a pious attitude underlay Bodin's unquestioning acceptance of the Hebrew chronology that the world was 5,500 years old and his rejection of the Egyptian contention that it was 10,000 years old. Yet, as we shall see, in spite of his preference for numerology, astrological considerations occupied a profoundly significant role in his work.

THE FOURFOLD THEORY OF HISTORY

The traditionalist belief that Bodin was a rationalist rests mainly on his rejection in chapter 7 of the *Methodus* of the 'Four Empires' theory of history, which found its authority in the Book of Daniel and which had recently been revived by the German Protestants. According to this theory, which has close astrological correspondences, world history moves through four complete phases or, in some versions, four phases preceded or followed by a fifth, a primordial or a future golden age, or perhaps both. This theory had found occasional favour through the medieval period, but in Bodin's time had been popularised by the German reformers, who argued strenuously that Protestant Germany was the fifth empire in the series and hence the culmination of God's plan in human history. Melanchthon's commentary on the Book of Daniel was published in Wittenberg in 1543, to be followed a year later by Luther's version. Brown has remarked that in the apocalyptic atmosphere of the times it seemed that 'nearly every Reformation leader wrote his interpretation of the book'.[27] The theory of the Four Empires was certainly accepted as the standard scheme of European Protestants, often with powerful political consequences. For example the millenarian Fifth Monarchy Men in the England of the 1640s were so-called because of their desire to bring the fifth empire, the reign of Christ, into being.

Contemporary French historians were perhaps duty bound to oppose a philosophy of history that gave such prominence to their powerful eastern rival and it is not surprising to find them denouncing it. That their attack was couched in terms of critical arguments has deceived modern historians into imagining that those who made these arguments were proposing rational systems as an alternative. For example, Collingwood cites Bodin's dismantling of the Four Empires theory as the principal evidence for the existence of a rational attitude in sixteenth-century historiography.[28] Franklin's argument that the criticism of the Germans by Melchior Cano, Jean Bodin, François Baudouin and Louis Le Roy was a major catalyst in the development of modern critical history represents the consensus opinion and has gained general acceptance.

Bodin's criticism of the Four Empires theory was indeed clear and reasoned in tone. He pointed out that the words of Daniel were too ambiguous to apply to contemporary events, that there had been more than four empires, and that, in any case, the Germans had no right to regard their own culture as the culmination of world history; he pointed out quite correctly that the colonial empires of the Spanish and Portuguese were bigger and the Turkish greater. He applied a similar logical barrage to destroy the classical theory of five epochs outlined in the eighth century BC in Hesiod's epic poem, the *Works and Days*.[29]

However, other evidence indicates that Bodin's criticism was motivated less by adherence to rational principles than by his own prejudice, including an element of anti-German feeling, a suspicion which was already current among his critics in the early seventeenth century. The Lutheran theologian Johann Quensted (1617–1688) complained that 'He [Bodin] vomits forth all sorts of slanders against the Germans. He is always boasting about himself and his people, but too ready to tread others into the earth'.[30] Such opinions appear to have been widespread, at least to judge from Bayle's report that 'The Germans complain much of him and abuse him'.[31]

Such opinions may hardly be accepted as impartial, yet are nevertheless evidence of the controversial impact of Bodin's work. Even Tooley, a modern observer, has argued that the reason that monarchy was Bodin's preferred form of government was that he was 'a patriot and a Frenchman', rather than on account of any rational evidence.

Allegations that Bodin's work owed much to prejudice are substantiated by his own revival of the ancient theory of three epochs, one which for over fifteen hundred years had stood at the centre of Judaeo–Christian historiography.[32] In other words, he was not opposed to the imposition of numerological constructs on history as a matter of principle, only to the German adoption of the Four Empires theory in particular. Bodin himself was taken by the idea that the number three was important in historical and political evolution, a fact which Collingwood failed to mention, let alone explain why reliance on this number had less to do with medieval fancy than did the belief in four or five epochs.

THE TRIPARTITE THEORY OF HISTORY

Like the fourfold theory of history, the threefold system is based on a unified theory of the cosmos in which space and time are completely interdependent and organised according to the same laws. The fourfold theory owes its origins to solar mythology, the movement of time through history being analogous to the passage of the sun through the four seasons. The threefold theory may be either lunar in conception, reflecting the threefold nature of the moon goddess, or an adaptation of the equation of historical phases with the three forms of the deity found in some eastern Mediterranean mythology and described by Plato: sky god (father), earth goddess (mother) and world saviour (child).

Bodin's theory, outlined in chapter 5 of the *Methodus* and Book 4, chapter 1, of the *Republic*, was based on division of all existence, including time and consciousness, into three forms (see Figure 8). There were three levels in the cosmos; a celestial world of the stars, an intellectual world of the mind and an elemental world of the birth and death of physical things. From this he projected three types of people, southern, temperate and northern, inhabiting six zones of

Levels of Consciousness and Being	Ruling Planets	Time	Space, Climatic Zones	Type of People	Biological Correlation	Society, Politics
		AD 2000	90°N			
Celestial World of the Stars	Mars, Moon (Sun)	Third phase	Frigid	Northern	Gall Bladder (Mars) Liver (Moon)	Development of industry, mechanization, democracy, warfare
		AD 0	60°N			
Intellectual World of the Mind	Jupiter, Mercury (Sun)	Second phase	Temperate	Temperate	Heart (Jupiter)	Development of the political arts
		2000 BC	30°N			
Elemental World of the Birth and Death of Physical Things	Saturn, Venus (Sun)	First phase	Torrid	Southern	Spleen (Saturn)	Piety, theocracy
		4000 BC	0°			

Figure 8 The division of time, space and consciousness by the number three in Bodin's political cosmology[33]

the world, three north of the equator and three to the south. In the northern hemisphere the torrid zone occupied latitudes 0 to 30 degrees north, the temperate zone 30 to 60 degrees north and the frigid zone 60 to 90 degrees north. In the southern hemisphere the zones occupied the equivalent degrees with the exception of the frigid zone, which came to an end at 75 degrees south, there being, Bodin claimed, no information for the polar region. The sceptic might be forgiven for finding this division of zones even more rigid than Ptolemy's, although in practice Bodin allowed exceptions on the grounds of local topography and climate. For example, the mountainous Swiss and Florentines had developed democratic forms of government, which were normally associated with northerners, on account of environmental factors which overruled the conditions arising from their habitation of the temperate zone.

In the common Christian version of the tripartite theory of history, the first epoch was that of God the Father, the period of the Old Testament, the second the era of Christ or God the Son, whose text was the New Testament, and the third and final epoch was that which followed the second coming, the era of God the Holy Spirit. Thus terrestrial history mirrored the divine trinity. This belief in three phases was devoutly held and had been given tremendous authority in the thirteenth-century millenarianism of Joachim of Fiore.

In Bodin's version, the first epoch, which lasted from around 4000 to 2000 BC, was dominated by southern peoples and marked by the development of religion, for which he believed the contemplative southern temperament was particularly fitted. The resulting state was theocratic. The second epoch, which lasted from 2000 BC to the beginning of the Christian era, was dominated by the temperate peoples and saw the rise of government and the political arts. The final epoch, which he believed was due to last until AD 2000, was dominated by the northern peoples, who excelled in mechanical invention and warfare.

There are three significant conclusions to be drawn from Bodin's adaptation of the tripartite scheme. Firstly he had broken with previous millenarian tradition by optimistically locating the current period of history in the third and final phase, rather than the second phase. By so doing he removed the apocalyptic fear, or in some cases, hope, that an imminent catastrophe would sweep away the current degenerate second phase to open the way for the triumphant and glorious third phase. This view may have reflected his ardent desire for political stability and rejection of revolution as a legitimate means of political change on the grounds that it represented an offence against the harmonious numerologically and astrologically regulated cosmos.

Secondly, he found partial agreement with his German critics in locating the Germans, as one of the north European peoples, as among the true representatives of the third and final phase. Clearly the argument was one of detail, Bodin wishing to broaden the definition of those who represented the culmination of history beyond the excessively narrow racial and religious bounds set by Luther, to include at least French dissenters such as himself. There may have also been some professional competition between Bodin and the Germans as to whose theory was true. Was history regulated according to the principles of the number three or those of the number four? This was the question.

Thirdly, by locating seventeenth-century Europe as the final phase of history Bodin contributed to the subsequent inflated notion that European culture and, amongst the north Europeans, Anglo-Saxon culture in particular, represented the high point of global civilization.

BODIN'S ASTROLOGY

In spite of his denunciation of Cardan's use of astrology, Bodin now revealed his own astrological inclinations. In a move which clearly reflected the contemporary Renaissance delight in pagan teachings and which might have been considered heretical were there not so many precedents in medieval history, Bodin ascribed planetary rulers to all the three epochs, arranging them in their descending 'Chaldean' order from Saturn to the moon, but excluding the sun, which 'like a fountain of light will be common to all'.[34] Accordingly the first epoch was ruled by Saturn, the second by Jupiter and the third by Mars. Continuing the sequence of planets, each epoch was given a second ruler, the first Venus, the second Mercury and the third the moon. The planets were more than the mere quantitative measuring points that Bodin's numerology might have suggested, and the celestial order was qualitatively completely mirrored in the terrestrial order.

Although he chose a tripartite system which had its origins in lunar mythology, the equation of the sun with all three phases of history embodied a belief that the passage of history through time as a whole reflected the annual journey of the sun around the earth. Bodin's application of planetary rulerships to two-thousand-year periods of history was in effect an extension of the widespread belief in the planetary rulership of small units of time, such as the hours of the day or the days of the week, to great periods of historical time. Hence the solar year becomes the model for the Great Year of history.

In keeping with medieval practice, the planets lent their qualities to their respective periods. These Bodin related directly to Chaldean tradition. Thus Saturn, signifying contemplation (according to Brown) or understanding (in Reynolds' translation), ruled the earth when religion and philosophy were born. Jupiter, planet of action and 'execution', was dominant during the second phase, bringing the rise of government and those political arts which were necessary to control men when the piety of the first age proved insufficient. Mars, planet of production and war, was the clear significator of the warlike and mechanically inventive north Europeans. In fact Bodin referred to these people as the 'children of Mars'.[35]

These assertions were justified by a series of geographical, cultural, historical and sociological observations. Evidence for Jupiter's rulership of the second epoch he found in the fact that thunder and lightning, ruled by Jupiter, originated in the second, temperate, zone. Thus climatic causes in their meteorological form were introduced to demonstrate the interdependence of space and time and their joint regulation by the number three. Mars could be shown to rule the third epoch by similar arguments. For example, Plato wrote that Mars ruled the arts and crafts, and according to Bodin this planet was therefore associated with craftsmen in their role as producers of goods. Was this, he reasoned, not the cause of the inventive genius of the Germans and Britons and of the fact that their technical assistance was considered vital in the mines and industry of the people of the middling zone, such as the Spanish and Portuguese?

Bodin placed the entire scheme in the context of a planetary body politic, again starting from a disagreement with Plato who, he claimed, equated soldiers with the heart, magistrates with the brain and common people with the liver. Rather, Jupiter ruled the heart, Saturn the spleen, Mars the gall bladder and the moon the liver, a system which differed from the usual scheme in which Jupiter ruled the liver and the sun the heart. The northern people therefore received the dual benefit of the moon, which nourished the elemental earth, regulating the tides together with all biological processes, and of Mars, which nourished the body via the gall bladder.

Further evidence was cautiously plucked from the doctrines of natal astrology:

> If then, we are to have faith in the astrologers, those who have Mars in the ascendant at their birth will be either soldiers or skilled workers . . . those who have the moon (prominently placed) in their horoscopes are said to be exceedingly strong and healthy.[36]

Such qualities were clearly demonstrated by the Scythians, whom Caesar declared to be particularly warlike and are therefore typical Martian subjects. Thus the individual enters Bodin's scheme as the possessor of a horoscope providing a connection directly to the heavens, mediated by but also bypassing the superior level of the cultural group or historical epoch.

The nature of the state itself owed more to climatic factors, that is to the totality of environmental factors from celestial to geographical and meteorological influences, than to cultural or individual ones, which in Ptolemy's scheme of historical change were inferior causes. For example, Bodin considered that the English failure to subdue the Scots was a consequence of the English inability to operate politically or militarily in the Scottish environment. Similarly he reasoned that even if the French ever managed successfully to invade England they would be unable to impose their own political system, which had evolved from conditions peculiar to France.

In his delineation of the types of state Bodin again found disagreement with Aristotle, a point which has been brought forward by traditionalists as further evidence of his progressive thought. Yet Bodin disagreed only with the letter of Aristotle's views, not with the substance, and did no more than replace Aristotle's scheme of six types of state with his own system of three. These were monarchy, the rule of the individual, aristocracy, the rule of the minority (his personal preference), and democracy, the rule of the majority. In addition to these legitimate forms each state had two degenerate forms, making nine varieties of state in all. There were six types of revolution between the legitimate states and eighteen between the degenerate. In addition, a state could be ruled by a type of government derived from another. Republican Rome, for example, was a democracy governed by an aristocracy. In the context of the times Bodin's theory was thoroughly conservative. He rejected the modern interest in the mixed constitution, which allowed for flexible analysis of each system of government on its own terms, preferring to see political organisation as governed by the same numerological principles which controlled the division of space and the passage of time. It was analysis of all human society in terms of the number three that was to open the door to comprehending human history: 'From this distribution, as it was, of all three peoples, we shall understand more plainly the power of nature.'[37]

Tooley makes a brave effort to maintain Bodin's progressive reputation by claiming that he was the first person to question Aristotle's theory of six states. Never mind the fact that Aristotle himself also divided states into two, four or seven types. To continue with the proposition that Bodin's theory of three states was innovative in any sense other than detail is to lapse into fiction.

The fact that Bodin's adherence to a threefold theory of historical evolution influenced a stream of thinkers from Giambattista Vico to Auguste Comte ('the founder of sociology') is indicative of his success in revitalising and extending this particular 'fancy' of medieval historiography. Unfortunately, too many historians have ignored Bodin's medieval antecedents. Tooley, for example, credits him as an influence on Vico and also argues that he recalled Hegel's division of cultural types into oriental, Graeco-Roman and Germanic. Again the reader is left with the entirely false impression that Bodin was an innovator. A myth may thus be served but misapprehensions concerning the development of historical thought are thus extended to the work of Vico and Hegel.

There is, of course a subtle distinction to be made between Bodin's impact on subsequent thought and his own views. He may have prompted certain later developments in various areas of intellectual inquiry without necessarily having been a progressive thinker himself. Unfortunately a circular argument has been developed in which it is argued that the consequences of Bodin's work were progressive. It then follows, so the theory runs, that his own work represented a substantial break with the past. Therefore we can safely ignore those aspects of his work which contradict this conclusion, presenting them as irrelevant medieval hangovers. Having doctored the evidence, the conclusion is justified: Bodin was a shining beacon of Renaissance reason in a world still dominated by the murky depths of medieval superstition. Such a line of reasoning is to say the least, anti-historical.

Bodin was a convinced believer in the essential historicity of myth, arguing, for example, that Hesiod's description of Jupiter's revolt against Saturn possessed a factual basis as an account of the social change that took place when the first epoch was transformed into the second.[38] His belief that Hesiod's myths were capable of historical interpretation further undermines the case that his criticism of the poet's five-epoch periodisation was based on condemnation of ancient superstition as a whole. Bodin's belief that myths could be taken as political metaphors, even if not literally true, is surprisingly modern, yet it makes sense only in terms of his serious application of a medieval astrological–numerological scheme to his theory of historical development. Once again Bodin's supposed modernism can be shown to have been a natural consequence of 'medieval fancy', rather than a reaction to it.

Bodin's role in the development of historical thought is undoubtedly more complicated than is assumed by Collingwood, Franklin and the traditionalists. If, as seems the case, he was deeply influenced by medieval astrological historiography, we are bound to consider his positive comments on astrology in addition to his criticisms.

Bodin was a devout believer in astrology. His references to natal horoscopes have already been noted, but his main interest was in the field then known as the study of revolutions, the interpretation of historical events in the light of the great planetary cycles, or revolutions. In spite of his technical criticisms of Ptolemy and Cardan he was in absolutely no doubt that historical change was governed astrologically, a belief which was firmly rooted in his acceptance of an ordered Neoplatonic universe:

> Seeing that there is nothing in this world which commeth to passe by chaunce or fortune, as all divines and the wiser sort of the Philosophers have with one consent resolved: Wee will here in the first place set downe this maxime for a ground or foundation, That the chaunges and ruines of Commonweals, are humane, or naturall or divine.[39]

In this scheme everything, every single event, had a purpose and a function together with a cause which itself may be traced directly to either human interference, climatic or geographical causes or divine will. As we have seen, human activity in both its individual and collective forms, together with the range of causes grouped together as climatic, were themselves related to astrological influences which, in the Aristotelian scheme laid down by Thomas Aquinas, mediated between God and earth. For God Bodin reserved the ultimate authority:

> I have, however, a firm conviction that [astrological?] regions and celestial bodies do not have the power to exercise ultimate control (a belief wrong even to entertain), yet men

are so much influenced by them that they cannot overcome the law of nature except through divine and or their own continued self-discipline.[40]

Bodin's astrology was aimed at enhancing freedom of choice through an understanding of the laws of nature and necessity as revealed in celestial cycles. 'All change', he wrote, 'is voluntary or necessary, or mixedly both'.[41] In the version of astrological causation worked out by Thomas Aquinas in the thirteenth century, necessary causes were the result of astrological influences and were felt through human physical desires and needs, the individual need to eat, reproduce and survive and the collective desire to make war or rebellion. Voluntary causes emanated from the soul which was in direct communion with God. It was therefore possible to mitigate or overcome inauspicious astrological omens and enhance auspicious ones through correct religious practice or a direct appeal to God through prayer. Of course, one could only do this once the astrological patterns had been read and understood.

Like Cardan and the majority of medieval historiographers since Abu Ma'shar, Bodin accepted that historical change was regulated by planetary cycles, beginning with the shortest term, the monthly lunar cycle, which became especially important if it culminated in an eclipse, and moving up to the long-term cycle of the Jupiter–Saturn conjunctions. His complaint was that as a result of the poor record of astronomical observation and accuracy there had to date been no authoritative work on the historical significance of these cycles. The situation was so bad, he claimed, that one astronomer might claim that a planet was retrograde while another might say it was direct in motion. Bodin's specific attacks on Ptolemaic rulerships and Cardan's astrological history, together with his general criticisms of the horoscopes for the world or for towns and cities, may therefore not be seen as indicating doubt in relation to astrology as such. As we shall see, his philosophical doubts concerning astrology's accuracy, arising from its inherent uncertainty, were solved by combining it with numerology.

THE REFORM OF ASTROLOGY

Bodin set out to complement his critique of Ptolemy and Cardan by demonstrating the relevance of astrological cycles through his own work. Like many other sixteenth-century scholars he drew lessons from the great conjunction of 1524 when Mars, Jupiter and Saturn united at the tenth degree of Pisces. All the other planets, as well as the Dragon's Head, Bodin reported, had either been in Pisces, a watery sign, or Aquarius, the sign of the water carrier, and great panic had ensued as astrologers forecast a deluge of biblical proportions. The embarrassing refusal of the flood to materialise produced a reaction against astrology. Bodin himself quoted this as the most serious of all recent astrological errors. Yet, he reasoned, if astrology was in principle true, it should be possible to avoid such mistakes, a work which could only be accomplished by going back to first principles.

> Yet doubt I not but that some more certain precepts might be given of the chaunges, and ruines of Commonweales if a man would enter into a certain account of the time past even from the begining of the world.[42]

Bodin defined his task. First, a chronology of events must be established. Secondly, this must be compared to planetary cycles, especially to eclipses and to the Jupiter–Saturn conjunctions. The correlations between terrestrial events and celestial cycles must then be related to number, which was both more reliable than astrology and superior to it. Finally the appropriate conclusions must be based on 'Most evident and manifest arguments' as opposed to the 'vain conjectures' which had formerly held sway. We can see how Collingwood accepted Bodin's inflated judgement of his own work at face value.

Bodin's published research along these lines is not extensive. We may take this as evidence that, contrary to his manifesto in favour of detailed research, he did little such work himself, preferring to follow the accepted astrological practice of selecting one or two items of evidence to prove the case. He did, however, bring forward certain anecdotal accounts. For example, he cited the Peloponnesian War as just one of many such events whose commencement coincided with a significant eclipse. There was, he concluded, no doubt that changes in commonwealths were defined by celestial cycles. Yet the brevity of his work, combined with the inaccuracies in dating noted above, make it difficult to see any superiority over Cardan's efforts.

Yet attention to chronology is said to be one of Bodin's great contributions to historical method. Perhaps historians have unquestioningly accepted Bodin's own claims to be the first to examine chronology without either studying his work or analysing his motivations. Indeed, the myth of the great innovator may have been originated by Bodin himself.

It does seem clear that Bodin's disputes with other authorities lacked any real substance. He rejected Aristotle's theory of six states, yet imposed his own version of three. He dismissed the 'nuptial number', derived from the number six, which, in Plato's *Republic*, determines the duration of historical epochs of 36,000 years. Yet he generated his own numerological cycle based on the number seven. He contemptuously attacked Ptolemy's geographical rulerships, yet joined him in arguing that cultural characteristics were derived from planetary qualities. He criticised Cardan's astrological history, yet his own differed only in detail.

Bodin's reputation as a progressive thinker is therefore derived from what he rejected rather than what he proposed, and when we examine his comments on astrology in full the nature of his contribution to Renaissance thought assumes a fresh perspective. If he was a supporter of medieval astrological teachings he nonetheless wished to reform those teachings. He may then be seen as one of a distinguished line of astrological reformers including Kepler and Copernicus.

Halbronn, for example, considers Bodin's astrological theories as an influence on Kepler, who, in the early years of the seventeenth century, made a determined effort to create a reformed astrology, abandoning the signs of the zodiac and Houses of the horoscope in favour of reliance on astronomically exact planetary cycles.

It is clear that Bodin was moving in this direction. For example, the doubts prompted by precession led him to reject the signs of the zodiac.

> Moreover, what they [the Chaldeans] have given us about the Signs of the Zodiac is altogether indefensible, since all parts of the Zodiac and whole signs have changed place since the time of their observation. For the first star of Aries, which occupied the first part of this constellation for six hundred years before Ptolemy, has arrived at the twenty eighth part . . .[43]

Precession, Bodin believed, had so altered the zodiac that it was futile to suggest that Augustus and Cosimo de Medici had anything in common as a result of both being born under Capricorn. Bodin's argument again exposes the weakness of his research, for it was Augustus' moon, not his sun, which was in Capricorn, although his statement that precession had totalled 17 degrees from the birth of the one to the other did nevertheless require an answer. He was, of course, ignoring the fact that the Ptolemaic zodiac used by European astrologers was fixed by the seasons rather than the constellations, the first point of Aries being defined by the sun's position at the spring equinox.

It may also be significant that the only two positive references to natal horoscopes in either the *Methodus* or the *Republic* both refer to planetary position in terms of diurnal motion, such as the rising of Mars, rather than in terms of the zodiac. It is tempting to see Bodin as an ancestor of those astrologers who placed more importance on diurnal position than sign location. It may not be stretching the point to argue that if Halbronn's suggestion concerning the influence of Bodin on Kepler can be substantiated, the latter's attempts to reform astrology owe much to the former's doubts over precession.

It was the absence of zodiacal reference points which made it necessary for Bodin to relate planetary cycles to number in terms of the periods of time between the conjunctions of any two planets under consideration. Again, this was hardly innovative, yet combined with a rejection of the zodiac did foreshadow Kepler's attempted astrological revolution. When we examine his work rather than his claims it becomes clear that Bodin was in no sense a conscious or genuine reformer of astrology, yet his work may have had consequences in subsequent reforming programmes. However, it must be said that Bodin's rejection of non-astronomical astrology, such as Ptolemy's geographical rulerships, did not prevent him from promoting similar non-astronomical planetary rulerships of cultural types and historical epochs. His astrology was therefore still based on the old idea of the doctrine of signatures and the great chain of being as well as on physical planetary influences.

Lest we should imagine that his approach was genuinely forward looking, we should take note of Bayle's comments, which first appeared in his *Dictionary* of 1697. According to Bayle, Bodin expressed the opinion that

> . . . comets are spirits who, having liv'd innumerable Ages on Earth, and being at last come nearer Death, celebrate their last Triumph, or are brought again into the Firmament as shining stars. This is attended with Famine and Pestilence etc. because the Cities, and the People lose the Governours who appeased the Wrath of God.[44]

Bayle was not sure how to interpret this belief, suggesting that perhaps Bodin was referring to dying angels rather than human spirits. Bayle's uncertainty is hard to explain, for Bodin was revealing quite clearly his acceptance of a major plank in the canon of the astral religion long perpetuated by Neoplatonists, one with which he cannot have been unfamiliar. Bodin's attempt to reform astrology was born of a desire to demonstrate certain of its fundamental truths. Halbronn writes that Bayle did not even consider Bodin a 'sincere critic' of astrology.[45] It would be much safer to call Bodin a critic, not of astrology, but of other astrologers.

The disservice committed by those modern historians who have suppressed any reference to Bodin's astrology takes on a new dimension when his place in the history of astronomy is denied. This denial may be traced back to the seventeenth century, judging from Tooley's comment that

> . . . the fact that he based his doctrine of environment on a cosmological system which was on the point of being abandoned at the very time he was writing partially contributed to the oblivion which was the fate of this part of his work.[46]

Of course, the *Republic* was published almost a century before astrology was firmly banished from intellectually respectable circles and did enjoy at least fifty years as a popular classic. Yet Tooley's view is broadly true. Bayle's intemperate description of Bodin as 'a credulous man and infatuated with astrology'[47] was written in 1697 and appears to have been the model for subsequent portrayals of Bodin as a great innovator in political and historical theory who unfortunately paid some credence to archaic medieval beliefs which, however, it would be better not to mention.

It is interesting to note that Bayle, one of the founders of the Enlightenment, was unable to cope with Bodin's astrological beliefs by any other response than a sneer. Paradoxically, a movement dedicated to the pursuit of reason and knowledge began its life by the censorship and exclusion from the realm of learning of what had only a century before represented high philosophical wisdom. In the many pages Bayle devoted to Bodin it was not even deemed acceptable to include the information about Bodin's astrology. It was permissible, however, both to exclude and condemn it without evidence or argument.

BODIN AND HERMETICISM

The reassessment of Bodin's historical reputation must involve a comparison of his astrology with that of his contemporaries, in particular with the learned Hermetic and Neoplatonic astral magic of men such as Marsilio Ficino, Pico della Mirandola, Henry Cornelius Agrippa and Giordano Bruno. Astrology, after all, has always contained many different traditions and schools of thought, often in competition with each other.

The evidence suggests that Bodin saw himself in complete opposition to these people on account of their overt paganism. To Bodin, the measure of what was true and what was not was whether God had approved it, witness his rejection of the Egyptian assessment of the age of the world in favour of the Hebrew.[48]

Frances Yates has shown how Bodin's last great work, *De la Démonomanie des Sorciers*, published in 1580, was, in addition to being a savage denunciation of witches which added fuel and respectability to the witch hunts, a bitter attack on Renaissance magic, particularly on Pico della Mirandola and Cornelius Agrippa.[49] According to Yates, Bodin launched his assault on Pico not for his use of Qabala but for his incorrect use of it. Pico himself was a severe critic of the use of horoscopes to make precise judgements, but as a disciple of Marsilio Ficino, the translator of Plato and the *Corpus Hermeticum*, he automatically accepted the doctrine of the divinity of the celestial bodies. He believed, for example, in the magical use of Qabalist letter formations to bring about the marriage of heaven and earth. Such practices were abhorrent to Bodin, who would no doubt also have found himself out of sympathy with such magically oriented luminaries of the astrological Renaissance as the English magus John Dee. Yet, as a Platonist and Pythagorean himself, Bodin could not attack the fundamentals of Renaissance Hermetic and astral magic, only those forms which departed from a Christian frame of reference. In fact he regarded both Pico and Agrippa as virtually diabolic.[50]

In spite of her revisionist attitude to the Renaissance, Yates adhered to the traditional view that 'Bodin's logic cut at the root of Renaissance magic with all its religious and cultural associations'.[51] Yet in the same breath she acknowledged Bodin's stern view that witches must die, an opinion which, like his attack on Pico and Agrippa, was derived from his Christian convictions and biblical authority. What sort of rationalist, it must be asked, believes intensely in the real existence of demonic witches and the reality of the witches' sabbath? Bodin clearly believed devoutly in the existence of that same magic which, according to Yates, he destroyed with his cutting logic. It is indeed difficult to see the consistency between Yates's stated account of Bodin's devout medieval beliefs and her conclusion that he attacked those beliefs. Perhaps Yates, who was clearly half way to accepting the real nature of Bodin's thought, was still inclined to accept the traditional interpretation of his work. Yet when Bodin denounced the work of Johann Weyer, Agrippa's protégé, for suggesting that witches were not infernal agents but merely deluded and silly old women suffering from melancholy, who was then the rationalist? In fact we must ask what sort of critical rationalist believed that the planets lent their qualities to historical epochs, and that historical chronology was based on Platonic, Pythagorean and Qabalistic speculation rather than on historical records? We come back to the possibility that Bodin's work was deeply rooted in medievalism, not a reaction to it.

Clearly both Weyer and Bodin adhered to elements of what modern historians describe as rational, logical thought, while explicitly accepting beliefs that those same historians condemn as irrational medieval fancies. In holding this balance, they were perhaps no different from many great scholars since the twelfth century, and scarcely more backward than those modern historians who impose their own *a priori* belief systems on their historical studies. Perhaps, in fact, the entire interpretation of the intellectual history of the Renaissance as the story of the overthrow of unreason by reason, with great forward-looking scholars pitted against the cultural inheritors of the backward medieval world, is a falsehood. Yet if so, it is one which has enabled historians to dismiss astrology as a medieval irrelevance which was eventually discarded by the logical Renaissance mind, rather than considering the possibility that it was a vital and integral part of Renaissance thought.[52] We are faced with a myth which has led to a fundamental distortion in our understanding of the history of ideas.

BODIN AS AN ARISTOTELIAN AND NEOPLATONIST

There is, then, as I have been arguing, an alternative view which suggests that Bodin was a conservative, an Aristotelian inclined Neoplatonist whose attacks on his free-thinking Hermetic contemporaries were motivated by a reactionary dislike of their fashionable paganism, and whose critique of German Protestant historiography was fuelled by support for an alternative which was equally abstract and archaic. Here is the irony. Bodin, who has been described as a brave rationalist rejecting medieval folly may equally be portrayed as a devout medievalist reacting against his free-thinking Renaissance contemporaries.

Amongst modern historians it has been Tooley who, although applauding Bodin's innovatory work, comes closest to conceding the depth of his commitment to twelfth-century Aristotelianism;

> One needs to be as near the middle ages in time, and in spirit, as Bodin was, to think and write of the state in relation to the cosmic process, at once rooted in it and reflecting it.[53]

When we examine the purpose and motivation behind Bodin's study of history and politics we find it differs little from that which drove the Roman chroniclers. If, as Bodin believed, history was the record of a series of recurrences, rather than a process of change, cyclic rather than evolutionary, its purpose was to enable men to avoid repeating the mistakes of the past once the same general conditions returned. The examples he relates from history are therefore cautionary tales, designed to enable men to 'acquire prudence'. In this he was of course, following a path trodden more recently by Machiavelli. Unlike Machiavelli, Bodin was deeply concerned with moral and ethical problems in government and, indeed, in all political behaviour. He also chose more examples from the past.

It is far from surprising that Bodin's history shared the same concerns as the Roman chroniclers, searching for the underlying occult laws which regulated historical change, teaching moral lessons in the process. What is instructive though is that his return to classical roots in his legal studies was, in Harmon's opinion, progressive, because he anticipated the modern school of sociological jurisprudence, in which the law has a social purpose, being important only if it is socially useful. Yet his astrological theories have been neglected because they went out of fashion in the seventeenth century. So, historical studies of Bodin's work are dominated by what is fashionable at a later time, not by what he said. Bodin's astrology went out of fashion, was therefore judged not a relevant field for historical research and considered of irrelevance in terms of the whole body of his work. 'It was therefore natural and inevitable', wrote Tooley, 'that his treatment of history should seem from our point of view to lack perspective'.[54] It is a dismal comment on modern historical studies that historians should so complacently admit their refusal to understand cultures and times apart from their own. We return to the belief, which is only now being discarded, that as astrology and other esoteric ideas are false, they are historically irrelevant. What a historian schooled in logical positivism regards as false in the present is therefore to be ignored in the past.

Hence Allen's dismissive statement that Bodin 'interlards the discussion with lengthy disquisitions on astrology and the magic that is hidden in numbers', which is symptomatic of the *Republic*'s boring and confused style. The contradiction between Tooley's simultaneous admission that Bodin's work cannot be understood in isolation from his cosmology and his curious cutting of astrology from his version of the *Republic* has already been noted. Yet Bodin's astrology was as absolutely central to his theory of history as were the celestial and other miraculous omens which pepper the Roman chronicles, bequeathing force and meaning to human actions.

Ironically, Allen concluded that

> . . . Bodin's claims to special honour consist, I think, in the fact that almost alone among sixteenth century thinkers, he made an honest attempt to construct a comprehensive theory of political society. All that we are rationally entitled to demand of such a system is that it should be coherent and intelligible and that it should not ignore or distort indisputable facts'[55]

A species of intellectual schizophrenia must be at work for Allen to make such a statement while clearly excluding Bodin's astrology from the body of work properly to be considered.[56] Tooley, whose fuller study of Bodin makes him a more reliable witness, admitted that Bodin mingled judgement of fact with judgement of value without distinguishing them. In fact, value judgements as well as celestial influences form a vital part of Bodin's political theory, which is no less coherent and intelligible for that. Indeed, it is astrology which makes Bodin's theory coherent. This, at least, is what he believed.

ASTROLOGY IN BODIN'S IDEAL STATE

Bodin's purpose, as is made clear in the title of the *Methodus*, was the comprehension of history. This, he also makes abundantly clear, was ultimately to be accomplished through the study of astrology and numerology combining in an analysis of planetary cycles. All history was to be understood in terms of cosmic cycles manifesting in terrestrial affairs.

Bodin's goal was to discover the secret of stability in a politically unstable world, a goal prompted by his experience of the uncertain times in which he lived. This all his biographers agree. He was 17 when Henry II came to power and persecution of the Protestants began in France. The wars of religion broke out in 1562, four years before the publication of the *Methodus*. The *Republic* itself was written during the midst of civil war. Indeed, peace was only restored by the Edict of Nantes in 1598, two years after his death. He therefore set out to establish the system of law, economy and political rights and duties which were essential to the smooth running of a just society. In so doing he is credited with the creation of modern jurisprudence, political economy, the concept of a state founded on a community of people rather than on monarchical power and governed partly by attention to individual political rights. What is unfortunately not stated is that all this was to be accomplished within the framework of a reformed and rigorous astrological numerology. He wished to extend the cosmic order into the political order, the correct organisation of which, he believed, must be accompanied by an understanding of the cosmic order as revealed through history. Indeed, Bodin's political and historical work may be viewed as little more than attempts to validate his cosmology.

Such a point of view opens up new avenues for understanding the totality of his work. For example, his political relativism, the belief that states evolve the form of government best suited to local geographical, environmental and cultural factors, receives added force when astrological influences are taken into account. A Saturnine theocracy, for example, is unlikely to survive amongst a Martial people such as the English. Each form of government has something to offer. Thus in spite of Bodin's personal preference for monarchy, he had to admit that democracy suited the Swiss temperament. A theory which Harmon wrote off as asinine from a different perspective actually preaches tolerance in a world where people are normally automatically hostile to political systems other than their own.

Bodin's desire for toleration arose out of his political experiences, as did his desire to reform astrology. Indeed, his reformed astrology was to serve a political purpose, to help solve the present religious wars and avoid future conflicts. His contribution to the history of ideas is thus intimately connected to the political history of the times. We can also see that the attempt to reform astrology was a response to the breakdown of the political community, parallel with his support of absolute monarchy as an alternative to the discredited and crumbling rule of the feudal lords which had climaxed so disastrously in the religious wars.

Bodin's discussion of universal time at the end of the *Methodus* harks back to the universalism of the Stoics, from whom he inherited his cyclical philosophy. Yet he did not share their belief in planetary necessity, allowing for the mitigation of astrological effects by divine intervention and human action. In Bodin's version (see Figure 7) historical causes descended from God to the individual. God was of course perfect, and the mathematical laws which regulated the universe were also perfect, or at least near perfect. Astrological cycles were less perfect but sufficiently so to be understood by observation as well as by pure reason. Society, however, is composed of men who have been afflicted by the Fall and is so imperfect that it cannot be understood through observation. Society must therefore be studied by reference to pure reason, that is numerology and astrology together with the law of God as revealed in the scriptures, mainly the Old Testament. The study of reason and the scriptures enables men to escape from the chains of the laws of nature, gaining freedom of choice in the process. The statesman who had gained such understanding would then be able to rule wisely.

Bodin was not enamoured of democracy, his favoured form of government being rule by a philosopher–king, since, under such rule, minorities would be better protected than if the ignorant majority were in control. Although he had little to say on the matter of natal astrology, it would not be far-fetched to attribute his concern for individual rights in matters of conscience and political rights based on property to an understanding of the uniqueness of each person based on a private pact with the cosmos sealed via the horoscope at birth. Theoretically, therefore, it is pointless for any Jupiterian state to impose its own religious opinions on a contemplative Saturnine individual who had already reached his own conclusions.

In all respects Bodin's attempt to maintain the political and social order was inseparable from his belief in cosmic order. His belief was that both should operate in harmony, and that when this happened peace and prosperity would be restored. Bodin's discreet mysticism, firmly rooted in the medieval world, thus becomes the inspiration for his work, not an embarrassing irrelevance.

If, on the other hand, we retain our central belief in Bodin's critical, rational outlook, we must accept the place of astrology and Platonic–Pythagorean numerology as an integral part of that outlook. It is just not compatible with a search for historical truth to censor those parts of his work which do not appear to the modern historical mind to be critical and rational, while emphasizing those that do. Perhaps the innovative consequences of Bodin's work in fields apart from astrology may be traced to a desire to maintain the medieval universe in working order throughout the turbulence of the sixteenth century. Such conclusions are lost when his theories are censored and simplified in order to provide support for a modern myth at the expense of an understanding of the many contradictions and complications in his work.

LOUIS LE ROY

Similar issues arise from a study of the work of Louis Le Roy when this is compared to his subsequent historical reputation. Le Roy was another of the other French historians who, along with Bodin, are traditionally described as rationalist rebels against medieval superstition.

Le Roy was born at Coutances in 1540 and, like Bodin, he attended the Collège de France. He was in fact heavily influenced by Bodin, but achieved a reputation as a renowned humanist scholar in his own right, his fame spreading through Italy, Germany and England, all of which countries he visited during the course of his studies. His career was capped in 1572, the year after Bodin entered Alençon's household, when he was appointed Regius Professor of Greek at the Collège de France. Four years later, in 1576, coinciding with the appearance of Bodin's *Republic*, he published his seventh and major work, *De la Vicissitude et Vanité des Choses en l'Universe*. In 1594 an English edition was published under the title *Of the Interchangeable Course, or Variety of Things in the Whole World*.

Franklin regarded Le Roy's rejection of the Protestant German Four Empires theory as a step in the development of modern criticial history as important as Bodin's criticism of the same scheme. Yet a reading of Le Roy's work renders the suggestion that his opposition to Protestant German historiography was based on critical rational convictions even harder to sustain than Bodin's. In fact, like Bodin, Le Roy had his own alternative with which to oppose the Four Empires theory. In his case this was explicitly and thoroughly astrological. He did not share Bodin's doubts concerning contemporary astrological practice.

Indeed, Le Roy opened his book with a survey of astrological factors. Clearly working in a traditional naturalistic Aristotelian–Ptolemaic framework, rather than in what was then the modern magical Hermetic mode, in that he was concerned with climate and geography rather than images or talismans, Le Roy nonetheless shared the same astrological heritage. His attitude was spelt out clearly and unambiguously: 'As character potential comes from the stars, so does collective potential. It is possible to deviate from destiny, but the course of events will automatically revert to it. The best thing is to wisely help destiny run its course.'[57] Le Roy argued that towns, cities and systems of government had their own cycles, rising and falling in patterns which in true Ptolemaic fashion were inextricably linked with those of geography, climate and the stars. He considered the cycles of the planets and the significance of the equinoxes and solstices; discussed the Arabic theories of the conjunctions of Mars, Jupiter and Saturn; considered the Platonic theory of the Great Year according to which the world year comes to an end when all the planets return to the places they occupied at their creation; and reported Berossus' theory that conjunctions of all the planets in Cancer denote destruction of the world by fire and in Capricorn destruction by water. The moon pulls the tides in a physical sense but is also related to the transition of types of government from monarchy through to aristocracy, oligarchy and democracy. The arts and sciences go through similar changes, but taking into account progression through time, their form is more like a wave than a cycle. Even climate is governed by the planets; the north wind is ruled by Jupiter, east by the sun, west by the moon and south by Mars.

Le Roy's work was clearly more explicitly astrological than Bodin's, a factor that must raise questions concerning his supposed role as a founder of modern critical history. For example, if his importance in this respect is accepted, what, we may ask, was the function of astrological thought in shaping modern historical method? Like Bodin's astrology, Le Roy's can be defined in relation to the intellectual climate of the sixteenth century. For example, Le Roy's Ptolemaic Aristotelianism contrasts with the magical hermetic Platonism of figures such as Marsilio Ficino, Giordano Bruno or Henry Cornelius Agrippa. In terms of the fashions of the time it is therefore quite possible to present Le Roy as a reactionary, hanging on to a safe and traditional view of astrological influences. Yet like Bodin he is presented as a progressive rationalist, criticizing medieval historiography from the supposedly advanced perspective of Renaissance humanism. This opinion is contradicted by a study of Le Roy's work, through which he appears, like Bodin, to be deeply immersed in medieval astrological historiography. The opening of

Le Roy's magnum opus is in fact a faithful summary of the historical perspective outlined some thirteen hundred years earlier in the *Tetrabiblos*, the fount of all astrological wisdom since the second century. If Bodin and Le Roy were rational it was only in opposition to their rivals' theories. If they adhered to critical standards of evidence the goal was to prove their preconceived ideas. In Bodin's case, the facts were adapted to conform to his pre-existent Pythagorean numerology.

Meanwhile, Le Roy, Bodin's younger contemporary, adopted classical second-century Greek astrology as the principal structure for historical analysis. It is true that Le Roy's section on astrology occupies only the opening pages of the *Interchangeable Causes*, but this is no evidence that he considered it as unimportant. He clearly regarded astrological effects as the superior cause, describing these as a necessary step before elaborating in more detail the inferior causes outlined in the Ptolemaic canon, such as geography, climate and culture.

CONCLUSION

A reconsideration of both men's work is clearly overdue, and with it a reassessment of the origins of what passes for modern critical history. Could it be that what modern historians have judged to be the irrational sits closer to modern historical practice than was once supposed? This would certainly be one conclusion if Bodin's and Le Roy's contribution to modern critical history was found to be based at least partly in medieval astrology. The view of Bodin and Le Roy as humanist critics of Renaissance and medieval unreason may indeed be derived from their work. Yet in Renaissance terms both men may also be described as conservatives rather than progressives, criticizing sixteenth-century Platonism and Protestantism from a medieval Aristotelian perspective.

The current state of the literature regarding both Bodin's and Le Roy's published work, as well as the trend in historical studies which they are supposed to have represented, is unsatisfactory. Some statements raise more questions than they answer. Brown, for example, regarded 'the concept of the cyclical development of political and artistic forms' as fundamental to Le Roy, as they were to Bodin, describing him as 'one of the most advanced spirits of his time'.[58] The implications of his judgement are profound, for as Manuel has made clear, concepts of cyclical development were closely tied to astrological doctrines, a point substantiated by the prominent role given to astrology by Le Roy. So, if Le Roy was indeed 'one of the most advanced spirits of his time', was this on account of his astrological beliefs? Most historians would argue that Renaissance scholars were advanced in spite of, not because of, the prevailing astrological beliefs of the time, a view which has been traditionally put either by ignoring these beliefs or belittling them.

Studies of Bodin's work in particular have located his contribution to modern historical method in a reaction against medieval historiography. Yet, as with Le Roy, we must be open to the possibility that his medieval affiliations exerted a positive, yet so far unacknowledged influence on modern historical thought. For example, Keith Thomas has concurred with Manuel in attributing the modern idea of a historical epoch to the Renaissance belief in astrological cycles.[59] Such opinions must await further research.

Brown followed accepted practice and assessed Le Roy's work by ignoring his astrological theories, much as Collingwood ignored Bodin's, and his judgement that Le Roy was progressive is sustained only by following the pattern of censorship established by Bayle. Medieval and Renaissance astrology were false and therefore irrelevant. Le Roy's cyclical theories are therefore precursors of what came after rather than the legacy of what came before. Ironically, in view of Bodin's supposed role as the founder of chronology, Brown rearranged the sequence of events, presenting Le Roy's work as the starting point of a new form of historical analysis rather than the continuation of a tradition at least two thousand years old.

The question is, then, whether the image of Bodin and Le Roy as two of the main founders of modern critical history is at least in part a fiction created by historians such as Collingwood, with a view to establishing a respectable lineage for what they proudly believed to be their own objective reading of history. It can be shown how Collingwood's great work on historiography, *The Idea of History*, does contain elements of myth making. Certainly his theory in relation to Bodin is based on only a partial reading of Bodin's work. As we have seen, elsewhere Collingwood's work is fatally undermined by an astonishing ignorance of classical historiography and its apocalyptic astrological theories.[60] As attention is paid to astrological theories of history, Collingwood's intellectual ancestors disappear, but so, too, in view of his failure to consider all the evidence, does his own claim to impartiality.

Some of those historians whom I have defined as revisionists in view of their readiness to acknowledge the importance of astrology in medieval and Renaissance culture find common ground with the traditionalists in regarding their subject as the study of a dead language whose implications for present-day historical thought are minimal. Some adopt a more enlightened attitude, yet the cumulative result has tended to be that the role and function of astrology in the past is still little understood and suffers from many misconceptions. A wide-ranging reassessment of the astrological historiography of the past may not be without consequences for our understanding of the development and nature of modern historical ideas.

Notes

1 Lynn Thorndyke, *History of Magic and Experimental Science*, 8 vols (New York, 1925).

2 > And the idea of epoch-making events has become a commonplace, and with it the division of history into periods each with its own peculiar character.
>
> All these elements, so familiar in modern historical thought, are totally absent from Greco–Roman historiography and were consciously and laboriously worked out by early Christians.
>
> R. G. Collingwood, *The Idea of History* (Oxford: OUP, 1946), p. 52.

Since I wrote this paper, the suppression of the history of astrology has been raised by Patrick Curry in *Astrology, Science and Society* (Boydell), pp. 1–4. The possible reasons are discussed by Halbronn, *The Revealing Process of Translation and Criticism in the History of Astrology* in P. Curry (ed.), op. cit., pp. 213–15. Halbronn's work, published in 1987, the year after this paper was presented, includes important comments on the significance of Bodin's astrological comments.

3 Eugenio Garin, *Astrology in the Renaissance*, trans. C. Jackson & J. Allen (London: Routledge, 1983), p. 16.

4 Keith Thomas, *Religion and the Decline of Magic* (London: Weidenfeld & Nicolson, 1971), p. 386.

5 Frank E. Manuel, *Shapes of Philosophical History* (London: Allen & Unwin, 1965).

6 See Julian Franklin, *Jean Bodin and the Sixteenth Century Revolution in the Methodology of Law and History* (London and New York: Columbia Press, 1963), esp. pp. 116–17.

7 Collingwood, op. cit., p. 57.

8 See Frances Yates, *Giordano Bruno and the Hermetic Tradition* (London: Routledge, 1971).

9 J. W. Allen, 'Jean Bodin', in F. J. C. Hearnshaw (ed.), *The Social*

and Political Ideas of Some Great Thinkers of the Sixteenth and Seventeenth Centuries (London: Dawsons Pall Mall, 1967), p. 45.

10 M. J. Harmon, *Political Thought from Plato to the Present* (New York: McGraw, 1981), p. 209. Harmon sees Bodin as the ancestor of nineteenth- and twentieth-century racism.

11 Arthur Marwick, *The Nature of History* (London: Macmillan, 1981), p. 30.

12 I realise that the use of the term 'irrational' has prejudicial connotations in modern usage. However, I need a word that will provide a contrast with what Collingwood described as rational historiography. By irrational we may describe a thought process derived from faith or *a priori* preconceptions, by rational one which allies itself with empirical evidence and proceeds via logical deduction. The difficulty emerges partly because the distinction between the two modes is often one of individual subjective judgement and because in many senses Renaissance and medieval astrology was clearly based on a carefully reasoned rational view of the universe. Indeed, some modern historians are arguing that medieval Aristotelian cosmology, which is irrational to many a narrow modern mind, was in fact good science. I am therefore in the position of applying a description to medieval astrology which allies me with Collingwood. However, I wish to argue that an irrational frame of reference need be no worse than a rational one; it is merely different. The religious, mystical and magical aspects of medieval astrology may indeed have been irrational yet still functioned as a perfectly acceptable path to understanding the nature of reality. Ironically the type of rational historiography epitomised by Collingwood contains features which may be described as irrational in the pejorative sense. That is, the refusal to acknowledge the role of astrology in Renaissance thought and the creation of the myth of Bodin the modernist, which may be ascribed to 'religious', rather than historical, motives (see note 55).

13 See, for example, Norman Cohn, *The Pursuit of the Millennium* (London: Mercury Books, 1962), p. 109.

Collingwood also acknowledged the similarity between medieval and modern millenarian beliefs:

> We have so far gone back to the medieval view of history that we think of nations and civilisations as rising and falling in obedience to a law that has little to

> do with the purpose of the human beings that comprise them, and we are perhaps not altogether ill disposed to theories which teach that large-scale historical changes are due to some kind of dialectic working objectively and shaping the historical process by a necessity that does not depend on the human will. This brings us into somewhat close contact with the medieval historians.
>
> R. G. Collingwood, op. cit., p. 56

14 Pierre Bayle, *An Historical and Critical Dictionary*, vol. 1 (Bobbs, US, 1965), p. 651.

15 Frances Yates, *The Occult Philosophy in the Elizabethan Age* (London: Routledge, 1979), p. 70.

16 Frederick Copplestone, *History of Philosophy*, vol. 3, p. 324.

17 Jean Bodin, *Six Books of the Commonwealth*, Book 2, chapter 3 (Arno, US, 1979).

18 Manuel, op. cit., p. 63.

19 Ibid., p. 138.

20 M. J. Tooley, *Introduction to Six Books of the Commonwealth*, p. vii.

21 Copplestone, op. cit., vol. 3, p. 324. According to Julian Franklin, Bodin's universalism was influenced by François Baudouin's proposition that history must be universal because God is as exalted in history as in nature, citing Baudouin's *De Institutione Historiae Universae et ejus cum Jurisprudentia Conjunctione Polegomeonon*, pp. 8–9, 11–12. See Franklin, *Jean Bodin and the Sixteenth Century Revolution* (Columbia Press, 1963), p. 117.

22 Copplestone, op. cit., citing Montesquieu's *Republic*, I:8.

23 Claudius Ptolemy, *Tetrabiblos*, esp. Books 1 and 2.

24 Manuel, op. cit., p. 60.

25 Jean Bodin, *Methodus*, chapter 5; *Republic*, Book 4, chapter 2.

26 Halbronn notes that Bodin's concern with astronomical accuracy lay behind his attack on August Ferrier's *Treatise on Astrology* of 1550. Ferrier's critical response in his *Advertissements à M Jean Bodin sur le quatrième livre de sa République* (1580) prompted a reply from Bodin under the pseudonym Réné Herpin. This bitter argument was terminated only by Ferrier's death. See Halbronn, op. cit., p. 208. For Bodin's views on the rate of precession see also note 42.

27 Brown, op. cit., p. 70; Bodin, *Methodus*, chapter 7.

28 Collingwood, op. cit., p. 57.

29 Hesiod's account of the five epochs of terrestrial history in the *Works and Days*, c. 750 BC, is the earliest written account of an epochal approach to history.

30 Cited in Brown, op. cit., pp. 71–2.
31 Bayle, op. cit., p. 658.
32 Bodin, *Methodus*, chapter 5; Brown, op. cit.
33 In some instances Bodin's tripartite classifications relate directly to each other. For example the three groups of planets, divisions of history, types of people and biological correlations are explicitly connected. However, the three levels of consciousness and being which formed the Platonic model for the other systems correlated only in part. The intellectual world of the mind correlates exactly with Jupiter and Mercury, the planets of wisdom. The elemental world connects with Saturn, the ruler of death and the planet which encompasses spirit in matter, but not with Venus. It is possible that Bodin intended astrological connections which are not now obvious on account of his disagreement in certain matters, such as the biological correlations with the planets, with astrological tradition.

Although he defined a type of state for each historical phase, he made no attempt to correlate these with his three main classifications, monarchy, aristocracy and democracy. This failure to produce a system of exact correlations has been held against him, even though to do so would have been at odds with his Platonic belief that all knowledge of the physical realm was by definition uncertain. His sole concern was to demonstrate the organising function of the number three in the entire universe.
34 In the Chaldean order, which had of course been debunked by Copernicus' revival of heliocentric theory, the planets are arranged from the moon to Saturn in order of their apparent velocity of travel around the earth. This order was also supposed to represent their distance away from the earth. Clearly Bodin had absorbed Copernicus' influence in some matters but not in others.
35 Bodin, op. cit., chapter 5.
36 Ibid.
37 Ibid.
38 Ibid.
39 Bodin, *Republic*, Book 4, chapter 2.
40 Ibid.
41 Ibid., Book 4, chapter 1.
42 Ibid.
43 Bodin, *Methodus*, chapter 5. In contrast with his earlier statement, Bodin here correctly assumed a rate of precession of 1 degree every seventy-two years. See also note 26.

44 Bayle, op. cit., citing Bodin, *Theatro Natura*, Book 2, pp. 221–2.

45 Halbronn, op. cit., p. 211. Interestingly, Bodin's desire to reform by returning to the roots foreshadows Newton's attempt to reform cosmology by returning to the roots of Judaeo–Christian theology, a programme which resulted in the removal of every astrological influence except comets. See Simon Schaffer, *Newton's Comets and the Transformation of Astrology* in Curry, op. cit.

46 Tooley, op. cit., p. xxxix.

47 Halbronn, op. cit., citing Pierre Bayle, *An Historical and Critical Dictionary* (Bobbs, US, 1965).

48 Manuel pointed out that Bodin obviously managed to find some truth in Egyptian and Chaldean chronology, managing to reconcile them with the scriptural version.

49 Frances Yates, op. cit., pp. 67–71. For a full account see Baxter in Sydney Anglo (ed.), *The Damned Art, Essays in the Literature of Witchcraft* (New York: Methuen, 1985).

50 Halbronn cites Bodin's frequent reference to Ibn Ezra and Maimonides, as in his 'Letter' on astrology published in 1555, to explain his concern with the proper uses of astrology, and by implication, magic. It did not matter, for example, whether astrology could or could not be used to cast the horoscope of Christ. What mattered was whether this was impious. Such an attitude would certainly square with the moral stance which was so important to Bodin's political philosophy. In the 'Letter' Bodin wrote that astrology was 'the most beautiful science in the world', but that problems arose from its abuse, the word 'astrologer' becoming synonymous with the word 'sorcerer'. As we have seen, Bodin added technical and historical inaccuracy to his list of the causes of astrological errors, but the concern with morality undoubtedly surfaced again in the *Démonomanie*. See Halbronn, op. cit., p. 208.

51 Frances Yates, op. cit., p. 71. Yates also noted that to be a politique could result in charges of magic or sympathy to magic. See *The Rosicrucian Enlightenment*, p. 110 (London: Routledge). No doubt Bodin had good reason for his discretion when he joined the Catholic League, but it is ironic that he was intolerant of some of his fellow astrologers. It would be in line with his general thinking to consider that their overt paganism would threaten the social fabric.

52 The conventional view is that astrology died out in the late seventeenth century after being proved false by the scientific

revolution. Since this paper was written Patrick Curry has argued that astrology in relation to England did not die out, but that it was banished from the intellectual establishment, retaining much of its public popularity.

53 Tooley, op. cit., p. xxxix.
54 Ibid., p. xxxiii.
55 Allen, op. cit., pp. 44–5.
56 The question of historical bias is of course necessarily raised by the disagreement of one school of historians with another. However, we tend to find an acknowledgement on each side that the other's conclusions are at least derived from reasonable interpretation of the evidence. I am arguing that as far as the history of astrology is concerned this has often not been the case, and that there are examples of distortion caused by refusal to consider the evidence. Apart from references such as that by Curry (see note 2), there has been no study of such bias. However, Eysenck and Nias have found evidence of bias against astrology today by both 'hard' scientists, such as physicists and astronomers, and 'soft' scientists such as psychologists. The authors, both clinical psychiatrists, describe such bias as religious in view of the fact that it is based on belief rather than on scientific investigation or verifiable evidence. It is reasonable to suggest that similar bias exists amongst historians. See Hans Eysenck and David Nias, *Astrology, Science or Superstition*, chapter 1.
57 Louis Le Roy, *On the Interchangeable Course*, p. 11.
58 Brown, op. cit., p. 20.
59 Keith Thomas, *Religion and the Decline of Magic* (London: Weidenfeld & Nicolson, 1971), p. 386.
60 Collingwood's belief that apocalyptic history was invented by the Christians was cited above. See the *Idea of History* (Oxford: OUP, 1961), p. 50.

Bibliography

Allen, J. W. (1926), 'Jean Bodin', in F. J. C. Hearnshaw (ed.), *The Social and Political Ideas of Some Great Thinkers of the Sixteenth and Seventeenth Centuries* (London).

Baxter, Christopher (1977), 'Jean Bodin's de la démonomanie des sorciers' in S. Anglo (ed.), *The Damned Art, Essays in the Literature of Witchcraft* (London).

Bayle, Pierre (1710), *An Historical and Critical Dictionary*, 4 vols (London).
Bodin, Jean (1555), *Six Books of the Commonwealth*, abridged and trans. M. J. Tooley (London, 1955).
Bodin, Jean (1606), *The Six Books of the Commonweale*, trans. Richard Knolles (London); facsimile edition ed. Kenneth Douglas MacRae (1962) (Cambridge, Mass.: Harvard University Press).
Bodin, Jean (1985), 'Method for the easy comprehension of history', trans. Beatrice Reynolds, *Records of Civilisation: Sources and Studies*, no. 37 (Russell Press, US).
Bodin, Jean (1946), *The Response to the Paradoxes of Malestroit*, trans. George Moore (Washington).
Brown, John L. (1939), *The Methodus ad Facilem Historiarum Cognitionem of Jean Bodin: A Critical Study* (Washington).
Cohn, Norman (1957), *The Pursuit of the Millennium* (London).
Collingwood, R. G. (1946), *The Idea of History* (Oxford).
Copplestone, Frederick (1950), *History of Philosophy* (London).
Curry, Patrick (1987), 'The decline of astrology in early modern England 1642–1800', PhD thesis, University of London.
Curry, Patrick (ed.) (1987), *Astrology, Science and Society* (Woodbridge: Boydell).
Eysenck, H. J. and Nias, D. K. B. (1982), *Astrology, Science or Superstition?* (London).
Franklin, Julian H. (1963), *Jean Bodin and the Sixteenth Century Revolution in the Methodology of Law and History* (London and New York).
Franklin, Julian H. (1973), *Jean Bodin and the Rise of Absolutist Theory* (London and New York).
Garin, Eugenio (1983), *Astrology in the Renaissance: The Zodiac of Life* (London: Routledge).
Grande Encyclopédie, La, vol. 22 (Paris).
Halbronn, Jacques (1987), 'The revealing process of translation and criticism in the history of astrology', in P. Curry (ed.), *Astrology, Science and Society* (Woodbridge).
Harmon, M. Judd (1964), *Political Thought from Plato to the Present* (London and New York).
King, Preston T. (1974), *The Ideology of Order: A Comparative Analysis of Jean Bodin and Thomas Hobbes* (London).
Le Roy, Louis (1594), *Of the Interchangeable Course, or Variety of Things in the Whole World* (London).
Manuel, Frank E. (1965), *Shapes of Philosophical History* (London).
Marwick, Arthur (1973), *The Nature of History* (London), first

published 1970.
Ptolemy, Claudius (1940), *Tetrabiblos*, trans. F. E. Robbins (London and Cambridge, Mass.).
Schaffer, Simon (1987), 'Newton's comets and the transformation of astrology' in P. Curry (ed.), *Astrology, Science and Society* (Woodbridge: Boydell).
Thomas, Keith (1971), *Religion and the Decline of Magic* (London).
Thorndyke, Lynn (1925–), *History of Magic and Experimental Science*, 8 vols (New York).
Tooley, M. J. (1953), 'Jean Bodin and the medieval theory of climate', *Speculum*, vol. 28, no. 1, Jan.
Walker, D. P. (1958), *Spiritual and Demonic Magic from Ficino to Campanella*.
Yates, Frances A. (1964), *Giordano Bruno and the Hermetic Tradition* (London: Routledge, 1971).
Yates, Frances A. (1972), *The Rosicrucian Enlightenment* (London).
Yates, Frances A. (1979), *The Occult Philosophy in the Elizabethan Age* (London: Routledge).

VI

THE ASTROLOGICAL BASIS OF SPENSER'S 'SHEPHEARDE'S CALENDER'

John Heath-Stubbs

Commentary

The idea of a shepherd's calendar would not be unfamiliar to the Elizabethan readers of the poet, Edmund Spenser. A perpetual *Kalendar of Shepheardes*, first translated from French in 1503, circulated in at least seventeen editions throughout the sixteenth and into the seventeenth century. The French original, *Le compost et calendrier des bergiers*, included practical advice for shepherds. There was also moral and religious advice; the Creed, Pater Noster and Ten Commandments were printed in it and it listed the deadly sins and cardinal virtues, with hints on how to avoid eternal damnation. It also explained the influence of the planets on the parts of the human body, and rules for good health, together with some other semi-astrological material.

'E. K.', a mysterious contemporary whose comments and glosses were published with *The Shephearde's Calender*, refers to this 'old work' which gave its name to the new poem. He also explains why the poem begins in January, instead of in March, the beginning of the astrological year, and then still the beginning of the civil year for most purposes. Soon after the publication of the poem in 1579, John Dee was working on the revision of the Julian calendar for the queen. Matters calendrical were in the air.

Each of the twelve eclogues is illustrated with a woodcut; it seems from his correspondence that Spenser was pleased with the artist's work. Each picture shows a rustic scene, with some characters in the poem, and each has the astrological sign of the month in the sky; for example, the second month, February, has the glyph for Pisces beside the two fishes, framed with clouds. (The 1911 de Selincourt edition of Spenser's works reproduces the woodcuts and the relevant correspondence.)

Letters between Gabriel Harvey and Spenser show that he was in touch with Dee's pupils, Philip Sidney and Edward Dyer. He belonged to a circle whose Neoplatonism included the Hermetic and Cabbalistic strands.

> Spenser more than once insinuates, that the soul of Chaucer was transfused into his body; and that he was begotten by him two hundred years after his decease.
>
> John Dryden, *Preface to the Fables* (1700)

If Spenser claimed a special link with Chaucer, certainly their successors agreed with him. Alastair Fowler (in *Spenser and the Numbers of Time*, p. 160) quotes *The Faerie Queene*:

> I follow here the footing of thy feete,
> that with *thy meaning* so I may the rather meete. [My emphasis]
>
> *The Faerie Queene*, IV ii 34

where Spenser acknowledges that he is taking over Chaucer's unfinished 'Squire's Tale'. Fowler makes an interesting point which emphasizes the quite exceptional relationship between the two poets over matters of hidden and subtle meaning. One cannot doubt the impression Chaucer's astrology made upon Spenser, who used its symbolism to such purpose.

Milton touches on the same point in *Il Penseroso*, a poem full of Platonic ideas, invoking peaceful contemplation and the higher Saturn:

> Or call up him that left untold
> The story of Cambuscan bold . . .

(referring to Chaucer's unfinished Tale)

> And if aught else great bards beside
> In sage and solemn tunes have sung,
> Of tourneys and of Tropheys hung,
> Of forests and enchantments drear,
> Where more is meant that meets the ear . . .

thus making the link with *The Faerie Queene*.

That last is a telling line, descriptive of much in both poets; and descriptive of the numerology and astrology underlying Spenser's poetry which has engaged recent critical attention. John Heath-Stubbs brings a poet's and a scholar's mind to bear upon the way Spenser used astrology in *The Shephearde's Calender*.

A. L. K.

It was about twenty years ago, a little after it had been published, that I read Professor Alastair Fowler's book, *Spenser and the Numbers of*

Time. This study is primarily concerned with Spenser's use of numerology in *The Faerie Queene*. Alistair Fowler also convincingly demonstrates that there is an astrological symbolism running through the poem as well. *The Faerie Queene* as we have it, consists of six books and a fragment of a seventh, the so-called Mutabilitie Cantos. This is only just short of a quarter of what Spenser had planned, that is to say the first part of twelve books, to be followed by a second part consisting of another twelve books, making twenty-four books in all.

Fowler, to my mind very convincingly, demonstrates that the extant books of *The Faerie Queene* correspond to the seven planets, not in the order of their apparent distance from the earth in the Ptolemaic system but in the way in which they are related to the seven days of the week – a system which probably goes back to Babylonian times.

Book I, the Legende of Holinesse, corresponds to the Sun. It is full of solar symbolism; and the Red Cross Knight, who is St George, the hero of this book, in some sense lives out the life of Christ, the Sun of Righteousness; while Una, who represents Truth of the True Church (in Spenser's view the reformed church) is the woman of Revelations, clothed with the Sun. She is also accompanied and protected by a lion. The Sun is, of course, the planetary ruler of the zodiacal sign Leo.

The second book, whose subject is temperance, is ruled by the Moon which acts as a mediating influence. The third book, the Legend of Chastity, has for its heroine Britomart whose name Spenser interprets as 'the martial Britoness'. She is therefore a Martian figure, Mars being the ruler of the third day of the week; but as a virgin warrior she also has characteristics of Pallas Athene, who, according to the system of Manilius, is the ruler of the sign Aries, more usually assigned to Mars.

The ruler of the fourth book is Mercury whose sign is Gemini. The subject of this book is friendship, and Fowler shows how the twins of Gemini are represented in this book by a number of dualities of friends. The book also closes with the revelation that Venus is in fact hermaphrodite, sexual love and friendship being ultimately the same. Hermaphroditus was the son of Mercury and Venus.

The fifth book is the Legende of Justice and corresponds to Jupiter. Artegall, the hero, has adventures which largely correspond to those of Hercules, Jupiter's son. The sixth book, Courtesy, is pastoral in character and very largely amatory so it naturally corresponds to Venus.

In the fragment of a seventh book of the Mutabilitie Cantos, the

Titan Mutabilitie challenges the order of Jove, maintaining that everything lies under her sway. The reply that is given to her is that although things seem to change they move cyclically and eventually return to their original place. The fragment ends with a vision of the eternal sabbath. Saturn, the ruler of Saturday, rules the sabbath. Fowler also shows that Spenser was familiar with Ptolemy's star catalogue, and that the number of the characters in each episode corresponds to the number of stars in the zodiacal constellation appropriate to the book.

There is a difficulty, it seems to me, in fitting this convincing scheme into a system of twelve and, finally, of twenty-four books. I asked Professor Fowler about this and he told me that he was confident that this could be managed, using the very complex multiplication of spheres which later Ptolemaic astronomy – that of Spenser's time – demanded. I suggested to him that if his interpretation were right it would be theoretically possible to predict the subjects and scheme of the completed poem. I hope I am not betraying a confidence if I say that he informed me that he had made such a predictive scheme and had deposited it in the Bodleian Library, not to be opened until and unless lost books of *The Faerie Queene* should come to light. He believed it might be possible that some lost material might be amongst the Essex papers.

Helena Shire in her *Preface to Spenser* postulates a scheme similar to Fowler's except that she sees Venus as primarily the ruler of the third and fourth books, though joined to the influence of Mars and Mercury respectively. Frances Yates in *The Occult Philosophy in the Elizabethan Age* gives another scheme which takes account of the Venetian, Francesco Giorgi, and his 'planetary–angelic–sephirotic' formulations which were influential in Elizabethan Neoplatonist circles (see especially her chapters 4 and 9).

'THE SHEPHEARDE'S CALENDER'

My reading of Alastair Fowler's book prompted me to wonder whether a similar scheme was not to be found in Spenser's earlier poem *The Shephearde's Calender*, published in 1579. There are two explicit astrological references in this poem in the August and November eclogues, but they are puzzling and will be considered later. Spenser has an astrological scheme in this poem and each of the twelve eclogues, corresponding to the twelve months of the year, contain references to the planetary rulers of the appropriate signs of the zodiac.[1]

First of all I should explain that the nature of this poem is a series of pastoral poems or eclogues. Pastoral poetry originated with the Greek poet, Theocritus, native of Sicily, who worked in Alexandria in the later part of the third century BC. The line of his successors[2] may be traced, via Virgil, Petrarch and Mantuan (1448–1516), who was very widely read in Spenser's time, a standard schoolbook for Elizabethan boys and an influence on the poet.

Spenser knew and used the Greek pastoral poets as well as Virgil, Mantuan, and the sixteenth-century French poet, Clément Mareau; but he claims as his English predecessors Chaucer, whom he called Tityrus, and William Langland, 'the shepherd who the ploughman played awhile'. He also took the name of Colin Clout, by which he designates himself in his poems, from another English predecessor, John Skelton.

Nevertheless Spenser's poems are highly original[3] and signalled the beginning of the great flowering of Renaissance poetry in England as much as Wordsworth's and T. S. Eliot's initiated the periods of Romantic and Modernist poetry.

The Shephearde's Calender is accompanied by a commentary by 'E. K.'. Who E. K. was is a matter of controversy: some have believed him to be simply Spenser himself, perhaps Edmundus Calendarius, but others have supposed him to be a friend and colleague, perhaps Edward Kirk, which I am inclined to believe. It seems to me that E. K.'s point of view is not always the same as that of Spenser – for instance, he is a more extreme Calvinist than Spenser is. It would also appear, if I am right, that E. K. misunderstood some of Spenser's astrological references.

A novel feature of this poem is the assigning of the twelve eclogues to the twelve months of the year. The poem's title is taken from a handbook for shepherds translated from the French. Helena Shire describes it as follows:

> This was 'an old book',[4] familiar to men of Renaissance Europe in print in many languages, in English *The Kalendar and compost of Shepherds, le compost et kalendrier des bons bergiers*. It was . . . a handbook for everyman 'the shepherd', bringing together all he needed to know for his physical, moral and spiritual wellbeing.
>
> Helena Shire, *Preface to Spenser* (1978), p. 98

Another original feature of Spenser's poem is the welding of some of the individual eclogues together by an ongoing story. This story has to do with the three-cornered relationship between Colin (Spenser himself), Hobbinol (his close friend, Gabriel Harvey, Cambridge scholar and Protestant pamphleteer) and Rosalind, who represents Machabyas Chylde, later to be Spenser's first wife. This three-cornered relationship, involving passionate friendship between men in tension with the love of a woman or sometimes two women, was to become a recurring theme in Elizabethan literature.[5]

THE TWELVE ECLOGUES OF 'THE SHEPHEARDE'S CALENDER'

I shall now consider the twelve eclogues of *The Shephearde's Calender*, beginning with the January one and attempting to show that each of them has references to the relevant zodiacal sign and its ruling planet.

In January the Sun enters Aquarius, whose ruling planet is Saturn, the bringer of melancholy and old age. Here we have Colin as the lover afflicted with the lover's melancholy, which springs from the cold influence of Saturn and apparently affects not only Colin but all his flock.

> Such rage as winters reigneth in my heart
> My life-bloud friesing with unkindly cold;
> Such stormy stouures do breede my balefull smart,
> As if my yeare were wast and woxen old;
> And yet, alas! but now my spring begonne,
> And yet, alas! it is already donne.
>
> Edmund Spenser, *The Shephearde's Calender*,
> Januarie Eclogue, stanza 5

It will be noted that Colin seems also afflicted with old age, though he is in fact young.

The February eclogue is mostly taken up with the fable of the oak and the briar, which the old shepherd, Thenot, tells to the young shepherd, Cuddy, as a warning to him not to despise old age. The fable is attributed to Tityrus – that is to say to Chaucer – and is meant to be in Chaucerian style. The oak is the tree of Jupiter and the Sun enters the sign of Jupiter in Pisces. However, the oak here stands for old age, as does the speaker of the fable; and the briar has the brashness of youth. So the oak has Saturnian as well as Jovian associations. According to Lilly, all trees that are prickly belong to Mars, which would include the briar (see *Christian Astrology*, p. 68, for trees of Mars; p. 64 for trees of Jupiter). This makes a link with the following Mars-ruled sign.

The March eclogue is closely modelled on a Greek original by Bion, one of the earliest followers of Theocritus, but it is transferred to a very English setting. Two boys, Willy and Thomalin, go beating the bushes which are as yet leafless, in search of birds; instead of a bird they disturb Cupid, who wounds one of them with his arrow. There are various mythological accounts of the parentage of Cupid, but that most commonly given him makes him the son of Mars and Venus. The sun enters Aries, whose ruler is Mars, in March and here we have Cupid the son of Mars, 'all in arms'.

In April the Sun enters Taurus, whose ruler is Venus. The April eclogue therefore continues and enlarges the love theme of Colin and his wooing of Rosalind. But Colin here is the youthful poet, not the afflicted melancholy lover of the January eclogue. His lyrics culminate in a song in praise of Eliza who is, of course, none other than Queen Elizabeth I. The song is one of the best and most successful of Spenser's lyrics. The Virgin Queen was never identified with Venus but with the Moon, Cynthia. The moon is in fact exalted in Taurus. The rose and the lilly, both flowers dedicated to Venus, are here associated with Eliza, the rose being the red and white Tudor rose and the lilly, or fleur-de-lys, representing the English sovereign's continuing claim to the throne of France.

In May, the Sun enters the sign of Gemini, whose ruler is Mercury. Spenser's May eclogue takes the form of a débat between two shepherds, Piers and Palinode. The occasion of their dispute is the May-day games which Piers – who takes his name from Piers Plowman – condemns and Palinode is prepared to tolerate. E. K. takes Piers to represent the reformed clergy and Palinode the popish clergy. But as I have already indicated, I think that E. K.'s point of view is slightly different from Spenser's, and that they should rather be identified with a Puritan and a moderate Anglican point of view respectively. The use of the débat form here suggests the duality of the twins. As in the fourth book of *The Faerie Queene*, this eclogue concludes with another fable, told by Piers. It is the story of the wolf and the kid, evidently a folk tale, with affinities with two well-known stories. One is that of the Three Little Pigs and the other the episode in Snow White when the evil queen disguises herself as a pedlar and tries to poison Snow White. It is a tale of trickery and theft, appropriate to Mercury, the patron of thieves.

In the June eclogue the love scene, Colin's wooing of Rosalind, continues, but as the Sun enters Cancer Colin suspects Rosalind of infidelity and his chaste passion for his friend Hobbinol now takes precedence over his erotic passion for her.

Hobbinol invites Colin to leave the hills, that is to say, Lancashire, for the dales or Cambridge, a watery spot which one may take to be ruled by the watery influences of the moon. There is a specific reference to the moon goddess in the following lines:

> But friendly Faeries, met with many Graces
> And lightfoote nymphes, can chace the lingring Night
> With Heydeguyes, and trimly trodden traces,
> Whilst sisters nyne, which dwell on Parnasse hight,
> Doe make them musick for their more delight:
> And Pan himselfe, to kisse their crystall faces
> Will pype and daunce when Phoebe shineth bright:
> Such pierless pleasures have we in these places.
>
> *The Shephearde's Calender*, June Eclogue

The fairies are also associated with the Moon and moonlight.[6]

In the July eclogue we come upon the first of Spenser's explicitly astrological references and at the same time on a puzzle.

> And now the Sonne hath reared up
> His fyerie-footed teme
> Making his way between the Cuppe
> And Golden Diademe:
> The rampant Lyon hunts he fast,
> With dogs of noysome breath
> Whose balefull barking bringes in hast
> Pyne, plagues, and dreery death.
>
> *The Shephearde's Calender*, July Eclogue

Part of this is perfectly clear: in July the Sun enters the sign of Leo, and this constellation is accompanied by the two constellations of Canis Major and Canis Minor, with their principal stars, Syrius and Procaion. Syrius rises with the sun at this time of the year and these so-called Dog Days were traditionally supposed to bring fever and plagues and particularly rabies among dogs. But the references to the 'Cuppe' and the 'Diademe' are very puzzling. These can only be the constellations Crater and Corona Borealis.

> *The Cuppe and Diademe*, be two signes in the Firmament, through which the Sonne maketh his course in the moneth of July.

> *Lion*, Thys is poetically spoken, as if the Sunne did hunt a lion with one dogge. The meaning whereof is, that in July the sonne is in Leo. At which time the Dogge starre, which is called Syrius, or canicula, reigneth with immoderate heate, causing pestilence, drougth, and many diseases.
>
> *The Shephearde's Calender*, July Eclogue, gloss by E. K.

Now the first of these statements appears simply to be wrong. The constellations of Crater and Corona Borealis are nowhere near the sign of Leo. Crater is a southern constellation and Corona Borealis, the Northern Crown, is a northern one. The eclogue itself is a debate between the shepherd, Thomalin, and the proud goatherd, Morrell, who sits at the top of a high hill. Morrell has been identified with Robert Aylmer, who had been among the Protestant exiles of Queen Mary's reign, was now the Bishop of London, and was regarded as a 'proud prelate' and a suppressor of Catholic recusants and Puritans alike. The poem is a piece of rhetoric of a traditional kind, debating the virtues of high and low, valley and hill; Morrell cites various sacred hills, among which are included Latmos, on which the sun was supposed to rise.

> Morrell:
> Besyde, as Holy fathers sayne,
> There is a hyllye place
> Where Titan ryseth from the mayne
> To renne hys dayly race
>
> *The Shepehearde's Calender*, July Eclogue

The poem concludes with an attack on the pride of the Roman clergy in particular. The theme of this poem is therefore primarily pride and height. If we think of the year as beginning in January, the transition from June to July gives us the central point of the sequence. Professor Fowler has shown in *Silent Poetry* that the mathematical centre of a poem written during the Renaissance period is liable to give us an image of the sun or of royalty, since the Sun is in the centre of the heavens and Christ, the Sun of Righteousness, was crucified in the centre of the earth.[7]

Therefore, although we are past midsummer's day, I think that Spenser wanted us to think here of the Sun riding at its highest point, shining as it were in its pride and therefore as nearly as possible equidistant between north and south, that is to say between the southern constellation of the Crater and the northern one of Corona Borealis.

Professor Fowler, in *Conceitful Thought*, suggests the following solution to the problem:

> A difficult passage: though Corona Borealis and Crater straddle the sun's ecliptic path, neither was in the July sign, Leo. (Crater was in Virgo, Corona in Libra.) Spenser follows an astrological schematic tradition such as Manilius' or Firmicus Maternus', giving paranatellonta or constellations that rise or set with the signs. Thus Hyginus *Poet.astron.* 3.4 connects Corona's setting with Leo's rising. According to Firmicus 8.10 and 8.11 Corona rises in 5° of Virgo, the sign to which precession had moved Leo by Spenser's time. Corona had moved too; but concerning extrazodiacal constellations Firmicus had the authority of literary tradition: c.f. the Sala dei Venti programme, in which Corona was still connected with Virgo (E. H. Gombrich *Symbolic Images* (1972) p. 111 and p. 113). Spenser's 'calendar for every year' may even assume a poetical astronomy with constellations occupying their ancient positions.
>
> Alastair Fowler, *Conceitful Thought*, pp. 69–70, n. 39

The August eclogue follows Theocritus in giving us a singing game which is here converted into an English rhyme-capping game. The Sun enters Virgo in August and the constellation Virgo was often identified with Astraea, the goddess of Justice, who left the earth at the end of the Golden Age. Elizabeth was very frequently identified with Astraea and her birthday was in this sign. The planetary ruler here is Mercury and this I think may be the clue to Spenser's poem; the singing contest is in fact a contest of eloquence, of which art Mercury was the patron, and the presence of Astraea may represent the justice of arbitration.

The September eclogue consists of a dialogue between Hobbinol and Diggon Davy. Ian Maclean in 'Spenser's Shephearde's Calender' in *A Study in Elizabethan Allegory* identifies the principal speaker in this poem, Diggon Davy, with Richard Davies, Bishop of St David's, a prelate of whom Spenser and Harvey approved for his support of the 'prophesyings' – free Bible-reading sessions of which the established authorities tended to be suspicious. A large part of this eclogue is taken up with an attack on the pride and corruption of the Roman clergy. It is a little difficult to connect this eclogue with the sign of Libra, whose ruler is Venus. I can only suggest that we should concentrate here not on the image of the planetary ruler, but on that of the sign itself, the scales. They may represent God's justice and in particular His judgement on a corrupt church. In *Paradise Lost* – and Milton was Spenser's greatest disciple – the sign of Libra is used as a symbol of God's justice when God hangs the sign in the heavens to put an end to the incipient conflict between the archangel Gabriel and Satan when the two encounter one another in Eden.

In October the Sun enters the Martian sign of Scorpio. This eclogue again deals with Colin as poet. But there is particular emphasis on his ambition to essay poetry of a higher kind, epic or tragic:

> Cuddie [=Colin]:
> O! if my temples were distained with wine,
> And girt in girlonds of wild Yvie twine,
> How could I reare the Muse on stately stage,
> And teach her tread aloft in buskin fine,
> With queint Bellona in her equipage!
>
> *The Shepehearde's Calender*, October Eclogue

Bellona, the goddess of war, was the sister or wife of Mars. We are to think here particularly of epic poetry, though the 'stately stage' and the 'buskins' point rather to tragedy. But epic and tragedy were essentially considered to be the same genre, differing only in that the one was narrative in form, the other dramatic. Since the time of Virgil it had become a tradition that the poet should start out with the humble form of pastoral poetry before passing on to the epic. Petrarch's eclogues had preceded his Latin epic, *Africa*. Spenser was to follow *The Shephearde's Calender* with his epic, *The Faerie Queene*.[8] Epic, at any rate up to Milton's time, dealt with 'wars, hitherto the only argument heroic deemed'. Therefore Mars, or Bellona, the ruler of the sign of Scorpio, is naturally its patron.

In the November eclogue we come upon another explicitly astrological reference, and again at first sight it would appear to be incorrect. Spenser writes:

> Colin: Thenot, now nis the time of merimake,
> Nor Pan to herye, nor with love to playe;
> Syke myrth in May is meetest for to Make,
> Or summer shade, under the cocket hay.
> But now sadde Winter welked hath the day,
> And Phoebus, weary of his yerely taske,
> Ystabled hath his steedes in lowlye laye,
> And taken up his ynne in Fishes haske.
>
> *The Shepehearde's Calender*, November Eclogue

E. K. adds the gloss, 'the sunne reigneth, that is, in the sign Pisces all November: a haske is a wicker pad, wherein they use to carry fish'.

E. K. is quite clearly wrong here, but was Spenser? The November eclogue is mostly taken up with an elegy for a lady called Dido. She has been variously identified, but E. K. says that her name is a secret. At first I thought it possible that Spenser had written this elegy earlier and incorporated it when he came to write *The Shephearde's Calender* because he wished to include an elegy in this eclogue since November is the month liturgically associated with the dead. The lady, I thought, might actually have died in February; Spenser had not noticed the reference to Pisces; for during November the sun moves into Sagittarius. But Scorpio would have coincided with the first days of November which would have included All Saints' Day (1 November) and All Souls' Day (2 November).[9] So Spenser wishes to associate his elegy for Dido with these festivals.

We now come to the last of Spenser's eclogues, that for December. The Sun now enters the sign of Capricorn, whose ruler is Saturn. This links up with the first eclogue, the one for January also ruled by Saturn. In both of them we see Colin oppressed by lover's melancholy, and with a sense of old age. In the December eclogue he seems actually to have become old in bidding farewell to youthful pastoral poetry. The December eclogue in some ways anticipates Wordsworth's *Prelude* in giving, though in miniature, the growth of a poet's mind. It is noteworthy that two significant episodes in Wordsworth's poem, the robbing of the raven's nest and the plundering of the nut tree (although I have no doubt they were actual events in Wordsworth's youth), seem to be literary echoes of Spenser's poem. Spenser writes:

> How often have I scaled the craggie Oke,
> All to dislodge the Raven of her nest?
> How have I wearied with many a stroke
> The stately Walnut-tree, the while the rest
> Under the tree fell all for nuts at strife?
> For ylike to me was libertee and lyfe.
>
> *The Shepheardе's Calender*, December Eclogue

For Spenser, in fact, is the great founder of a tradition of mainly Protestant visionary poetry which runs through Milton to Blake, Wordsworth and onwards to Yeats. It is also noteworthy that in this eclogue he refers to his own astronomical studies:

> I learned als the signes of heaven to ken,
> How Phoebe fayles, where Venus sittes, and when.[10]

The study of astronomy which included astrology was part of the quadrivium, so anyone who had been at university would have some knowledge of it; and to understand almost any poetry from the Middle Ages to the seventeenth century some knowledge of it is essential.

My own knowledge of astrology is very sketchy but I hope that the foregoing may have shown that such studies were very much integral to Spenser's work not only in *The Faerie Queene* but also in *The Shephearde's Calender*.

Notes

1 See Helena Shire, *A Preface to Spenser* (1978), pp. 100–3, where the woodcuts illustrating each month are reproduced, with the appropriate sign shown in the heavens.

2 The majority of Theocritus' idylls are idealised scenes from the life of the shepherds in Sicily. (Sicily had been settled by immigrants from Arcadia and it is for this reason that the word 'arcadian' has become synonymous with pastoral innocence.) Though idealised they also contain a strong realistic element. Later workers in this genre progressively moved it further from reality towards the portrayal of a purely imaginary and artificial world. An element of allegory entered in, especially with Virgil, whose eclogues had references to the political events of his own day, particularly to the death and deification by his successor, Augustus, of Julius Caesar. The form never wholly died out during the Middle Ages and was revived by the humanists of the Renaissance. Petrarch (1304–74) introduced into his eclogues an element of ecclesiastical satire, attacking the corruptions of the church of his day. This was a perfectly natural thing for a Christian writer of pastoral poetry to do, since both Old and New Testaments are full of pastoral imagery. Petrarch's poetry was written in Latin; so was Mantuan's, also an ecclesiastical satirist. Mantuan was the favourite poet of Holofernes, the pedantic schoolmaster in *Love's Labour's Lost*. Spenser's English predecessors as pastoralists were Alexander Barclay (1475–1552) and Barnabye Googe (1540–94).

3 See F. W. Bateson, *Critical History of English Poetry*; he compares the importance of their publication with that of the *Lyrical Ballads*

by Wordsworth and Coleridge in 1789, and T. S. Eliot's *Prufrock and Other Observations* in 1916.

4 Helena Shire continues: 'It gave a regime of diet for the season, a tree of the virtues and vices (with penalties) . . . it taught him to find his way by the stars and showed in diagrams how his body was constituted and conditioned by celestial powers of planet or zodiac sign.' *Op. cit*.

5 We find variations of this, for example in Lyly's *Alexander and Campaspe* (1584), and in Shakespeare's *The Two Gentlemen of Verona* and *The Merchant of Venice*. Shakespeare's sonnets are highly original and doubtless contain an autobiographical element, but it is against this convention, I am convinced, that we ought first of all to read them before treating them as historical documents and endeavouring to identify the persons involved, as A. L. Rowse among others has attempted to do; his methodology seems to me to be extraordinarily naive in this respect.

6 Titania, their queen in Shakespeare's *Midsummer Night's Dream*, takes her name from a title of the moon goddess, who, according to Hesiod, was a daughter of the Titan, Hyperion. Keats knew this when he wrote in *Ode to a Nightingale*: 'And haply the Queen Moon is on her throne, Clustered about with all her starry fays.'

7 Thus the mid-point of *Paradise Lost* gives us the image of the Messiah and his chariot overwhelming the hosts of Satan. The mid-point of Gray's *Elegy Written in a Country Churchyard* is an image of inverted royalty: 'Some Cromwell, guiltless of his country's blood.' To these I would add among others Collins' *Ode on the Poetical Character*, where the mid-point of the poem has the image of the 'bright youth of day', that is Apollo.

8 The tradition continues more or less with Spenser's successors. Milton's earlier poems up to and including *Lycidas* are all roughly pastoral in character. Pope represents himself as inheriting his pipe from Colin (Spenser). He certainly wished to proceed to an epic poem, though his projected 'Brutus' was never written. Blake's *Poetical Sketches* and his *Songs of Innocence*, and Wordsworth's *Lyrical Ballads* may in some sense be considered as pastoral essays preceding an epic ambition. Many of Tennyson's early poems show the influence of Theocritus, but his own epic was in fact to be a series of idylls – the *Idylls of the King* – rather than an epic in the full classical or Renaissance sense of the word. The last of the poets in this tradition was W. B. Yeats, who tells us that his earliest work was a play in which he

endeavoured to combine the styles of his two favourite poets, Spenser and Shelley. Fragments of this play survive as 'The Song of the Happy Shepherd' and 'The Sad Shepherd', the two poems with which his *Collected Works* opens.

9 That Spenser, in spite of his Puritan leanings at this time, was conscious of the ecclesiastical calendar, is borne out I think by Alexander's essay on Spenser's *Amoretti* in *Silent Poetry*, edited by Alastair Fowler. Dunlop points out that this series of sonnets is linked to the church's lectionary, as witness the most celebrated, 'Sonett for Easter Day'.

10 The next stanza tells us that Spenser had also studied the tides, the 'power of herbs, both which can hurt and ease', and soothsaying based on the flight of birds (December Eclogue, lines 83–90).

VII

KEPLER'S BELIEF IN ASTROLOGY

Nick Kollerstrom

Commentary

Johannes Kepler (1571–1630), the famous German astronomer, is a most significant figure for historians of astrology. Apart from his important discoveries in astronomy, and his introduction of three minor aspects into the practice of astrological interpretation, his views about celestial influence upon human beings in general are individual. They are neither deterministic nor dogmatic, as Nick Kollerstrom shows.

There is a letter from Kepler to Johan Herwart, which Nick Kollerstrom drew to my attention, in which Kepler speculates about planetary influences upon a man's character at birth. He goes on to consider his own horoscope and dwells on the effects of Saturn as he has experienced them.

> Letter from Johannes Kepler to Johann Herwart, April 1599.
>
> Here is another question: how does the conformation of the heavens influence the character of a man at the moment of his birth? It influences a human being as long as he lives in no other way than that in which the peasant haphazardly ties slings around pumpkins; these do not make the pumpkin grow, but they determine its shape. So do the heavens: they do not give a man morals, experiences, happiness, children, wealth, a wife, but they shape everything with which a man has to do. And yet, from the constellation of the birth of a man, the heavens take an infinite number of forms during the course of his life. They never remain the same; so the constellation at birth is a passing one. Now how can something be active which doesn't exist? It is active in so far as it had that position once . . . Would there perhaps be some mark of this position on human bodies, or is it related to the light and in this way impressed on the proper soul? And how would it imprint on the soul its destiny which is a nothing? All this would be confirmed by experience, and indeed by the experiences of those who are by no means stupid . . .
>
> In my case, Saturn and the sun work together in the sextile

> aspect (I prefer to speak of what I know best). Therefore my body is dry and knotty, and not tall. My soul is faint-hearted and hides itself in literary corners; it is distrustful and fearful; it seeks its way through harsh brambles and becomes entangled in them. Its habits are similar. To gnaw bones, to eat dry bread, to taste spiced and bitter things is a joy to me. To walk over rugged paths, uphill and through thickets, is a holiday treat for me. I know no other way of seasoning my life than science; I do not desire any other spice and I reject it if it is offered to me. My fate is precisely similar to this attitude.
>
> From 'Johan Kepler in seinen Briefen', ed. M. Caspar and W. von Dyck (Munich, 1930); trans. M. M. M., printed in J. B. Ross and Mary Martin McLaughlin (eds), *The Portable Renaissance Reader*, Viking Penguin, 1968.

Interpreting the sun–Saturn sextile in his horoscope Kepler presented a self-deprecating picture of himself and yet one which shows that 'to taste spiced and bitter things is a joy to me' – he is reconciled to this quality. He delights in his predilection for long walks over rugged terrain (see engraving on p. 61). All this is traditional. Kepler recognizes in himself the tendency to choose what is difficult. There is no self pity in his analysis.

The following passage from Cornelius Agrippa supplements this view of Saturn, emphasizing the intellectual side.

> Besides, seeing he [Saturn] is the author of secret contemplation, and estranged from all public affairs, and the highest of all the planets, he doth, as he withcalls his mind from outward business, so also make it ascend higher, and bestows upon men the knowledge and presages of future things. And this is Aristotle's meaning in his book of Problems. By melancholy, saith he, some men are made, as it were, divine, foretelling things to come: and some men are made poets.
>
> Cornelius Agrippa, *Occult Philosophy*

The mind ascending higher is often seen as the Capricornian higher aspect, while 'bestowing upon men the knowledge' is seen as the Aquarian one, both symbolized by their glyphs. Agrippa traces the association between melancholy and prophecy and contemplation back to Plato.

In William Lilly's *Christian Astrology* (1647) these last ideas dwindle to ' . . . he is profound in imagination, in his acts severe, in words reserved . . . ' (when well placed). The busy practitioner might not expect many such among his clients, perhaps.

Nick Kollerstrom shows that Kepler's view of the effects of planetary conjunctions on political matters leave scope for initiative rather than for submission to fate.

A. L. K.

> The soul of the newly-born baby is marked for life by the pattern of the stars at the moment it comes into the world, unconsciously remembers it, and remains sensitive to the return of configurations of a similar kind.
>
> Kepler, *Harmonices Mundi*, chapter 7

Kepler's lifelong attempt to recast astrology within a harmonic–Pythagorean framework has relevance today. As the year 1987 saw the first visible supernova since Kepler's star of 1604,[1] this seems an appropriate time to re-examine the achievement. Very few of Kepler's works have been translated into English down the centuries, which has permitted a radically one-sided interpretation of his work to flourish. In recent years, however, modern translations of one of Kepler's seminal works on the theory of how astrology works have appeared,[2] which have made available for the first time to English readers a perspective on what he really believed. That one of the great creative founders of modern science struggled for decades to relate together astronomy and astrology is a matter of no small importance. Was it indeed the case, as one scornful academic has argued, that 'Kepler's remedy [that is, his proposed reform of astrology] was one of those that in the end kill the patient'?[3]

Historians seem agreed that Kepler's beliefs have had small effect upon posterity, being against the tide of events:

> Kepler's defence of astrology . . . seems to have been entirely without effect upon later generations.[4]

Another expressed the view that Kepler's rationalizations

> could not endure nor gratify in an age of expanding experimentation, in an age of telescopes, magnetism, static electricity, microscopes, egg and sperm cells, the vacuum, atmospheric and gas pressures, etc. Hence they proved very shaky supports and were worth no more than straws to drowning men. They stopped with Kepler or with men like Fludd. With the passing of that generation they are never heard of again.[5]

Like Ptolemy, Kepler regarded the twin themes of astronomy and astrology as being of equal interest and value – but he was the last of this tradition. He was, quite simply, the last Western astronomer of note to believe in astrology. After him the abyss opened up, which he would surely have regarded as a more terrible thing than the religious disputes of his day. He was employed as a 'mathematicus', which term related both to astronomy and astrology; it did not have the abstract meaning of today. As Kepler is known to all astronomers for the three laws of planetary motion which he discovered, so is he today known among astrologers for the three new aspects which he formulated.

In his presidential address to the British Astronomical Association in 1979, Leslie White said of Kepler that it was not generally appreciated that 'throughout his troubled life until his death in 1630, his inspiration and his most magnificent ideas came directly from Pythagorean cosmology'.[6] These beliefs of his are normally dismissed in the history books as mere vestiges of a medievalism from which he was regrettably unable to free himself – in striking contrast to his more modern contemporary, Galileo. In 1601 Kepler wrote *De Fundamentis Astrologiae Certioribus*, and then, in 1619, *Harmonices Mundi*. The former is of especial interest to us, as being in the form of an extended introduction to his yearly almanac, written in Latin and being somewhat a bid for the post of imperial mathematician at Prague – in which he was successful. It gives, as he says, 'what one may state and defend on physical grounds concerning the foundations of Astrology and the coming year 1602'. The latter opus, which took twenty years to compose, was a grand five-point synthesis of geometry, arithmetic, music, astrology, and astronomy. It has never been translated into English and is today, alas, remembered merely because his third law of planetary motion is contained in it.

'TERTIUM INTERVENS' – 'THIRD MAN IN THE MIDDLE'

In 1610 he published his *Tertium Intervens* or 'Third Man in the Middle', wherein he defined his position over the gathering storm of controversy between astrology and astronomy. The title page referred to 'Star-gazing superstition', but also warned 'theologians, physicians and philosophers against throwing out the baby with the bathwater, and thereby maltreating their profession'.[7] They would be, he claimed, *maltreating their profession* if they threw out astrology, or rather the kernel of truth which he believed that it held.

At this time he was the imperial mathematician under the Emperor Rudolf II at Prague. He had risen to the post after the death of the astronomer, Tycho Brahe, in 1601. Previously he had worked in Graz, Austria, teaching secondary school mathematics. It was there that he commenced preparing yearly almanacs and cast horoscopes. In 1595 an odd notion came to him. To quote Carl Sagan's account, slightly dramatized from contemporary evidence:

> Kepler was a brilliant thinker and a lucid writer, but he was a disaster as a classroom teacher. He mumbled. He digressed. He was at times utterly incomprehensible. He drew only a handful of students his first year at Graz; the next year there were none. He was distracted by an incessant interior clamour of associations and speculations vying for his attention. And one pleasant summer afternoon, deep in the interstices of one of his interminable lectures, he was visited by a revelation that was to alter radically the future of astronomy. Perhaps he stopped in mid-sentence. His inattentive students, longing for the end of the day, took little notice, I suspect, of the historic moment.[8]

The strange notion which then dawned upon Kepler was the idea that the five Platonic solids, nesting one inside the other, could specify the relative distances of the six planets in their orbits round the sun. (He was by this time committed to the Copernican, sun-centred universe.) Only one person had astronomical observations accurate enough to test this model, and that was Tycho Brahe; and, to quote Sagan again, 'by chance, at Rudolf's suggestion, he [that is Brahe] had just invited Kepler, whose mathematical fame was growing, to join him in Prague'. This belief meant a lot to him, even though his later discovery of elliptical orbits was somewhat to demolish its credibility.

The two of them must have had some interesting conversations together. It was the view of Tycho Brahe that: 'Those who deny the influence of the planets violate its clear proofs, which it does not become people of sound judgement to contradict.'[9]

In the vast transition from the closed Ptolemaic world to the infinite Copernican universe, the two shared the conviction that, though many traditional beliefs would have to be jettisoned, the fact of celestial influence could be demonstrated. As Kepler inscribed on the title-page of *De Fundamentis*, 'Discover the force of the heavens O Men: once recognised it can be put to use'.

'DE FUNDAMENTIS'

This work, whose title is variously translated as 'On Giving Astrology Sounder Foundations' or 'On the More Certain Fundamentals of Astrology', gives quite concisely Kepler's view of how and the extent to which astrology works; in a manner which, in the view of the present writer, has not yet been improved upon. Justifying his presentation of an almanac he said, in the foreword,

> For he who will please the crowd and for the sake of the most ephemeral renown will either proclaim those things which nature does not display or even will publish genuine miracles of nature without regard to deeper causes is a spiritually corrupt person . . . With the best of intentions I publicly speak to the crowd (which is eager for things new) on the subject of what is to come.

Possibly with undue optimism, he invited his patron to compare his forecasts with political events, 'For only those who are concerned with politics in a rational way will be able to judge correctly the success of these forecasts'.

His early work had attempted to explain aspects by relating them to three-dimensional solids but this didn't really get very far. His later work derives more completely from musical intervals. He explains the five aspects Ptolemy used and the three new ones of his own by taking various fractional lengths of a string, as with a violin string, and looking at which ratios give pleasing harmonies and which do not; but even this doesn't work perfectly and he spends a lot of time looking at two-dimensional plane figures and their degrees of symmetry. As a mathematician, he discovers a couple of new such combinations – 'tessellations' or regular figures that lock into each other on a plane surface, and he uses the angles which they form to explain which harmonies are astrologically important and which are not. So, there are a lot of diagrams in his work showing regular figures in terms of the angle made against the zodiac. He asserted that 'No more than 8 harmonic ratios arise from comparing the regular plane figures', adding that he hoped one day to be able to demonstrate this. These give him the eight aspects of conjunction, opposition (1:1), trine (1:2), square (1:3), quintile (1:4), biquintile (2:3), sextile (1:5) and sesquiquadrature (5:8). So there is a slight difference between Kepler's approach to harmonics and that which the late John Addey developed:[10] Kepler seeks to show

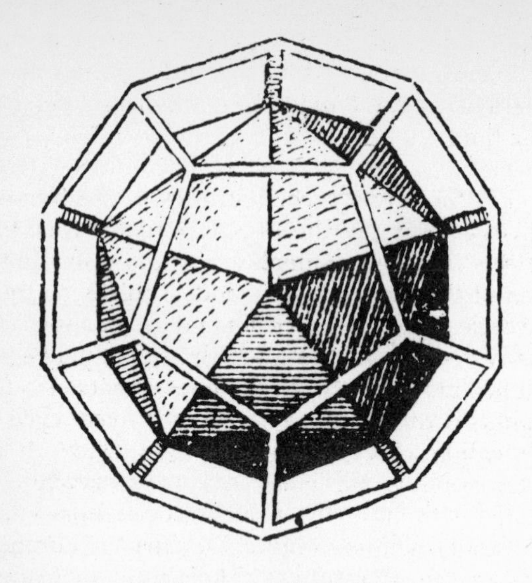

Figure 9 Dodecahedron
From Harmonices Mundi, *Book V*

that there are a limited number of aspects that actually work in astrological terms.[11]

Concerning the three new aspects which he discovered, the quintile (72 degrees), the biquintile (144 degrees) and the sesquiquadrate (135 degrees), he claims to have detected their effect through years of weather observations. Their effect was a matter of empirical inquiry as much as anything else in the natural world; in this view he differs radically from other founders of modern science in the seventeenth century. He had a collection of 800 horoscopes, and claimed also to have taken daily weather observations over a period of some sixteen years.

De Fundamentis describes the effects of the sun and moon and the planets in terms of their light, the influences of the moon upon humours etc., and then comes on to his view that 'Earth has a vegetative animal force, having some sense of geometry'. The earth is stimulated by the geometric convergence of rays formed round it. The world-soul is sentient but not conscious. As a shepherd is pleased by the piping of a flute without understanding the theory of musical harmony, so likewise earth responds to the angles and aspects made by the heavens but not in a conscious manner. Eclipses, he says,

> are so important as omens because the animal faculty of the Earth is violently disturbed by the sudden intermission of light, experiencing something like emotion and persisting in it for some time.

He surmises that there are 'cyclic journeys in the humours of the Earth', and gives as example 'the 19 year period of the Moon' which sailors say affects tides – presumably the 18.6-year nutation cycle, that is rotation of the lunar nodes – and 'if this is so the laws and periods of the cycles should be investigated by collating observations made over many years, something which has not yet been done'. In recent years it has indeed been shown how climate effects, harvests and tidal heights do vary with such a nineteen-year cycle.[12]

Astrologers will be relieved to hear Kepler's view that, 'If astrological predictions about a particular year prove mistaken I think they should be treated with indulgence, such is our ignorance of causes'. In February (of 1601), Venus conjunct Mercury 'will bring turmoil to the conditions of the atmosphere. Their influences are about as contradictory as those of Saturn and Mars.' Then in March, 'there will be thunder due to Sun opposing Mars, although Mars' latitude detracts from the force of this aspect', yet 'The clustering of aspects adds force to it, thus there will be unnatural warmth'. In April, 'there will be rain at least two days before and after the Full Moon, since the planets are all aspected to one another'. Because of Saturn and Mars at quintile in May, 'There follows the most delightful mildness with moisture'. That may be the first account of the effect of a quintile! Jupiter and Mars come together in July and 'This will give clear skies and great heat'.

Lunar aspects come and go too quickly to create weather, he explains; however body humours are affected by them:

> let the physician, if he can, refrain from treating a seriously weakened patient when the Moon is in a powerful aspect. For every aspect is of itself a natural purgation. But if strong purges are needed let him on the contrary choose powerful aspects. Indeed, the whole business of crises depends upon the return of the Moon and its configurations with the planets, and it is vain to seek explanation for it elsewhere.

This view is of interest in view of the modern finding that hospital operations conducted during the full moon period are associated with greatly increased amounts of bleeding.[13]

The last, political section of this 1601 calendar contains an affirmation on transits: 'almost every motion of the body or soul or its transition to a new state occurs at a moment when the figure of the heavens corresponds to its birth figure . . . '[14] This comment is *à propos* the Jupiter–Mars conjunction coming up, where he says it would be usual for astrologers to predict the death of some outstanding military leader. Not wishing to 'slander the heavens, by asserting that they have been framed so as to kill men', he explains that 'this movement leads to disaster for those who are ill disposed, but in the same way it draws on to great things those who are stronger by reason of their age or state of health. We may see each of these alternatives this year, but there is no necessity for them to occur.'

For the Mars–Saturn conjunction in September, he recommends that, if 'there is a risk of civil discord, let there be no assemblies in August and September – let them be dispersed, by an early removal of the causes of discontent, or let some new matter be proposed . . . ' On the other hand, if a bold deed is to be undertaken, which 'requires persevering effort', this time would be suitable, adding: 'For it lies in our power to affect how these things turn out; it is not a matter of complete necessity.' In the next paragraph he adds that this conjunction occurs 'when these planets are rising over Poland' (?), and since the previous solar eclipse 'will be deepest in Muscovy and Poland, and since there is already war in those parts, I think that these are signs of disaster for that region'. Regrettably, I have been unable to check up on this prediction. He concludes, 'If, meanwhile, a secure peace is established, there will be absolutely no danger from the effects of the heavens alone'.

A COMPOSER OF CALENDARS

Kepler went on producing calendars for three decades, from 1595 to 1624. In the city of Graz he worked as 'district mathematician and calendar maker' and gained his initial renown from the accuracy of his first predictions: he predicted a winter of severe cold and an invasion by the Turks, both of which came to pass. The composing of calendars was for him a way of making money, and yet he feared lest it should compromise his scientific reputation, writing to Maestlin that 'There is much therein which must be deliberately pardoned, or else it injures my reputation with you'. The prognostications were expected to include such things as war and pestilence, weather and harvest, the religious and political upheavals, and when to sow or bleed or purge and the like. 'Many of the rules of this Arabic art amount to nothing', Kepler said (to Maestlin). He only printed some 500 copies per year. Kepler's biographer, Caspar, referred to the calendar makers, 'of whom there were very many', indicating that it was a practice in some demand.

Of especial interest – for persons such as the present writer unable to read old German – would be the English translations of Kepler's prognosticums for 1603 and 1604. In 1603 many such works were printed about the Jupiter–Saturn conjunction of that year: this event, which occurs every twenty years, had just moved into a fire sign of the zodiac. The conjunction recurs in the zodiac signs of one element for ten consecutive conjunctions, that is for two centuries, so what could this entry into a new element portend? Previously the transition of this conjunction-sequence into a new element had been seen as portending the rise of Charlemagne, and before that it was in the time of Christ. Apart from Kepler's own works, what of note could be about to happen?

Yet more awesome was the appearance the very next year of a new star, extremely bright, in fact sparkling and rainbow hued, right next to the Jupiter–Saturn conjunction, when it was also conjunct Mars! The four stars glittered in the constellation Ophiucus (the Serpent bearer), and the imperial mathematician was asked to interpret it.[15] He was more interested in scientific observation of the new star, but everyone wanted to hear about what it signified. His 1604 work, *De Stella Nova*, gives a discourse on signs and their interpretations, but he there appears far from convinced as to what meaning could be assigned to the spectacle.

The new supernova came to be called 'Kepler's star' though he had not discovered it. It is noteworthy that the only two 'new stars' ever seen in the West – that is supernovae or stars exploding within the Milky Way galaxy and therefore visible to the naked eye – are named after Tycho Brahe and Kepler.[16] One earlier one may have been seen in the time of Hipparchus, but there are no others. These two astronomers spent twenty tempestuous months together. The most accurate astronomical data ever made became accessible to the one person capable of interpreting them. Brahe found the situation very trying because his world system had an unmoving earth and Kepler would never accept this. It is easily forgotten that at the turn of the seventeenth century Brahe's system, where the earth rotated daily but otherwise did not move, was more widely accepted than either the Ptolemaic or the Copernican systems. It was a pragmatic compromise. Brahe was handing his data over to a man who was going to demolish the credibility of his world system, and instead enthrone the sun at the centre of things. He needed Brahe's data to do this. However, the two maintained a deep mutual respect.

Kepler as the imperial mathematician found himself on occasion grilled by the people of Prague over his astrological views and weather prophecies. From 'those of the lower classes with straightforward and active minds . . . I get such a working over that I might as well call them my teachers', he noted. On one occasion his biographer Caspar tells how, when a few sextile aspects were in prospect,

> Kepler swore 15 days before, in front of doubters, that there would be wind and rain on that day. In due course, on the day in question, came a fierce gale, driving black clouds, so that at noon it was as dark as half an hour before sunset. Amazed, the people asked themselves what was happening. Then the cry grew loud, 'Kepler comes'.[17]

His 1618 'prognosticon' predicted that the month of May would 'bring great upheavals to the world', and in that historic month two Prague councillors were thrown from a window, and the Thirty Years' War broke out. The 1618 calendar contained the remark that 'if a true comet should appear in the heavens' then the calendar writers would have to 'sharpen up their pens'. In that year, no fewer than *three* comets made their appearance, one having an especially bright tail. It was evident to all that this was an omen concerning the war that had broken out, as the emperor confronted the rebellious Bohemians, but of what kind? Persons waited to hear whom Kepler would side with, whether, as he put it, he was 'fox or hare'. After all, he was a staunch Protestant in a Catholic court and this was a religious war. It was for just this reason that he disapproved of making predictions, as it appealed to superstition in a way that enabled people to be manipulated. His belief in comets as omens seems to have been as follows: though such belief in omens was superstition, the Deity had some regard for popular superstition and so could arrange for comets to appear in the appropriate places and times to have a suitable message.

On the subject of making predictions, we may note that when the renowned General Wallenstein anonymously requested his horoscope, Kepler appended to the horoscope the words: 'I have only devised horoscopes when I was sure that my work is intended for somebody who understands philosophy, and is not afflicted with contradictory superstition.' (He apparently understood that it was intended for Wallenstein.) To be sure, Kepler was criticized when Wallenstein was killed on 25 March 1634: on being asked for some future predictions in 1624 by Wallenstein he did give them, but they ended with the date of March 1634, which he said, 'will entail a terrible confusion in the country which will affect him'. The dire question was asked, had this prediction been self fulfilling, as the general had always been so dependent upon astrologers?[18]

TWO NOTABLE CORRESPONDENTS

One of Kepler's regular correspondents, the physician Georg Brengger, noted in a letter to Kepler in 1608:

> You say you have confirmed by meteorological experience that there exist the additional aspects quintile, biquintile and sesquiquadrature. I myself should like to see an example of this observational material, for with a number and variety of aspects always occurring, so that one is unsure to which of them one should ascribe a change in the atmosphere, I do not know how I should make an observational test, or even whether I should find it possible to do so.

To this Kepler replied,

> In 1600, when from 23 April until 2 May, New Style, there were no primary aspects, and Magini's tables showed Saturn and Jupiter to be at quintile, on 1 May there was a very heavy fall of snow both in Prague and in Styria for Ferdinand's wedding, and the jousting had to be cancelled. From observing the heavens, it was found that during these same days Saturn and Jupiter were 72° apart. Tycho's students made the check on my behalf with Tycho's quadrant.

The majority opinion today would assuredly be in favour of Kepler's correspondent's view.

Kepler's correspondence with Robert Fludd does not touch on astrology directly, yet remains of a general interest concerning the nature of symbolism; it shows a disagreement between Fludd's pictorial-cum-occult view and Kepler's mathematical-cum-rational position. They had both composed treatises on the subject of 'harmonices Mundi' but from very different viewpoints. Fludd (Hermetic–cabbalist and London apothecary) claimed that 'Kepler is concerned with the external movement of things, but I with the internal and essential processes of Nature'. Kepler maintained that Fludd's Hermetic analogies were 'dragged in by the hair', adding that 'Without mathematical demonstrations I am like a blind man'. This correspondence was discussed by the physicist Wolfgang Pauli,[19] and more recently has been reviewed in the Cambridge University Press publication, *Occult and Scientific Mentalities in the Renaissance*.[20]

THROWING OUT THE ZODIAC?

> Inasmuch as the soul bears within itself the idea of the zodiac, or rather of its centre, it also feels which planet stands at which time under which degree of the zodiac, and measures the angles of the rays that meet on the earth; but inasmuch as it receives from the irradiation of the Divine essence the geometrical figures of the circle and (by comparing the circle with certain parts of it) the archetypal harmonies (not, to be sure, in purely geometrical form but as it were overlaid or rather completely saturated with a filtrate of glittering radiations), it also recognises the measurements of the angles and judges some as congruent or harmonious, others as incongruent.[21]

That statement occurs in his great work, *Harmonices Mundi*, and shows a somewhat Platonic attitude, whereby the soul has a pre-existent concordance with the geometry of the heavens, so that it can in some way sense the impressions which it makes.

Yet it is certainly true that Kepler sometimes dismissed the zodiac; indeed he only reached the new aspects because of this attitude. While for Ptolemy the five kinds of aspect were all formed between zodiac signs, that is they had to be multiples of 30 degrees, Kepler was prepared to ignore this limitation and thereby develop his three new aspects.

What were Kepler's grounds for dismissing the zodiac? For example, were they based on the fact of precession, whereby the zodiac divisions have moved away from their original stellar references? One hopes that more of his works will be translated into English. Mathematically he viewed the number twelve as the most perfect number for dividing up the circle. He apparently found the triplicities of the zodiac more acceptable than the individual signs, as shown by his discussion of the Saturn–Jupiter 'great conjunctions' moving through the different elements (see Figure 10).

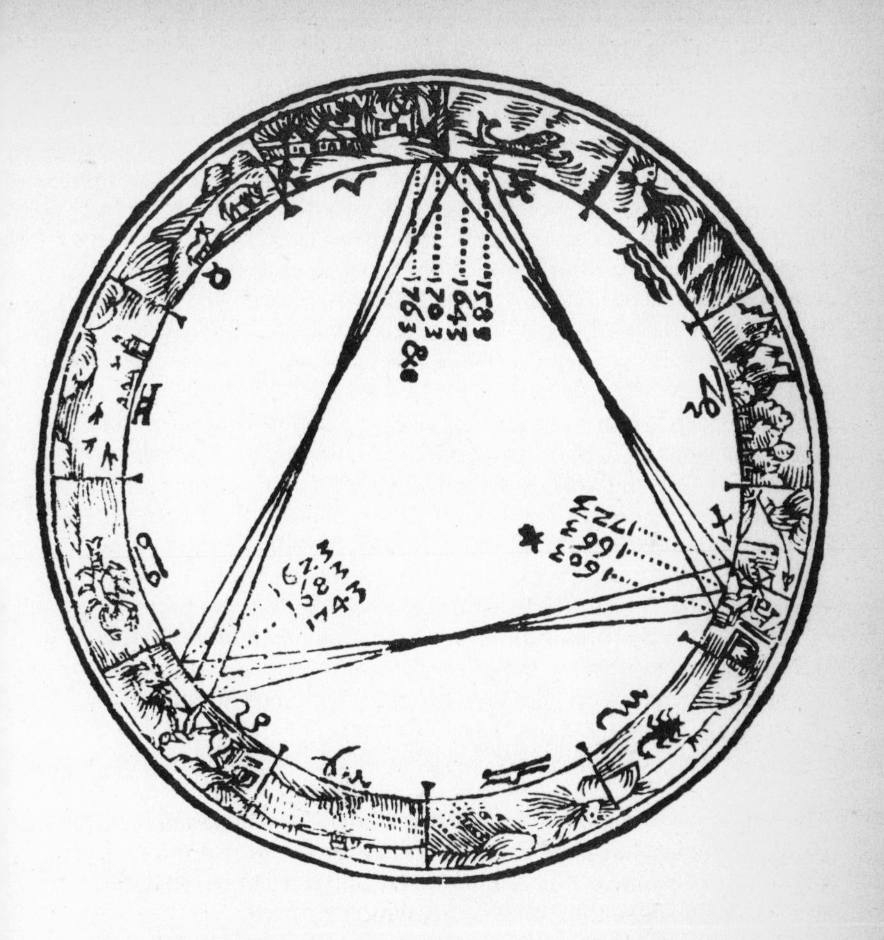

Figure 10 De Trigono Igneo. This figure from De Stella Nova *shows a sequence of Jupiter–Saturn conjunctions, which occur every twenty years, from 1603 to 1763. It shows the process of entering the three fire signs, and how this had fully occurred from 1663 onwards. Great predictions were made on the basis of this, which happens only every 800 years. It happened previously, Kepler pointed out, at the time of Christ. Tycho Brahe had expressed the view that this was only the seventh such since the world began, and so was a special epoch. Of interest are the zodiac sign images Kepler has drawn round the side; the figure has been enlarged to twice the size of the original.*

In 1606 Kepler wrote to an English scientist (Harriot) saying, 'Ten years ago I rejected the division into 12 equal parts, the houses, the dominations [i.e., rulerships], the triplicities etc, all of that, keeping only the aspects and transferring astrology to the science of harmonics'.[22] He rejected much of traditional astrology in his attempt to recast it in a heliocentric world. For example, in a mood to oppose astrological determinism, he boasted that 'An astrologer will search in vain in my horoscope for the reasons why in 1595 I discovered the relationship between the heavenly spheres', etc. But, on the other hand, he wrote to a friend: 'Regard this as certain, Mars never crosses my path without involving me in disputes and putting me myself in a quarrelsome mood' (to Fabricius in 1602). Should we conclude from this that he was prepared to blame the heavens for his temper, but not to allow it credit for his discoveries?

'HARMONICES MUNDI'

> Now because 18 months ago the first dawn, 3 months ago broad daylight but a very few days ago the full sun of the most highly remarkable spectacle has risen – nothing holds me back. I can give myself up to the sacred frenzy, I can have the insolence to make a full confession to mortal men that I have stolen the golden vessels of the Egyptians to make from them a tabernacle for my God far from the confines of the land of Egypt. If you forgive me I shall rejoice; if you are angry, I shall bear it; I am indeed casting the die and writing the book, either for my contemporaries or for posterity to read, it matters not which: let the book await its reader for a hundred years; God himself has waited six thousand years for his work to be seen.

This exclamation (in *Harmonices Mundi*, Book V) is normally viewed as Kepler rejoicing over discovering his third law, that the cube of planetary orbit radius is proportional to the square of orbit period – though with some puzzlement that the mere discovery of a mathematical relationship should get him into such a state. However, a modern scholar has pointed out that

> the cause is in the success of the harmonic archetype, which now, thanks to the period–radius law, can give a full account of the observed structure of the planetary system . . . Kepler seems to be proclaiming his own success in the task at which

> Ptolemy failed, namely to give a true account of the harmony of the world, expressed in musical consonances, astrological aspects and the motions of the planets. Astrological harmony is an integral part of Kepler's work as it is of Ptolemy's.[23]

He discovered Ptolemy's *Harmonica* in 1617, saying that it afforded him an 'especial increase of his passionate desire for knowledge and encouragement of his purpose' – so perhaps the 'golden vessels of the Egyptians' referred to Ptolemy's studies in Alexandria. The apprehension that his endeavour might have to wait some time for readers who could understand it may have been justified.

> But now, Urania, there is need for a louder sound while I climb along the harmonic scale of the celestial movements to higher things where the true archetype of the fabric of the world is kept hidden.

This seems a suitable position in which to leave Johannes Kepler, as he articulated the polyphonic song of the solar system in Book V of *Harmonices Mundi*. He expressed the hope that it would inspire musicians and one wonders whether it did so. For example, Venus and earth in their periods expressed the ratio 5:8 which as a musical sixth he saw as quite a pleasant ratio. (There are exactly five inferior conjunctions of Venus every eight years.) 'The agreement is frighteningly good' was the verdict of the astronomer, Fred Hoyle, concerning the tie up between musical ratios and planetary velocities as Kepler described it, and he added, 'One wonders how many modern scientists faced by a similar situation in their work would fail to be impressed by such remarkable numerical coincidences . . . '[24] While astrology is by its nature earth centred,the music of the solar system is for Kepler heard as it were from the sun, because the relative speeds of the planets – between aphelion and perihelion, their points nearest to and furthest from the sun – interweave to give the consonant, that is harmonious sounding intervals. One modern scholar has observed that Kepler's 'elaborate polyphony turns out to be in excellent agreement with observation', and that there has been 'no advance upon Kepler's explanation of how the system originally came by its resonances'.[25]

CONCLUSION

Leibniz referred to Kepler as 'that incomparable man', whom 'the fates had watched over that he might be the first among mortals to publish the laws of the heavens, the truth of things, and the principles of the gods'.[26] However, the mechanical philosophy which developed in the seventeenth century was opposed to his way of thinking. It took his three laws of planetary motion, it used his ephemerides tables, which were more accurate than any previously published by 'nearly two orders of magnitude'[27] – and forgot the rest. The consequence was that, to quote the science historian Bernard Cohen, writing in 1975:

> At the present time, not a single one of Kepler's greatest works has ever been completely translated into English, French, Russian, or Italian. And only in recent years have any of Kepler's writings whatsoever been published in complete English versions.[28]

The first Kepler biography of any note to appear in English was the 1959 translation of Caspar's magnum opus. One section of *Harmonices Mundi* is now available in English, along with the science fiction work, *Somnium*, about a journey to the moon. Then in 1975, quatercentenary celebrations were held in various parts of the world, celebrating Kepler's achievements, and a large English volume was published by the journal *Vistas in Astronomy*. For the first time, a tolerable amount appeared in English, permitting evaluation of the man's beliefs and achievements. An essay such as the present one, based upon source material in English, could not have been composed at all prior to the 1980s. Part IV of *Harmonices Mundi* was characterized by Kepler as being 'Astrological, on the causes of Aspects'. Its tanslation would be of interest, as also would be that of his *De Stella Nova* and *Tertium Intervens*.

Notes

1 Kepler's star of 1604 was a galactic supernova, that is an exploding star in our galaxy. The 1987 supernova was an explosion in a daughter galaxy to the milky way, one of the Magellanic Clouds, visible in the southern hemisphere. Other supernovae in between these two were in other galaxies and so only visible telescopically.

2 J. V. Field, 'A Lutheran astrologer: Johannes Kepler', *Archive for History of Exact Sciences*, vol. 31, (1984) pp. 190–268, contains a translation of *De Fundamentis Astrologia Certioribus*. See also an earlier translation of *De Fundamentis* entitled 'Johannes Kepler's on the more certain fundamentals of astrology' by Bruce Brackenridge and Mary Rossi in *Proceedings of the American Philosophical Association* (1979).
3 G. Simon, 'Kepler's astrology: the direction of a reform', *Vistas in Astronomy*, vol. 18 (London: Pergamon, 1977), p. 446.
4 J. V. Field, 'Astrology in Kepler's cosmology', in Patrick Curry (ed.), *Astrology, Science and Society* (Boydell, 1987), p. 169.
5 M. Grabaud, 'Astrology's demise', *Osiris*, vol. 13 (1958), p. 253.
6 L. White, 'Pythagoras', presidential address, *Journal of the British Astronomical Association*, vol. 90 (1980), p. 123.
7 Max Caspar *et al.* (eds), *Gesammelte Werke*, vol. 4 (Munich, 1937), p. 147.
8 C. Sagan, *Cosmos* (1980), (London: Futura, 1983), p. 57.
9 Lecture by Brahe at the University of Copenhagen, 27 September 1574, *Oratio de Disciplinis Mathematicis* (quoted in Sven Svensson, *Dynamic Astrology* (Spearman, 1983), p. 12).
10 J. Addey, *Harmonics in Astrology* (Fowler, 1976).
11 The smallest aspects that could be effective Kepler ascertained by looking at polygons of decreasing 'nobility', that is degree of symmetry, and this he found reached a limit at 'configurations which hesitate between power and powerlessness, namely the 24° arc from the pentekaedecagon [fifteen-sided] and the 18° arc from the icosigon [twenty-sided]' (*Harmonices Mundi*, Book IV, proposition XV). Field comments 'The lowest grade of configurations which are definitely accepted as aspects is that of the decile [36 degrees], tridecile [108 degrees], octile [45 degrees] and trioctile [135 degrees] aspects' (op. cit., 1984, p. 218).
12 M. Gauquelin, *The Cosmic Clocks* (Owen, 1969), p. 103.
13 E. Andrews, 'Moon talk, the cyclic periodicity of postoperative haemorrhage', *Journal of the Florida Medical Association*, May 1960, pp. 62–6.
14 J. Kepler, *De Fundamentis*, section LXXV, 1602.
15 On 17 October 1604, when Kepler saw this new star, it stood at 22 degrees of Sagittarius, merely 3 degrees from the ecliptic, with Jupiter at 20 degrees, Mars at 25 degrees and Saturn at 12 degrees of the same sign.
16 'Tycho's star' of 1572 was in a spiral arm at the edge of our galaxy, while 'Kepler's star' was a supernova near to its centre.

The explosion of 1054 which formed the crab nebula would have been at least as bright and visible in daylight; however, no European records exist of its sighting, an indication of the prevalent belief that the heavens were immutable. Book II of Pliny's *Natural History* describes the new star seen by Hipparchus.

17 M. Caspar, *Kepler*, English translation (Collier-Mac, 1962), p. 172.
18 For a discussion see A. Beer, *Vistas in Astronomy*, vol. 18 (London: Pergamon, 1978), p. 408.
19 W. Pauli, 'The influence of archetypal ideas on the scientific theories of Kepler', in C. Jung and W. Pauli, *The Interpretation of Nature and the Psyche* (London: Routledge, 1955).
20 B. Vickers (ed.), *Occult and Scientific Mentalities in the Renaissance* (Cambridge: CUP, 1986), ch. 3, p. 153, ch. 5, pp. 177–229 and ch. 8, pp. 284–90.
21 *Harmonices Mundi*, Book IV (quoted in W. Pauli, op. cit.).
22 Letter to Harriot, 1606, quoted in Vickers, op. cit., p. 267.
23 J. V. Field, 'Astrology in Kepler's Cosmology' in P. Curry (ed.), *Astrology, Science and Society* (Boydell, 1987), p. 168.
24 Quoted in A. Beer, 'Kepler's astrology and mysticism', *Vistas in Astronomy*, vol. 18 (London: Pergamon, 1975), p. 408.
25 J. V. Field, op. cit., p. 290.
26 G. Leibniz (1689), 'Essay on the causes of the motions of the heavenly bodies' in *Acta Eruditorum*, quoted in I. Bernard Cohen, 'Kepler's century', *Vistas in Astronomy*, vol. 18 (London: Pergamon, 1975), p. 12.
27 O. Gingerich, 'Kepler's place in astronomy', *Vistas in Astronomy*, vol. 18 (London: Pergamon, 1975), p. 262: 'The fantastic improvement of nearly two orders of magnitude in the prediction of planetary positions . . . '
28 I. Bernard Cohen, op. cit., p. 5.

VIII

SOME VARIETIES OF ELECTIONAL ASTROLOGY

Annabella Kitson

Commentary

The notes which follow sketch the philosophical assumptions behind this genre and exemplify some of the ways in which it has been used, with special reference to its English heyday in the seventeenth century.

As the notion of 'elections' is not nowadays as familiar as other kinds of astrology, these notes are intended as a preliminary to the analysis by Derek Appleby of the foundation of St Paul's Cathedral, which he studies as an election.

In the seventeenth century we find a whole range of objects for election. Elections are made for personal reasons, important or trivial; for affairs of state; for buildings for the community. Some are made using sophisticated astrology, others with simple observation of the moon. They are used – very interestingly – to choose the best moment to start a piece of work, or to gain favours of many kinds, and also in medical astrology.

Sometimes elections – and, indeed, astrology generally – serve a subsidiary but vital role in deciding the moment for magical work, alchemy, and the making of talismans. Elias Ashmole, the great practitioner of electional astrology, wrote in his *Theatrum Chemicum* that 'By Elections we may Governe Order and Produce things as we please . . . ' I think it will be clear that he did not apply this only to alchemical processes for which elections are made. It may well be that the association between magical processes and astrology has coloured the way it has been seen; this may apply particularly to electional astrology, the kind used in such processes.

It seems that from ancient times elections have not always been clearly distinguished from horary questions. Mr Pattie, in 'Greek Astrology' in this book, quotes the *Prorogations* of Dorotheus of Sidon, which he takes it 'are answers to specific questions put by worried clients'. They include 'What sort of slave will this be . . . ?' and 'What price will I get . . . ?' (which appear to be horary questions), together with such questions as 'When is it best to build a building?' which has the answer 'When the Moon is increasing in computation and in light . . . ' with several conditions, in effect stating principles of electing.

Eugenio Garin quotes *Speculum Astronomiae*,[1] giving a distinction between making 'a judgment on the thing concerning which the interrogation was made with radical intention, namely, whether it shall be accomplished or not . . . ' (a horary matter), and choosing 'a praiseworthy hour to start some task for someone whose nativity is known . . . ' (an election).

Garin comments upon ' . . . the separation, which is so wide as to be almost a contradiction, between the doctrine of the interrogations [interrogationes equals eroteseis] as a presupposition of the "elections" [electiones equals Katarchai], and the theoretical endeavour made by Ptolemy in the doctrine of birth'. This touches on the divide between the purist followers of Ptolemy, for whom the birth moment means that 'the fate is sealed once and for all', at birth, and those who thought that through 'interrogations' man could 'choose his own star'.

Notes

1 Eugenio Garin, *Astrology in the Renaissance* (London: Routledge, 1983), pp. 37–8 and especially p. 123, n. 8.

> Some natural tears they dropped, but wiped them soon;
> The world was all before them, where to choose
> Their place of rest, and Providence their guide.
> John Milton, *Paradise Lost*, Book XII The expulsion from Eden

Electional astrology is the art of choosing, according to astrological principles, an auspicious moment for a deed, or for the inception of a project.

The importance of a good beginning is a powerful notion; it raises hopes of a good outcome. Symbolic moments are recognized today even by the most sophisticated: the placing of a crown on a monarch's head, the signing of a treaty, the words 'I now pronounce you man and wife' at a wedding, the launching of a ship or the beginning of a new year. Modern journalism stresses such moments. There are more private times, such as first entering a new house, which also elicit good wishes. What are good wishes exactly, if not a covert suggestion that the mind influences events?

Underlying all astrology is the philosophical belief that a universal sympathy unites heaven and earth. An ancient and elaborate system of correspondences between celestial and earthly things was recapitulated by Cornelius Agrippa (1486–1535) in his *Three Books of Occult*

Luna, the moon; at her feet, Cancer, the crab, the sign of her dignity. (Engraving, 'Seven Planets' series, the Master 'I. B.' of Nuremburg, 1529.)

Philosophy. This circulated widely and was translated into English by John Freake and published in London in 1651.

> Seeing there is a Three-fold World – Elementary, Celestial and Intellectual – and every inferior is governed by its superior, and receiveth the influence of the virtues thereof, so that the very Original and Chief Worker of all doth by

> angels, the heavens, stars, animals, plants, metals and stones convey from Himself the virtue of His Omnipotency upon us, for whose service He made and created all these things: Wise men conceive it no way irrational that it should be possible for us to ascend by the same degrees through each World, to the same very original World itself, the Maker of all things and First Cause, from whence all things are and proceed; and also to enjoy not only these virtues . . . but . . . to draw new Virtues from above.
>
> Cornelius Agrippa, *Occult Philosophy*

Agrippa has described a chain of being which links stones via stars to the First Cause. By giving minute details of the correspondences between planets and the terrestrial things they rule he shows how man may aspire to 'draw new virtues from above', and he relates all this to the Platonic theory of ideas (Chapter 11): 'Platonists say that all inferior bodies are exemplified by the superior Ideas.'

A mastery of these correspondences – the grammar of astrology – was essential to the interpretation of any horoscope, natal or otherwise. If, like Marsilio di Ficino and the Neoplatonists, one wished to 'draw down' virtues from the heavens, one must know with what terrestrial things to court these benefits, reinforcing the strengths or mitigating the weaknesses of a nativity in this way. Electional astrology, in this not unlike such astral magic procedures, is a deliberate courting of benefits.

This was not a supine kind of astrology, nor one that could be objected to as deterministic since it involved an exercise of the will. The basis of electional astrology is a calculated effort to modify the future favourably.

ELECTIONS BY LUNAR PHASE

> To everything there is a season, and a time to every purpose under the heaven:
> A time to be born, and a time to die; a time to plant, and a time to pluck up that which is planted;
> A time to kill, and a time to heal; a time to break down, and a time to build up . . .
>
> *Ecclesiastes*, chapter 3, i–iii

However worldly wise and sophisticated the author (perhaps a Phoenician?) of *Ecclesiastes* may have been, and however pessimistic his view, it cannot but intrigue the student of lunar astrology that the preacher mentions *twenty-eight* 'times' that God decrees for the series of contrasted activities. (The mystery of the author of the book of *Ecclesiastes* is discussed by Robin Lane Fox in *Pagans and Christians;* he suggests its Jewish writer lived in the later third century BC.)

Perhaps the most ancient and elementary kind of election was the practice, in general use among country people for centuries in many cultures, of mating and weaning cattle and planting and cropping according to the phases of the moon. In England as late as 1653 William Ramesey wrote that such practices were too common to mention. Nicholas Culpeper in his *Directory for Midwives* advised that babies should be weaned at a year, at an appropriate stage of the moon.[1] Lady Arabella Stuart wrote a letter in 1587 which shows that she observed the right phase for cutting her hair. The basic symbolism of the moon in barren or fruitful signs, and waxing and waning phases, is still applied to this day in magazines on popular astrology, which advise non-astrologers on nail and hair trimming; for example, if the hair is to grow quickly it should be cut when the moon is waxing in a fruitful sign, and so on.

Many such routine practical elections must have been made by direct observation of the moon by country people. In the Middle Ages the Arabic practice was followed of referring rather imprecisely to twenty-eight 'days of the Moon', which does not exactly satisfy either the 27.3 day sidereal cycle (the moon as seen against the constellations viewed from the earth) or the synodic moon–sun cycle of 29.5 days.[2] They would recognize perhaps that when she appears largest in the sky, at perigee when nearest to earth, she is also moving fastest round earth. A fast moon was always a desideratum. The 'days of the Moon' were counted from the moment of each sun/moon conjunction. In various cultures and at various times they were numbered 28, 29, 30 or even 31.

Virgil asks, as his first petition to the muses:

> Give me the ways of wandering stars to know
> The depths of heaven above, and earth below,
> *Teach me the various labours of the Moon,*
> And whence proceed the eclipses of the Sun . . . [my emphasis]
>
> Virgil, *Georgics*, II, 475, trans. John Dryden

This lends an aroma of rustic elegance to notions which in one usage were matters of agricultural planning and in another provided a time structure for magical procedures. The differentiation of these days according to a system of appropriate activities or 'labours' provided guidance when choosing the moment at which they could best be performed – the moment to elect, in fact.

Elias Lévi (Alphonse Louis Constant, born about 1810) gives in his *Transcendental Magic* the 'special characters of all the days of the moon, distinguished by the twenty-two Tarot keys and by the signs of the seven planets'. I quote this to show how the lunar tradition survived in magic practice – might be said to have been taken over by magicians and perhaps thereby discredited at an early stage.

Lévi's first day of the moon stands for the Tarot Magus:

> The first day of the Moon is that of the creation of the Moon itself. This day is consecrated to mental enterprises and should be favourable for opportune innovations.
>
> Eliphas Lévi, *Transcendental Magic*, trans. A. E. Waite

The twenty-ninth day (the Fool of the Tarot) 'is a day of failure and miscarriage in all things'.

Whatever the occult associations given for the day, each one is characterized as propitious or otherwise. But Lévi does not deal with practicalities. His 'days' are related to the moon/sun synodic cycle, which ends when the moon has caught up with the sun, having passed the degree of the previous conjunction.

While seventeenth-century people might respect the days of the moon for many practical purposes, the astrologer in general appears to lose interest in differentiating phases. Favourable requirements were usually a fast moon, increasing in light, well placed and aspected as, ideally, other heavenly bodies would be. The medieval view that a waning moon increased the force of the malefics remained implicit. New moons, full moons and eclipses retained their importance.

THE MANSIONS OF THE MOON IN ELECTIONS

Another very ancient lunar system is the consideration of the twenty-eight Mansions of the moon, related in early times to fixed stars. Unlike the phases, which related to each successive conjunction, the Mansions were fixed in the zodiac, supposed to start from 0 degrees of Aries (but affected by the precession of the equinoxes over the centuries).

The Arabic tradition and the Western one have twenty-eight equal

Mansions, giving each 12 degrees 51 minutes 26 seconds on the ecliptic. (There are variations elsewhere in number and extent.) The moon, whose speed from apogee to perigee varies by about 20 per cent (two to two-and-a-half days spent in each sign), therefore spends varying times transitting the different Mansions. Astrologers such as John Dee were not altogether satisfied with this equal division. He experimented with other arrangements for reasons connected with his interest in magic and the cabbala.

Alexandre Volguine[3] has studied the Mansions extensively in *Lunar Astrology* (1974) which includes much material from *Picatrix* – a miscellany of astral magic which Alphonso X had had translated from Arabic into Castilian in 1256. It was later translated into Latin and circulated widely as *Picatrix*; it was certainly known to Pico della Mirandola and Marsilio di Ficino.

Volguine gives various oriental and occidental interpretations for the Mansions; these require some disentangling as there is sometimes advice on Mansions in nativities, or horaries, or about what magical works the moon's transit of a Mansion is suitable for; for the purposes of elections not magical we learn which are suitable or otherwise for various activities. For example, Mansion four is favourable for work, manufacture and small trade and unfavourable for real estate, building and everything to do with mines.

Obviously, using these two systems of lunar phases and Mansions, the one dependent on the last sun/moon conjunction, the other fixed in the zodiac, would involve a great deal of calculation and precise knowledge of the moon's motion over short periods of time. This may or may not always have been harmonized with the findings of ordinary planetary considerations, which themselves demanded accurate tables.

It is interesting that Chaucer in his *Treatise on the Astrolabe*[4] promises that Part IV (which, if ever written, did not survive) would show the motion of the moon for every hour of the day. Other astrological calculations depend upon finding where celestial bodies are at a given moment; elections are different, requiring a review of a whole range of positions in order to choose the most propitious combination within the time constraints the client gives. An hourly view of the moon's position would be specially helpful for electing with Mansions.

Chaucer's 'Franklin's Tale' provides a classic example of contemptuous attitudes to lunar Mansions when associated, as they are here, with magical operations. There was a time when literary critics, anxious to dissociate Chaucer from sympathy with astrology, suggested that the Franklin voiced the poet's views. In fact, like other *raconteurs* in the *Canterbury Tales*, the Franklin delineates his own character in telling his tale.

What we do have is a mass of technical detail, amusingly inconsistent with a contempt for and lack of interest in lunar astrology. Knowledge of Mansions is distanced to some 'Oold felawe' at Orleans 'That hadde thise moones mansions in mynde'. The magical task is to make the rocks on the coast of Brittany disappear – a tidal, and so a lunar, matter; but the first move is to *elect* the moment for the magical procedure, by calculating when the favourable Mansion would be transitted by the moon:

> 'So atte laste he hath his *tyme yfounde*.' [My emphasis]
> 'The Franklin's Tale', line 1,270

We are told by the Franklin how the magician located his first Mansion in the zodiac and then that he found which Mansion the moon was in:

> And Knew ful weel the moones Mansion
> Accordaunt to his operacioun . . .
> 'The Franklin's Tale', line 1,289–90

In other words, he elected the appropriate Mansion for the magic he was to perform – a veil is drawn over the magical 'observaunces' which make the rocks disappear and which, I would emphasize, are the chief object of the Franklin's disapproval. The passage has often been glossed and is worth close study. Chaucer mentions, appropriately, the by his time old-fashioned 'Tolletane' (Toledo) tables, rather than the Alphonsine ones, and refers to parts of the magician's astrolabe. Robinson points out in his notes that the approximate date of the magical operation has been put at a time when the full moon would be in the fourth term of Cancer, an extremely powerful position.[5] We see that election of the moon Mansion was combined with attention to the degree and sign of the moon in the zodiac. We are meant to understand how laborious the process was.

'The Franklin's Tale' places lunar astrology significantly: associated with magic, in a distant country long ago, treated with ostensible dismissiveness ('I ne kan no termes of astrologye') by the prosperous, affable and not simple Franklin. However, it also enshrines the moon's Mansions forever in a charming and morally engaging tale, which certainly gives a very informative account of how to go about electing according to this method.

ELECTIONS IN NICHOLAS OF LYNN'S MEDICAL ASTROLOGY

The source for this subject is Nicholas of Lynn's *Kalendarium*.[6] Nicholas was a contemporary of Chaucer, whose use of his *Kalendarium* has been discussed on pages 81–4. Sigmund Eisner's edition includes and translates from Latin the canons at the end. It seems these medical canons were regarded as valuable long after the *Kalendarium* as such was obsolete as there are manuscripts containing them on their own in an early sixteenth-century hand.

Nicholas's tables allowed people to find the time of the exact sun/moon conjunction, that is the new moon, to hours and minutes, and similarly the opposition or full moon. The seventh canon explains the tables of solar and lunar eclipses – these are said to be inaccurate. The ninth canon gives the sign the moon is in at any time. All this was vital for medical elections.

Canons eleven and twelve deal with electing for a time to bleed the patient and to give medicine. The considerations are largely lunar. Nicholas quotes two striking anecdotes as warnings against neglecting them. He quotes Campanus who says a man 'inexperienced in the stars' bled himself in the arm when threatened with quinsy; he did this when the moon was in Gemini, the sign associated with the arms, with fatal results. Another man had an ulcer on his penis which was incised when the moon was in Scorpio (ruler of 'the secrets') and he died within the hour. Bloodletting was risky during the first and third quarters of the moon, when the humours are flowing from the interior to the exterior of the body.

One sees how general electional principles carry over into this specialized variety when the 'qualities' of signs (fixed, movable [now cardinal], and common [now mutable]) are considered. If the moon at the beginning of an illness is in a moving sign it is 'quickly changeable', if in a fixed sign it is permanent, and if in a common sign its duration is average. This corresponds to the duration of various things elected for, as we shall see later in relation to journeys, buildings and so on.

The moment chosen for compounding the medicine must also be elected, for 'medicines have almost as much power from the time they were compounded as from the material of which they are made'. Herbs were gathered at elected times.

Canon twelve explains that apart from the four bodily humours the body has four powers: attraction, retention, digestion and expulsion. Attraction flourishes in heat and dryness, so medicine which favours this should be given when the moon is in a hot, dry sign – and so forth.

Quoting the *Centiloquium*, supposedly by Ptolemy, and commented on by Haly, Nicholas says that one should never give purging medicine when the moon is visible with Jupiter.[7] This is because medicine is not natural to the body and Jupiter is the friend of all things natural and promotes them, working against the medicine.

The medical canons end with a detailed explanation about decumbiture horoscopes, that is those set up for the moment when the patient becomes sick – the inception of the illness.

The philosophy behind Nicholas' medical astrology acknowledges the patient's place in the chain of being – we might say in his physical and spiritual environment. It seeks to treat him as an individual – his own nativity is sometimes involved – but also as a part of the cosmos whose bodily humours are affected by the moon, and whose purging might offend Jupiter unless that planet were discreetly below the horizon.

ELECTIONS FOR MONARCHS

Turning from lunar astrology and from specialized applications of electional techniques, we find that electional astrology in general was in good standing with the establishment. It was not criticized by the church because it was not deterministic in its doctrine, but was an exercise of free will. Rulers and people who controlled the timing of important events made use of electional advice. John Dee set the date of Elizabeth I's coronation.

The medieval attitude is illustrated by 'The Man of Law's Tale', which concerns an election which never was but certainly should have been made for the emperor's daughter.[8] What we are presented with is a sketchy view of the horoscope for the moment when the weeping Custance starts her voyage to her wedding with her unsuitable bridegroom. This is an event map of course, from which the disastrous outcome might be inferred. The Man of Law is horrified at the extraordinary recklessness of a father sending a daughter on such a voyage without framing an election.

> Imprudent Emperor of Rome, allas!
> Was ther no philosophre [astrologer] in al thy toun?
> Is no tyme bet than oother in swich cas?
> Of vyage is ther noon eleccioun,

Namely [not even] to folk of heigh condicioun?
'The Man of Law's Tale', lines 309–13

Voyages and weddings and suchlike hazardous proceedings were exactly the moments for which elections were mandatory. The folly here is compounded by the fact that the emperor, unlike poorer folk, would certainly have an accurate nativity for his daughter, desirable – some said essential – in making an election.

What we are told of the horoscope of Custance's ill-advised departure suggests that it is the time of day, not so much the date, that is unsatisfactory. For it is the diurnal movement that has sent the planets, as always, on through the Houses (clockwise on the horoscope, not anticlockwise as the planets progress through the signs of the zodiac from day to day).

O firste moevyng! crueel firmament,
With thy diurnal sweigh that crowdest ay
And hurlest al from est til occident . . .
'The Man of Law's Tale', lines 295–98

Thus the ascendant is in an unfavourable sign; the lord of the ascendant, instead of being well placed in an angle, has moved it seems from the first to the gloomy twelfth House. The fast-moving moon is in a weak position. Mars, the lesser infortune, has 'slayn this marriage'. We are not told how, but the outcome is full of Martian cruelty by a hostile mother-in-law. Any reconstruction of the event horoscope is purely speculative – we are simply meant to understand that the moment does not satisfy the essential conditions of an election and bodes ill.

Chaucer introduced into 'The Man of Law's Tale' his astrological explanation of the disasters that follow – it is not in his source. Does the rebuke to the emperor have any ulterior motive, given Chaucer's tendency to make veiled topical allusions?

As to Chaucer's source on elections, two manuscripts of the Tale have a quotation in the margin, copied from the *Liber Electionum* of Zael (Zahel, an early ninth-century astronomer, known as Judaeus Sahl ben Bishr ben Habib). Zael wrote that a good choice will be made if the person electing understands what is appropriate for the stars to give for the purpose in mind.[9] So an election should be tuned to the purpose, and to the individual, whose nativity should be known; for there should be the right relationship between the natal sign and the planet ruling the matter elected for. We shall see that Zael continued to be influential in England.

Chaucer frequented court circles at a time when astrology and the occult were fashionable there.[10] Richard II commissioned an illuminated manuscript which dealt with the occult and included a text on physiognomy and a geomancy which was close to the one Chaucer used when writing 'The Knight's Tale' – indeed, Chaucer reproduces the same mistake to be found in the king's manuscript. We know that John of Gaunt, who dominated the court for much of the reign, was Nicholas of Lynn's patron.

Richard II had many advisers not approved of by his critics, but they did not include an official court astrologer. Was there an unofficial one? Who that might have been is open to speculation. There seems to have been an English tradition of *not* having a court astrologer. Even Elizabeth I, who constantly consulted John Dee at Mortlake, did not install him – or pay him regularly – and she did consult others. But Dee elected her coronation date. In politically dangerous times a court astrologer would have been vulnerable. Monarchs seeking electional advice are apt to be secretive: we know about such advice to Charles II because Ashmole's secret notes were deciphered.

I have dwelt upon Chaucer's pointed insertion of his own passage on an astrological election for a fictional emperor's daughter because this is a special category which left little documentary trace. Royal nativities, solar returns, event maps, may be identified by inferring their dates from planetary positions, but an uninscribed electional horoscope does not declare its purpose even if it survives; indeed, it may cause confusion by being taken for an actual event map, with which it would not necessarily be identical, given the probabilities of delay at, say, a coronation.

One approach is to analyse identified event horoscopes or reliable data and see if they conform to known contemporary principles of electing to an extent beyond chance. This is what Derek Appleby does in his study of the re-founding of St Paul's Cathedral.

CARDAN AND BONATUS ON ELECTIONS

Jerome Cardan, the famous Italian mathematician and writer on the occult sciences, set Edward VI's horoscope and Guido Bonatus, the Italian astrologer, dedicated his *De Astronomiae Tractatus* (1550) to the secretary of state, Sir William Paget.[11] Both writers were to be very influential in England as elsewhere. Their work was translated and published in English in 1676 by Henry Coley (latterly William Lilly's amanuensis) and edited by Lilly.[12]

Coley introduced Bonatus in *The Astrologer's Guide* by relating how he elected a moment for Guido Earl of Mountserrant to break out of a siege and defeat his enemy, at the cost of a wound of which he was forewarned. Of his 146 considerations perhaps No. 141 is the most interesting. It begins by discussing the gifts bestowed on men by the fixed stars, and argues that the fixed stars as agents, and men as patients, are not well matched. The stars move so slowly that men are not suitable to receive their 'impressions'.

From this he concludes that one should use the fixed stars in the foundation of cities, but planets in the erection of houses, because of their relative duration. Castles are very lasting, but not equal to cities, which are successively rebuilt. Lilly adds his own note at this point, on the 'gifts of the planets' in nativities.[13]

Cardan has a group of aphorisms concerning elections:

> 6. The best election a man can make is the place of his habitation: for if the Ascendant of the City he dwells in be the place of his Ascendant, he will have his health well, if the Mid-Heaven, he will come to preferment, if it be the place of the Sun in the Nativity, he will undoubtedly obtain honour and dignities, if of Jupiter he will grow rich; if of the Moon he will be very happy in most respects there.
>
> *The Astrologer's Guide, Anima Astrologiae,* pp. 97–9, 4th edn, 1986

Cardan says if you wish something to be kept secret you should do it when the moon is under the sun's beams; this conflicts with lunar astrology, which gives such times an evil reputation, but perhaps he refers to dark deeds.

Another very general injunction which, like the choice of city, rather stretches the term 'election', is that we should avoid important dealings with people whose nativities are unsympathetic to ours. This refers to synastry, or horoscope comparison when considering relationships between people.

> Make no new clothes, nor first put them on when the Moon is in Scorpio, especially if she be full of light and beheld of Mars, for they will be apt to be torn and quickly worn out.
>
> *The Astrologer's Guide*, p. 98

The symbolism of Mars, ruler of knives and malefic, is clear, related to things torn. The first putting on of clothes is much discussed. We shall see that this was an obsession with Elias Ashmole.

Like Bonatus, Cardan deals with building: one should not begin when the moon is in Scorpio (her Fall) or Pisces (both watery signs) or when the moon or lord of the fourth House applies to a retrograde planet 'for it threatens that such edifice shall soon fall or be ruined'. Retrograde planets signified delay and were generally negative (though much later some people said that the retrograde effect was apparent, not actual, and so not important).[14] The fourth House, at the bottom of the chart, is associated with foundations. We see how the moon, on which phases and Mansions were based in earlier days, is still pre-eminent and must always be well placed and free from afflicting aspects from unfriendly planets.

As to journeys, there is an interesting piece of symbolism: we should avoid having the significator (or planet who rules the matter) in water signs if evil planets are *elevated above them*, for this means bad weather and tempests which are, of course, above one in the sky. One should visualize the querent, standing with his head in the tenth House, the tempest raging round him; lower down, floods or dangerous seas, suggested by water signs. (Compare this with Nicholas of Lynn saying that the *wrong planet elevated* may make one vomit as the elevated planet draws the matter upwards in the body.) This is a kind of symbolism which is different from that of aspects and planetary attributes but is harmonized with it.

The tone of much of Cardan is expansive and more optimistic than that of medieval treatises. There is a sense of alternative possibilities: if the town does not suit you, move; if the man is disagreeable, deal with someone else. If business presses and the election is not ideal, try other methods: 'If you cannot *fit the Moon* to two planets that you have occasion for at once, *join her* to some fixed star that is of the nature of them both.' These emphases suggest a greater control of events and there are obvious historical reasons why this should be in the atmosphere.

> Indeed we ought generally to avoid the society of a person the Lord of whose Ascendant is an infortune and joined with the Dragon's Tail [the Moon's South Node] or any malevolent Fixed Star, for unless there be a great agreement between our Nativities they will do us some mischief, though perhaps against their will.
>
> *The Astrologer's Guide*, p. 98

The Dragon's Tail had a sufficiently evil reputation for the groundlings to get the point when Edmund refers to it in his famous anti-astrology speech in *King Lear*. Bosola, too, in Webster's *Duchess of Malfi* (Act 2, scene iii) gives it an evil name.

We shall see that Elias Ashmole took Cardan's rules even further: approaching a new solicitor he considered the man's nativity in relation to his own solar revolution.

ELIAS ASHMOLE AND HIS ELECTIONS

> By Elections we may Governe, Order and Produce things as we please: Faber quisque Fortunae propriae.
>
> Elias Ashmole, *Theatrum Chemicum Britannicum*, 1652

Elias Ashmole applied electional astrology to a remarkable range of concerns; indeed, this range goes some way to delineate the man. But perhaps we should infer that there was an element of astrological research in this: keeping precise records he could later assess the success of his elections, just as with his many event horoscopes he could consider their outcome. As with other activities, hindsight was a necessary learning tool. This had to be balanced against a frequently very urgent wish to promote his interests by any means he could.

C. H. Josten, in his edition of Ashmole's autobiographical and historical notes, presents a very detailed view of his subject's life and work – exceptionally so since he has deciphered some extremely intimate stenographic notes.[15] The dates, inscriptions and annotations of horoscopes Ashmole cast at the time of events are most valuable, illustrating horaries and elections.

Here is an example:

> 18 Dec. 1650 (MS Ashm. 374, f. 89^{v}) in cipher
> Inside a horoscope for 8.30 a.m.;
> 'About this time I first put on my purple
> shagged gown/'
>
> *Elias Ashmole*, p. 560

There are many other entries about the putting on of clothes at various times, and in cipher; not all have horoscopes, but the times are given to the minute and according to the system used by astrologers of reckoning from noon to noon, so that '19 hours' means 7 a.m. the following day. This suggests that horoscopes may have been lost.

On 5 June 1647 there is a cipher entry that he bought and put on his Spanish leather black belt and, forty minutes later, his 'cloth suit trimmed with gold/ and also the coat/ Libra 23 ascending/' – a suitably Venus-ruled sign for such grandeur, no doubt intended to charm.[16]

A man is never a hero to his valet, and here we peer over his shoulder rather voyeuristically as he stands at his looking-glass. He was a self-regarding man, but no doubt he thought advancement depended on good impressions – not least upon the well-to-do women he courted in hopes of a rich marriage.

Like John Aubrey, Ashmole elected for the signing and sealing of leases. He set up such an election for 10.30 a.m. in October 1651.[17] Elections would often be frustrated by circumstances, but their analysis might give us a view of his technique.

Journeys for himself and others are often elected for.[18] There is an example where two elected moments are considered and found 'bad'. He takes account of the planetary rulers of the day and the hour.[19] If a journey *has* to be made within a few days, then the variables at disposal are these, changing daily and hourly.

In January 1647 Ashmole notes an 'election to have Mr Baker lend me some money'. Propitious moments for asking favours or making transactions are traditionally sought. Another variety, frequent with Ashmole, is where he elects for starting a piece of work. In June 1647 he began to make an index for William Lilly's *Christian Astrology*:

> About 10: after noon I began to make an index of this book Aquarius ascending Moon applying to the sextile of Mercury who was Lord of the hour/ she being in the 7. house/ Mercury descending into the 5./ Moon separating from the square of Saturn lord of the ascendant and applies to Mercury. I had been long in determining to do this but did not go about it till now. But now Moon entering Virgo and being slow in motion, and reception between Mercury and her, and he very slow, I believe I shall go through it speedily./
>
> *Elias Ashmole*, p. 451

Aquarius, the sign associated with astrology, ascends. Mercury is emphasized as the planet of writing (Ashmole's own very Mercurial horoscope, which Lilly greatly praised for this quality, caused him to represent himself in notes with the glyph of that planet). The moon links the lord of the ascendant with Mercury, and she enters Virgo, a sign associated with attention to detail, and one where Mercury (writing) rules.

ASHMOLE ELECTS FOR HIS WEDDING

Ashmole's first marriage had been a love match. He was 32 when he married Lady Manwaring, née Forster. She was rich, 52, and had a disease which they both feared might infect him. However, according to Anthony Wood, her property was the foundation of his fortune.

Three horoscopes were set up for the wedding.[20] One for '16 November 1649, 8H 0' A.M. the time elected for my 2d marriage/ I went to be married about 15' before 8: Moon â [separating from] trine of Mercury, ad [applying to] a sextile of Venus Saturn and Jupiter'. (In notes he used the glyph for Saturn when referring to his wife, as he used Mercury for himself.) Annual revolutions and nativities with different data survive for her. Two other elections for 11 a.m. on 14 and 16 November were struck out and the uncomfortably early hour was the one chosen. Ashmole, who rose in the small hours to make talismans against rats, would always rise betimes for a favourable start.

The election he used gave good aspects between the moon and the benefics, Venus and Jupiter, and to Saturn. He was willing to take the Saturn side of the marriage for the sake of the money and social standing it brought him. Later Lilly said that directions for that year from Ashmole's nativity ought to have been considered, and were unfavourable for a marriage at that time – but it seemed that any contra-indications would have been ignored, so necessary was the marriage. Lilly described Lady Manwaring as[21] 'very handsome and of a goodly structure, Low, merry and chearful, but accidentally very much Saturnine', also as 'a person of great animosity'. He indicates that Ashmole did not have much 'content' in the marriage, which was putting it discreetly.

There is a note that the wedding ring was put on two days before the marriage – tried on, perhaps – at 3.35 p.m. Such a timing could be precisely controlled while church ceremonies are subject to the vagaries of others. But if this moment was significant for Ashmole no horoscope survives.

ELECTIONS FOR THE CASTING OF TALISMANS

On 9 July 1661 Dr Thomas Hyde, Reader of Hebrew at the Queen's College, Oxford, and later librarian of the Bodleian, wrote to Ashmole:

> I have likewise enclosed an account of what I have met with concerning Telesms: and chiefly such things as may direct to the making of them: I did on purpose neglect to multiply examples, because you told me you were sufficiently stored with them already. Had not some leaves been wanting, I could have furnished you with the making of a Telesm under each planet, whereas now we are forced to be content with only some of them . . .
>
> Quoted by C. H. Josten, *Elias Ashmole*, vol. 3, p. 835

Dr Hyde was an orientalist who gave Ashmole this material from Islamic sources, and promised to show him illustrations to help him 'to go more expeditely about the making of them [the talismans]'.

Twenty years later Dr Hyde writes again:[22] 'I have here sent you an account of some Talismans extracted out of Arabick bookes . . . ' (letter dated 13 September 1681). The earlier letter shows that Ashmole, who had done some research of his own, wanted practical advice from Dr Hyde's sources. His earliest record of casting horoscopes for this purpose is dated 18 July 1650:

11 a.m. 'S(igils): against Flyes and Fleas'
2.17 p.m. 'S(igils): against Flyes'
3.15 p.m. 'S(igils): against Fleas, Flyes, Caterpillars and Toades'
4.30 p.m. 'S(igils): against Flyes, Fleas & Caterpillars'.[23]

All this was for the driving out of vermin.

These operations were performed under a conjunction of Saturn and Mars, and Ashmole notes: 'The Figure of the Caterpillars & Flyes Fleas & Toades, were all made in full proportion, in litle, & cast off in Lead [Saturn's metal]. without Characters.' C. H. Josten explains that the 'efficacy of sigils [also called 'Lamins' and 'telesmes'] was supposed to depend not only on the celestial constellations at the time they were cast, but also on the invocation of certain angels, and on the use of proper suffumigations'. Ashmole's notes survive, as does his annotated copy of J. Gaffarel's *Unheard-of Curiosities concerning the Talismanical Sculpture of the Persians* . . . (London, 1650).[24]

In 1681 Ashmole was casting talismans for rather different purposes. Perhaps the most interesting record is the following:

7 Apr. 1681
Horoscope for 6.45 a.m.:

> 'Election to cast sigil of Jupiter and Venus'
> Underneath:
> 'I began to cast the 5 Gemini ascending/ but the metal sputtered and burnt my fingers and the sigil came not/ Mars behold[s] the ascendant with square/ [aspect]
> 'Those cast about 6H.45'. before noon/ were for a continued health and favour with great and good men and women/
> 'Those cast about 7: were to strengthen and enlarge memory, fancy and tongue, and wit/ to assist and encourage a search into mysteries and learning/.'
>
> C. H. Josten, *Elias Ashmole*, vol. 4, p. 1,679

I notice he chose an ascendant close to his own natal degree rising. He is courting the favours of the two benefics, Jupiter and Venus, presumably using their planetary metals, tin and copper, just as he used lead for Saturn to frighten the rats. The purposes he gives are particularly significant.

He makes a great number of elections for sigils in 1681 for Jupiter and for Jupiter combined with Venus and or the moon, and for all three, often for the purposes in the above example. He discards with Mars on the mid-heaven and with planets in the unfavourable Houses, sixth, eighth and twelfth; or, for example: 'I made no use of this time/ because the South Node was in the Ascendant and Saturn in the 6:.' He usually records the planetary ruler of the hour, considering both natural and artificial hours, which overlap.[25] On 5 August 1681 there was a conjunction of Jupiter and Venus. He began casting at 5 a.m. and recorded a large number of talismans made. He is not confident of the efficacy of all these because of the contra-indications he lists, 'But because it was so near the conjunction [of Jupiter and Venus] and Jupiter and Venus in the Fourth/ I ventured'.

Ashmole profits by a Saturn/Mars conjunction in December 1681 to cast more talismans in the shape of rats: eight rats between 2.37 and 2.59 a.m. and seventeen between 5.35 and 6.45 a.m., on the basis of two elections; next day, after suffumigating them in Mars' natural hour, Ashmole records where he places them in kitchen, scullery and cellar. His reputation for disposing of vermin stood high.

It has to be remembered that the many elections for the different purposes exemplified here are to be found among a much vaster number of Ashmole's horary questions and event data both public and private. The question is, did electional procedure for magical purposes influence practice in the other categories?

ASTROLOGY IN THE SERVICE OF CHARLES II AND HIS COURT

Letter of recommendation from Sir Edward Nicholas, to the lord high treasurer of England: 'Mr Elias Ashmole . . . one whom his Majesty makes use of in several particular Employments . . . ' October 16, 1660.[26]

Ashmole's biographer, C. H. Josten, writes:

> On three occasions in 1673 Ashmole's astrological advice was sought on political questions. The Lord High Treasurer, Lord Clifford, apparently had taken him into his confidence. Ashmole noted for 11 January that, in the evening, he 'sat with the Lord Treasurer 2 houres.
>
> *Elias Ashmole*, pp. 188–9

> At the end of October 1673 Charles II himself requested Ashmole's astrological advice on his future relations with Parliament.
>
> *op. cit.*, p. 189

In the spring of 1670 Ashmole recorded a series of horoscopes for various parliamentary events, beginning with the king's speech on 14 February and the developments which followed.[27]

There was mounting tension between the king and Parliament about the Declaration of Indulgence. On 15 January 1673, at '8 Hours 15 Minutes p.m.', Clifford put an horary question asking in effect if the Declaration of Indulgence would upset the granting of money to the king by Parliament.

There were other such questions on the king's relationship with Parliament. It is clear from correspondence that Ashmole sought Lilly's advice, which was very diplomatically given:

> To Elias Ashmole, 30 October 1673
> I have seriously waighed and considered your profound judgment, upon the figure sent mee, and I am very glad of the honor his Majesty did you, but more satisfied at your prudent and well grounded answer. . . .
>
> *Elias Ashmole*, p. 1,350–1

(Lilly goes on to make a number of his own astrological interpretations.) It is evident that their astrological advice to Charles II, Lord

Clifford and others was based upon horary questions, and the nativities and annual revolutions which Ashmole possessed for the people concerned. They were also close observers of events, Ashmole from his consistently royalist stance, Lilly from his ambiguous parliamentarian point of view. These differences had not unduly upset their symbiotic relationship over the years. Lilly's expertise was mediated to the court by the suave and acceptable Ashmole.

Knowing Ashmole's extensive interest in and practice of electing, one asks what the electional element was in their advice. There is an interesting – and as usual rather breathless – letter from Lilly, dated 23 October 1673, when the king's speech to Parliament[28] was in contemplation for 27 October:

> The Caball of Presbitery begins I see early; its now in Yorks power to ingratiate himself forever. but what God hath decreed must stand – The Tayle of the Comet in 1664 begins, so Saturn in Aries. and the last Comet of 167 – *Cunctando restituet Rem* – so now, Carolus, *Cunctando* may effect *idem*. – Moon next promiseth well – provided Moon ad conjunction of Jupiter at 2H P.M. that aspect bee not elapsed before his Majesty make his speech – nihil timendum . . .
>
> *Elias Ashmole*, p. 1,346

Lilly sees that delaying tactics have been successful in the past, so Charles may, by delaying 'effect the same'. He points out that the king should make his speech before this application of the moon to Jupiter has 'elapsed'. *Cunctando* was an apt word for the repeated prorogations of Parliament. Lilly's advice was electional, within tight constraints.

Four days later the king spoke at 10.50 a.m. He prorogued Parliament yet again.[29]

Even for a king there are constraints within which the electing astrologer must operate. Parliament would not assemble in favourable small hours such as Ashmole might use for his talismans!

WILLIAM LILLY AND ELECTIONS

Lilly seems to have been rather reticent about electing. In so comprehensive a textbook as *Christian Astrology* he writes:

> I know it will be expected I should have wrote of Elections . . . But as for Elections, me thinks he can be no ingenious

> Astrologian, that having studied or well entred into this my Booke shall not be able (*ad libitum*) to frame his own Figure of Elections, let the quaere be what it will.
>
> *Christian Astrology*, B3[30]

In his collection of aphorisms 'for better judging any Horary Question', No. 28 slides from considering qualities of signs in which significators are found, in what seems to be an horary context, to:

> From hence we begin Foundations of Houses and Townes when significators are fixed; . . . but in a thing wherein we desire a mediocrity [an average speed] we *elect* common signes. [My emphasis]
>
> *Christian Astrology*, p. 300

(An aphorism of Cardan is here combined with Bonatus' sixtieth consideration.) This is not to suggest that Lilly did not practise elections, but to show that as a genre electing was not always precisely differentiated in early modern times, any more than it was long ago.

We know that Lilly drew a horoscope for the laying of 'the first stone of the Royal Exchange' by Charles II (see the Introduction to 'The Founding of St Paul's Cathedral' in this book). In that paper Derek Appleby presents a table of the 'Yeeres of the Planets', taken from *Christian Astrology*. But Lilly there gave them separately, among the attributes under the heading of each planet.

Soon after the publication of Lilly's *Christian Astrology* in 1647, William Ramesey's *Astrologia Restaurata* appeared. It included a comprehensive section (Liber III) on elections – 181 folio pages, perhaps cornering the market for this topic. This seems to have been influential on the class for which it was intended, though the book as a whole did not and was not meant to compete with Lilly's.

We shall see that it gives much advice on the kind of elections Ashmole used: indeed, if Ashmole left records of the greatest gamut of electing practice in his time, Ramesey amply provided for such a reader.

WILLIAM RAMESEY ON ELECTIONS IN HIS 'ASTROLOGIA RESTAURATA'

'For eschewing evil and for choosing good'.

William Ramesey (1627–75/6) was the son of David Ramsay (*sic*), the famous clock and watch-maker to the royal family. Ramesey qualified in medicine at Montpellier and became a physician-in-ordinary to Charles II. He was admitted M.D. at Cambridge by royal mandate.[31]

He emphasizes, in keeping with the tradition, the need for the natal horoscope in making elections, adding that the annual revolution (solar return) should be studied too. Zael, Bonatus, Messahalla and Dariot are quoted as saying that if the nativity is unknown, respect may be had to the time of the client's request. By his time astrologers would be dealing with many clients without accurate birth data. (Perhaps this partly accounts for Lilly's preference for horary techniques.)

Ramesey was, of course, a royalist. His tastes and the times are reflected in his writing, which generally has a masculine, upper-class tone. He dismisses Haly's first House elections for weaning as unlikely to interest his readers. His material is set out with introductory remarks to each section, and several chapters on each House and its appropriate elections. (In what follows the number in brackets indicates the House concerned.)

The 'making of friendship between bretheren and others at variance' (third) was no doubt apt in years of civil strife. Feasting (fifth) leads to advice on how not to be offensive in one's cups. The seventh House (dealing with the opposition) includes 'on making peace, suppressing or encountring rebels'; but for storming castles or towns one needed to know the ascendant of their foundation – a problem which gave astrologers difficulty in various continental wars. One elected to find out 'the scope of whisperings or clandestine practices between any two . . . and of [a time] for playing chess to win . . . '[32] In a way fishing, teaching dogs to hunt and training falcons are adversarial matters too. Electing the moment to release prisoners (twelfth) was no doubt a chancy matter at that time; in an era of kidnapping it does not seem so remote an idea.

Like Nicholas of Lynn (see p. 179) Ramesey cautions against incising a part of the body when the moon was in the sign that ruled it. Another sixth House election is for bathing, whether 'for health or cleanliness', or for depilatory purposes. To bring water to a house with piping was fourth House; like 'tillage' it had to do with the earth and foundations.

Ramesey congratulated himself on avoiding marriage. But electing to beget a boy or girl was important to clients of all classes for social and dynastic reasons (fifth, children). Logically he deals next with christenings, for which he says he takes over Arabic rules for circumcision – perhaps a rather arbitrary cross-cultural proceeding.

Children also figure in the first House; 'putting children to nurse, to school or a trade'.[33] We have to remember that Manilius placed 'fortunes of children' in what corresponds to the first House.[34] Ramesey goes into some detail on the planet which signifies each profession and so must be 'fortified' in the election by favourable placing and aspects: Mars for the physician (emphasizing the surgical role) and Mercury for apprenticeship to an astrologer, for example. The putting of a child or a young man to a trade was indeed momentous, considering the influence of masters on apprentices. Career elections also come up in the tenth House, as one would expect; so does 'obtaining favours of Kings and Grandees'; and 'Electing [in the political sense] Kings and Nobles and of their beginning their Rule of Government'.[35]

There was an ingenious way of electing to make a will (eighth House) so that it would have to be changed, presumably postponing its ultimate purpose.

Remembering the elections we know to have specially interested Ashmole, we find that Ramesey lays particular emphasis on the buying and putting on of apparel, with minute details of suitable and unsuitable degrees and signs for the significator's place; various medical and cosmetic matters; borrowing and receiving of money; and all kinds of communication, writing letters, sending messages.

'If you do anything you would not have revealed begin when the Moon is in Scorpio under the earth.' Transcriptions of Ashmole's cipher notes do 'reveal' many covert proceedings – alas, they could not all be begun under the prescribed conditions! (Ramesey quotes this dictum from the 'Ancients'.) Under the ninth House we find detailed recommendations for 'learning sciences such as Music'. In the eleventh House of hopes and wishes are matters for which Ashmole also made talismans: accomplishing anything hoped for, gaining good repute and the love of friends. His 'great and good men and women' for whose favours he made talismans, perhaps come under tenth House, 'Grandees'.

On his title page Ramesey has these words: '*Astra regunt homines, sed regit astra Deus*'; the stars rule man but God rules the stars. This is a succinct statement of philosophy which he does not much develop. It also served to counter the objection that astrology is deterministic. He refers briefly to *anima mundi*, the soul of the world, and what he says Zahel called the 'Rem subtilem (subtle matter) of the signs and their significators'. But his gift lay in providing his contemporaries with a conspectus of electional possibilities, presented so that people would see how they might apply them.

One may surmise that Ashmole supplemented the usual electional techniques of his time with the making of talismans for various reasons: intellectual curiosity and an intensity of desire to achieve. Favours and financial success were an essential means of gaining the kind of intellectual life he wanted, and his second wife and her relations had to serve his purposes. Her wealth helped him to acquire the books, manuscripts and rare objects which supported his studies.[36] The less attractive, self-serving side of his nature is compensated for by his will to accumulate and set in order those acquisitions for posterity; to retrieve, record and preserve what might have been lost for ever of spiritual and aesthetic traditions.

Turning back to Lilly and his statement that any 'ingenious Astrologian' would be able to frame an election, we may see that he has some justification if that 'astrologian' had his own tenacity and command of the subject. His advice to clients would take account of electional considerations, but mostly in the undifferentiated way I have referred to, it seems. Correspondence suggests that Lilly was usually consulted about advice given by Ashmole to the court, and that he did not hesitate to pass on useful information.[37] His autobiography shows that he sometimes backed up his astrology with personal intervention on behalf of his client. The stars incline, they do not compel, was his motto ('*Non cogunt*' is inscribed on his portrait); passive acceptance was not his style, but I do not think elections for personal matters interested him.

ELECTIONAL ASTROLOGY AND ITS PLACE IN THE ART

It may be argued that the divinatory element in electional astrology is at a minimum compared, say, with horary. The skill of electing lies in the translation of what is hoped for via the planetary symbolism and the House symbolism into a day and time that will be auspicious, to put it briefly; whereas in horary astrology there is much more interpretation. It looks as if Ashmole coped with electing but needed Lilly's help with interpretation sometimes. Perhaps this was partly why Ashmole took to making talismans – only partly, however, I suggest, since his motivation was complex.

Like medicine, casting talismans, and magic generally, alchemy is an endeavour where astrology plays a somewhat ancillary role, providing an enabling language which sometimes in its long history has veiled trade secrets, and at other times expressed the *hypokeimenon* – the essential unity of all things – which both disciplines at their best aspire to celebrate.

It might be thought that such uses of electing should be left to one side, as they came to be before long; but I think these 'marriages' astrology contracted affected its history in several ways. First, there was perhaps an inflow from Ashmole's (to him) new oriental sources, which might modify electing techniques and pass into what I can only call 'ordinary' electing; next, there was the guilt by association which identified all astrology with the 'black' arts. (It is horrifying to consider what was lost when orders were given for manuscripts containing figures or diagrams to be burnt in universities because of such associations.) A process of dissociation led to the discarding of various elements in interpretation; a good example of this is the rejection of moon Mansions which we found as early as Chaucer, when they were associated with electing for a moment to make the rocks disappear in 'The Franklin's Tale'. I suggest that an example of how talisman-making may have influenced Ashmole's other electing is his exceptional emphasis upon the natural and artificial hours. Ashmole's records provide starting points for detailed research on the history of the craft of astrology, based on thorough analysis of his horoscopes and their inscriptions.

There is no doubt Ashmole had supreme faith in elections and used them to an obsessive extent. I do not think he used them as a substitute for deciding when to act, but rather as a means of refining the art; driven by intellectual curiosity and intense ambition he wished to act always in the way most favourable, and in the way that attuned him most completely to celestial influences.

I have not touched on his electing for the founding of buildings as that is discussed in what follows.

Notes

1 Bernard Capp, *Astrology and the Popular Press* (1979), p. 289.
2 Simon Best and Nicholas Kollerstrom, *Planting by the Moon* (Astro Computing Services, 1981).
3 Alexandre Volguine, *Lunar Astrology*, trans. John Broglio (A.S.1 Pubs, US, 1974), passim.
4 F. W. Robinson (ed.), *Works* (Oxford: OUP, 1974), p. 544. All Chaucer references are to this edition (but in the earlier printings

of John H. Fisher, *Complete Poetry and Prose of Geoffrey Chaucer*, the editor gives helpful astrological notes).

5 Ibid., p. 725, note to line 1,252 of 'The Franklin's Tale'.
6 Sigmund Eisner (ed.), *The Kalendarium of Nicholas of Lynn* (Scolar, 1980), p. 10. The canons containing medical material, nos 11 and 12, are on pp. 206–23.
7 Ibid., p. 212.
8 See J. C. Eade, *The Forgotten Sky* (Oxford: OUP, 1984), p. 126, for a detailed discussion of the passage. The suggestion that Chaucer was not fully aware of electional astrology and its applications is surprising.
9 Eugenio Garin, *Astrology in the Renaissance* (London: Routledge, 1976; translated into English, 1983), chapter 2, and n. 8, p. 123.
10 H. M. Carey, 'Astrology at the English court in the later middle ages', in Patrick Curry (ed.), *Astrology, Science and Society* (Boydell, 1987). Robinson, op. cit., p. 677, notes to line 2,045 of 'The Knight's Tale'.
11 Keith Thomas, *Religion and the Decline of Magic* (Weidenfeld & Nicolson, 1985), p. 343.
12 Guido Bonatus and Jerom Cardan, translated from the Latin by Henry Coley; edited by William Lilly in *The Astrologer's Guide, Anima Astrologiae*, 4th edn, facsimile of 1886 edition (Regulus Pub. Co., 1986).
13 Lilly, op. cit., p. 68.
14 This was A. J. Pearce's view in his *Textbook of Astrology* (1911), where he has a section on elections (p. 423). (He does not give many sources and his references to Ramesey do not suggest that he knew the original edition of *Astrologia Restaurata*.) Despite his view of retrograde planets, the idea of delay still attaches to them.
15 C. H. Josten (ed.), *Elias Ashmole (1617–1692), His Autobiographical and Historical Notes, his Correspondence, and other Contemporary Sources relating to his Life and Work*, edited with a biographical introduction, 5 vols (Oxford: OUP, 1966). See p. 9 for a discussion of Ashmole's writing in cipher. We are warned that before 1679 entries are not to be regarded as records of contemporary events: 'all notes of an earlier date were compiled from memory, or from such texts as a cipher diary which Ashmole kept between 1645 and 1649, from the *dates, inscriptions and annotations of horoscopes he had cast at the time of the events* [my emphasis], and probably also from lost sources of the same kind.' The horoscopes are not published but can be examined in

the MSS, and data and often some astrological commentary are published here. These volumes are an enormously rich source for the history of techniques.

16 Ibid., vol. 2, p. 446.
17 Ibid., vol. 2, p. 590.
18 Ibid., vol. 2, p. 362.
19 See glossary in this book.
20 Ibid., vol. 2, p. 494 ff.
21 Ibid., loc. cit., n. 3.
22 Ibid., op. cit., vol. 4, p. 1,692.
23 Ibid., vol. 2, p. 537.
24 Ibid., n. 3.
25 See glossary in this book.
26 Ibid., vol. 2, p. 797.
27 Ibid., vol. 1, p. 173.
28 For the continuing interest in horoscopes for the king's speeches to Parliament, see the introduction to Patrick Curry's paper on 'Astrological Periodical Literature' in this book.
29 Josten, op. cit., vol. 4, p. 1,347.
30 All references in this book are to the 1985 facsimile edition of *Christian Astrology* (1647).
31 Keith Thomas, *Religion and the Decline of Magic* (London: Weidenfeld & Nicolson, 1971), p. 360; Bernard Capp, *Astrology and the Popular Press* (1979), p. 326; Dictionary of National Biography; Ramesey, William, *Astrologia Restaurata* (1653–4), passim, and esp. Liber III.
32 Ramesey, op. cit., Liber III, section 8, chapter 8. This third book of *Astrologia Restaurata*, although bound with the first two books, has a separate dedication to 'Henrico Perrepoint, Marquis of Dorchester'.
33 Ibid., Liber III, section 2, chapter 1, p. 132.
34 Ibid. See Prudence Jones's paper on 'Celestial and Terrestrial Orientation' in this book.
35 Ibid., Liber III, section 11, p. 196.
36 Of course, Ashmole held office in the government, which was another source of income later.
37 For example of Ashmole consulting Lilly, see Josten, op. cit., vol. 4, p. 1,341, where Ashmole models on Lilly's notes his reply to Sir Robert Howard's question on relationship between king and Commons. For Lilly's City information see ibid., vol. 4, p. 1,348. He comments '*Bonum omen*' on the East India Company's unanimous vote to lend the king money; and (p. 1,349)

on news that the king and queen will dine in London the same comment, with ' – *Cunctando* – ' added, referring again to the king's delaying policy.

THE FOUNDATION OF ST PAUL'S CATHEDRAL AFTER ITS DESTRUCTION IN THE GREAT FIRE OF 1666

An Astrological Investigation

Derek Appleby

Commentary

In the years after the Great Fire of 1666 there was a vast amount of building and rebuilding in London. St Paul's was to be built on the site of the ancient cathedral which had been destroyed; it was the first Protestant cathedral in these islands; its architect was Christopher Wren.

We have seen the traditional emphasis on electing a propitious moment for building; and we know Elias Ashmole's intense interest in electing, and in the accurate recording of events (see 'Electional Astrology' and the sections on Ashmole). When I noticed Ashmole's record of the founding of St Paul's it occurred to me that it might be an elected date and time.

> 25 June 1675 (MS. Ashm. 1136, f. 53)
> 6H. 30' A.M.: the Foundation of St: Paule's
> Church London, Layed.
> C. H. Josten (ed.), *Elias Ashmole . . .*, vol. 4, p. 1,432

(St Paul's, Covent Garden, was founded 16 September 1633, so there is no confusion there; Ashmole did not record the time of that occasion.) Anthony Wood[1] says that despite what Ashmole recorded, ''Tis said' that it was 28 June 1675. A note to Sir William Dugdale's *History of St Paul's Cathedral* (1658) – that is the earlier cathedral – gives 21 June and this has been taken as correct by later writers. I note that Dugdale left London on 22 June, so if there was a change of plan he might not have known. On 21 June 1675, William Lilly wrote: 'Wee had great store of hail and stormes at Hersham . . . ' Perhaps bad weather delayed the founding.

In considering which date was correct, we note that Ashmole (who knew Sir Christopher Wren) gave the *time* as well, and had a motive for accuracy; Dugdale was out of London; Anthony Wood says he speaks from hearsay. I offered all the data to Derek Appleby for him to test.

Wren liked his head mason to have the honour of laying the foundation stone; at the early hour chosen probably no grandees would attend. The builders would want to profit by the long June day. It may be of interest to look at an account of the founding of the Royal Greenwich Hospital, now the Royal Naval College. This was more formal perhaps.

> 30th June 1696 I went with Select Committee of the Commissioners for the Fabric of the Greenwich Hospital, and with Sir Christopher Wren, the Surveyor, where with him I laid the first stone of that intended foundation; precisely at five o'clock in the evening after we had dined together. Mr Flamsted the King's Astronomical Professor *observed the punctual time with instruments*. Note that one of the workmen in helping to place the stone, being a corner large stone, grating his fingers against the gravelly bank, some drops of blood fell upon it. We afterwards returned to London. [My emphasis]
>
> J. S. de Beer (ed.), *Diary of John Evelyn*, (1955), vol. 3, p. 249.
> (The editor noted that it was the 'Grand' Committee, and that Flamstead was Astronomer Royal, not Professor.)

In view of Ashmole's known position as astrological adviser to Charles II, especially in the electional line, it is worth quoting another foundation record he kept:

> 23 Oct. 1667 (MS Ashm. 242, f. 78)
>
> Astrological notes with a horoscope, inscribed by William Lilly:
>
> 'King Charles his position of the first stone of the Royal Exchange. Oct: 23 – 1667, 23h. 7. A.M. per Esq Ashmole et Dominum Bernard'
>
> C. H. Josten (ed.), *Elias Ashmole*, vol. 3, p. 1,112

A second horoscope, 'in Lilly's hand and of the same event but for 42 minutes later, . . . is inscribed "false". A third one, in Francis Bernard's hand, is preserved . . . '

(Note that '23h. 7. A.M.' would of course mean 11.07 a.m. the following morning.) C. H. Josten notes a suggestion that 'Charles II perhaps laid this foundation stone "in true Masonic form" and that for this reason Ashmole, the freemason, was asked to determine the most propitious time for the ceremony'. (See *op. cit.* n. 4).

It seems that what we have is an accurate event map together with two attempted elections which, given the timing constraints of royal occasions, were not used to the minute. We know that Ashmole had nativity and solar returns for the king, and both Lilly and Bernard worked on the horoscope for the City of London; all these might be among the considerations in electing such an important moment.

In the following paper Derek Appleby, an expert on traditional astrology, analyses the St Paul's data according to the traditional principles of electional astrology as applied to a building intended to have great religious and ceremonial significance.

An election, if fulfilled, becomes one with the horoscope of the foundation. Astrologers relate this ('radical') map – as they would a nativity for a person – to the events in the life of the building; this is done both by progressing the planets, etc., in the radical map, and also by noting the transits to it made at the times of later events. Derek Appleby has selected the bombing in the Second World War – which the cathedral largely escaped – the funeral of Admiral Nelson and the marriage of the Prince and Princess of Wales.

Unfamiliar terms will be found in the glossary at the end of the book.

I am most grateful to the librarians of St Paul's Cathedral and Lambeth Palace libraries for their help in researching the foundation date.

A. L. K.

Note

1 A. Clark (ed.), *The Life and Times of Anthony Wood*, vol. 2 (Oxford, 1892), p. 317.

Three alternative dates have been proposed for the laying of the foundation stone of Sir Christopher Wren's St Paul's Cathedral. In my opinion the date taken from Elias Ashmole's diary must be the correct one – if, as we infer, the moment was elected.

In fact the chart for this date is intricately balanced astrologically, as I shall demonstrate; but first let me point out a key feature and compare it with the two alternatives:

25 June 1675: note the position and condition of the moon; she is

St Pauls Cathedral
Foundation
5 July 1675 6AM30
(NS)
51N31 0W6

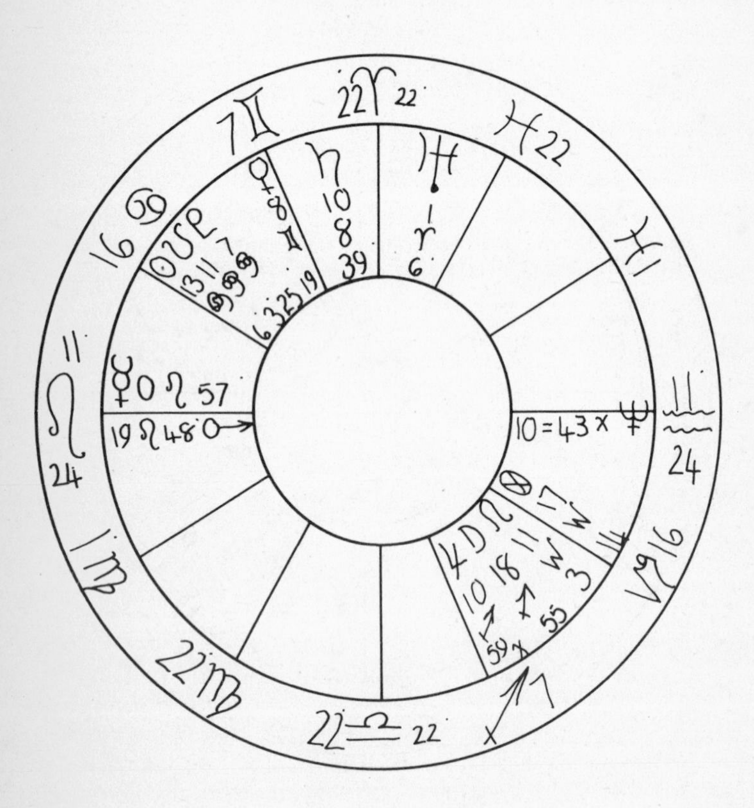

Figure 11 Horoscope based on Ashmole's data
[Old Style date: 25 June 1675]

St Paul's Cathedral Foundation
5 July 1675
6AM17
51N31 0W6

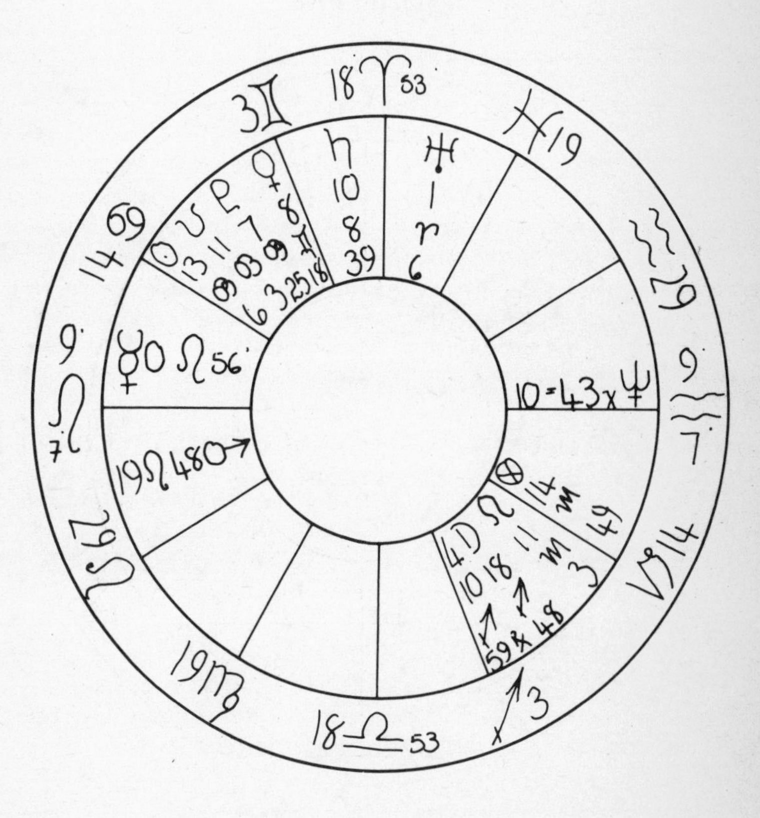

Figure 12 Horoscope based on Ashmole's data

separating from a conjunction of Jupiter, and applying to a trine of rising Mars, thus translating the light of Jupiter to Mars.

28 June 1675: this date is based upon Anthony Wood who noted the data given by Ashmole, but added ''Tis said that the stone was laid on 28th June'. I cannot see an astrologer selecting a moment when the moon is void of course and weak by sign.

21 June 1675: other authorities quote this date, but again I cannot imagine an astrologer electing a moment when the moon has no aspect but an application to a square of Mercury.

ASHMOLE'S DATA

Given the options available to an astrologer, he will attempt to cast about to find a planet with which he can fortify the foundation moment. With Jupiter the most dignified planet in the chart, it is possible that the astrologer might seek to let him rise or sit at the mid-heaven. This he could not do if he wished to preserve the translation of light with Mars, for by the time Jupiter rose the moon would have advanced beyond the trine of Mars. Alternatively, Mars may be allowed to rise and translate the virtue of Jupiter to him.

Why allow a planet to rise at all? When speaking of the planets' 'greatest years', Lilly says, under Saturn:

> The greatest [number of] years he signifies=465; his greater 57, his mean years 43, his least 30. The meaning whereof is this: Admit we frame a new building, erect a town or city, or family or principality is begun when Saturn is essentially and accidentally strong, the astrologer may conjecture the family, principality, etc., may continue 465 years in honour, etc., without any sensible alteration. Again, if in one's nativity Saturn is well dignified, is the Lord of the geniture etc., then according to nature he may live 57 years; if he be meanly dignified, then the native but 43; if he be Lord of the geniture and yet weak, the child may live 30 years hardly more.

So, if we are to lay the foundation stone of a great cathedral, we would like one of the planets to be well dignified, so that we can tap into its 'greatest years' potential.

We cannot get Jupiter at the ascendant without the moon becoming void of course; and Jupiter's greatest years are 428. If we put the sun on the ascendant (greatest years 1,460) we lose the stability (it is a fixed sign) and magnificence of Leo (the royal sign) rising. Aside

	Greatest	*Greater*	*Mean*	*Least*
Saturn	465	57	43	30
Jupiter	428	79	45	12
Mars	264	66	40	15
Sun	1,460	120	69	19
Venus	151	82	45	8
Mercury	450	76	48	20
Moon	320	108	66	25

from Jupiter, the best-conditioned planet is Mars, and his greatest years are 264. So we decide on Mars for around the material time he will be lord of the mid-heaven.

We can protect Mars with the virtue of a powerful Jupiter by translation of light. Also, Mars is in reception with the sun, for Mars governs the watery triplicity (as ruler of Scorpio, a water sign); and the sun rules Leo. This, then, is our key pattern: Mars, lord of the mid-heaven, rising in Leo, in mutual reception with the sun, lord of the figure, and receiving the virtue of Jupiter through a translation of light.

We have other dignities for good measure. Venus rules Taurus and Saturn governs the airy triplicity by day; thus Venus and Saturn are in reception.

The sun occupies the terms of Mercury and Mercury the sign of the sun, thus Mercury and the sun enjoy reception.

Jupiter is in his own terms; the moon in face.

I only have one small quarrel with Ashmole's data: if I had gone to all the trouble of setting up this election I would have ensured that the actual exaltation degree of Aries, 19 degrees Aries, was at the mid-heaven, for I would not only have that degree, but the moon and Mars form a very close Grand Trine in Fire with the mid-heaven.

During the Second World War St Paul's was spared the total destruction visited upon neighbouring buildings by enemy bombing; during the great fire of 29 December 1940, it stood like a beacon in the midst of total devastation, but it did suffer direct hits from high explosive bombs, which wrecked the high altar and north transept and destroyed most of the glass. This, no doubt, was the most traumatic experience to befall St Paul's since the laying of the foundation stone. Let me recall the words of Lilly describing the effect of a planet's greatest years: 'Admit we frame a new building, erect a town or city, etc., when a planet is essentially and accidentally strong, the astrologer may conjecture the building may so continue so many years in honour etc., without any sensible alteration.'

You will recall that the astrologer went to some trouble to fortify the planet Mars, and his greatest years are 264. Add 264 to 1675 and you arrive at 1939, the year war was declared. Fire and destruction were poured down upon the cathedral, but it survived when all about it did not; so there maybe something valuable in bringing the virtue of Jupiter to the key fortified planet in the election.

PROGRESSIONS FOR THE WAR

The astrologer must always attempt progressions and transits for important events upon a radical chart. Unfortunately, I have not got the dates for the direct hits upon St Paul's, but I have taken the date of the terrible fire, and since the culmination of bombing upon London was apparently 10 May 1941, the date I have taken will be within six months of the event.

The progressed sun is square progressed Pluto; the astrologer would not have known about Pluto, but it makes sense to me that this planet was involved at a time of devastation. Also, the progressed mid-heaven was conjunct the north node.

Transits: I can find no convincing transits save one (I am hampered by not knowing the exact dates of the bombing): I have demonstrated elsewhere how potent the influence of transitting Uranus was for England at the time of the Battle of Britain and the

Table 1 Progressions for the Terrible Fire, Second World War, 29 December *1940*

Progressed Sun 6 Aries 54 square progressed Pluto, 6 Cancer 47
Progressed MC 12 Capricorn 41 conjunct north node, 11 Capricorn 3

Progressed Mars 25 Aquarius 21 (seventh House)

Transitting Uranus:							
in Taurus	23 Jan.	22 Feb.	23 Mar.	24 Apr.	25 May	27 June	1941

Progressed sun 6 Aries 54 square progressed Pluto 6 Cancer 47

Solar eclipse	7 Aries	27.3.1941
New moon	7 Capricorn	28.12.1940

Blitz, and it interests me that Mars by progression had moved to 25 degrees 21 minutes of Aquarius, in the seventh House of enemies and war; throughout the first six months of 1941, Uranus by transit was squaring the progressed Mars from Taurus in the Tenth, being exact in May.

It may have been fortuitous that the transitting moon at noon on the day of the great fire was conjunct Fortuna.

Perhaps the most fascinating pattern is this: the progressed sun squares Pluto for the year; a solar eclipse falling within eight minutes of arc of the progressed sun on 27 March 1941, and, on the day before that great fire, a new moon opposed to Pluto.

OTHER GREAT MOMENTS IN THE LIFE OF THE CATHEDRAL

As is clear from the radical chart, St Paul's Cathedral, known as the parish church of the Commonwealth, is a place of high ceremonial (Leo rising, moon/Jupiter in the Fifth). I therefore decided to look at one grave and one joyous moment in its history.

The Funeral of Admiral Lord Nelson

The admiral was accorded the honour of being buried in the cathedral, and the ceremony was a tremendous affair. The coffin had been brought in a water procession from Greenwich and landed at Whitehall steps. The drums of the volunteer corps who were to line the streets beat to arms an hour before dawn. It was as dazzling a sunlit day in January as could be remembered in London. The great bell began to toll at 8.30 by which time most ticket holders were in their seats and every window on the route from the Admiralty was filled. At last the sound of fifes and muffled drums playing the Dead March from *Saul* gave notice that the procession was in motion. It was so long that the Scots Greys leading the procession had reached the cathedral before the officers bringing up the rear had left the Admiralty. It was 2.00 p.m. before the coffin was borne into the cathedral. It had been foreseen that darkness must fall before the service ended. Within, the choir appeared dimly lit, although many torches had been employed, but an effect of extraordinary brilliance had been achieved beneath the dome, and exactly above the bier, by the introduction of a temporary chandelier of 130 lamps. The last stages of the state funeral, designed by the College of Arms, arrived. Garter King-of-Arms lifted up his voice to proclaim the styles and

Table 2 Progressions for Nelson's Funeral

Progressed ascendant 11 Scorpio 4 opposition Saturn 10 Taurus 39
Progressed Sun 20 Scorpio 32 square Mars retrograde 19 Leo 48
Progressed Mercury 10 Sagittarius 40 conjunct Jupiter retrograde 10 Sagittarius 59

	Transitting Jupiter	24 Sagittarius 43	
	New Moon	28 Sagittarius 46	21.12.1805
	Radical Moon	18 Sagittarius 48	
	Progressed Moon	18 Virgo 42	
8 a.m.	Transitting Moon	19 Virgo 0	

titles of the departed. The officers of Lord Nelson's household broke their white staves and handed them to Garter to be cast on the coffin, about to be lowered by machinery into the crypt.

This was possibly the greatest funeral yet seen by the cathedral, and you may feel it makes sense that the progressed ascendant (now moved to the fourth House) is opposing Saturn. It was a great ceremonial occasion: the progressed Sun is square that Leo Mars. Progressed Mercury is conjunct radical Jupiter in Sagittarius. Transitting Jupiter has moved to 24 degrees Sagittarius and the previous new moon, which was a solar eclipse, falls conjunct within 4 degrees (also the degree of 1066 Uranus, ever an important degree for England). It was an occasion of immense public interest: see how the progressed Moon (signifying the people) is square to the radical Moon; and during the course of the day the transitting moon passes over the progressed Moon.

The Wedding of Prince Charles and Lady Diana Spencer

This was a joyous ceremonial occasion, possibly the greatest wedding the cathedral had yet experienced. Progressed Sun conjunct progressed Saturn – a state occasion. Progressed Mercury at the mid-heaven, sextile progressed ascendant in the seventh (House of marriage). Progressed Jupiter has moved to 22 degrees of Capricorn, and the previous full Moon, 17 July 1981, which was a lunar eclipse, fell at 24 degrees of Capricorn.

The general public followed the ceremony in their millions.

Table 3 Progressions for the Wedding of Prince Charles and Lady Diana

Progressed sun 16 Taurus 28 conjunct 16 Taurus 11
Progressed Mercury 22 Aries 13 conjunct MC 22 Aquarius 15

Progressed Jupiter	22 Capricorn 13	
Lunar eclipse	24 Capricorn	17.7.1981
Transitting Mercury	23 Cancer 22	

Wedding ascendant 7 Libra 56 trine Venus radical 8 Gemini 19

Transitting moon at the actual time of the marriage was conjunct radical sun in Cancer, and transitting Mercury opposing the eclipse degree and progressed Jupiter.

It was a musical extravaganza: the ascendant of the wedding chart is trine radical Venus in Gemini.

I rest content with this chart for St Paul's Cathedral.

Notes

For the 'years of the planets' see William Lilly, *Christian Astrology* (1985), pp. 60, 64, 68, 72, 76, 80, 83.

Translation of light: 'Translation of light and nature is, when a light [fast-moving] Planet seperates [*sic*] from a more weighty one, and presently joynes to another more heavy; and its in this manner, Let Saturn be in 20 degr [*sic*] of Aries: Mars in 15. of Aries, and Mercury in 16 of Aries; here Mercury being a swift planet seperates from Mars, and translates the virtue of Mars unto Saturn. Its done also as well by any aspect as by conjunction.' (William Lilly, *Christian Astrology*, p. 111.)

Bibliography

Oman, Carola (1947) *Nelson* (London: Hodder & Stoughton).

IX

THE REVOLUTION OF 1688

Derek Appleby

Commentary

As an astrologer approaching the subject, Derek Appleby sets the bloodless, so-called 'Glorious Revolution' of 1688 in an extended – indeed, a chronologically vast – context. The Declaration of Rights in February 1689 was a statement, drawn up by the 'convened' Parliament, of the unconstitutional acts of James II, who had fled to France. William III and James' daughter, Mary II, were proclaimed joint sovereigns after their acceptance of this Declaration, which later became part of the Bill of Rights. It attacked James II for attempting to subvert the Protestant religion, for levying money without parliamentary consent, and for maintaining a standing army in peacetime. It thus justified the offer of the throne to William of Orange and Mary, who were both grandchildren of Charles I.

The Declaration of Rights was a significant moment in the life of the country and of the monarchy, marking progress towards parliamentary government. The settlement of 1689 did not contain the seeds of universal suffrage, an idea which had been advanced by the Levellers and was contained in the amended 'Agreement of the People' in 1647 (Christopher Hill, *The World Turned Upside Down: Radical Ideas during the English Revolution*, 1985). It was an idea which long lay dormant. However, the Declaration was an historic moment in the development of Parliament's power, in its relations with the monarchy, and in what flowed from that development.

The horoscopes of King Edgar's coronation (referred to as '973') and of William I's ('1066') are viewed as foundation charts of the monarchy and the people, and so may be related by progression and transit to later events, as one might relate an individual's horoscope to his or her life events.

As the revolution arose from politico–religious dissension, Derek Appleby considers these problems as they arose in earlier reigns. Mars rules the ninth House of religion in the 973 chart (the *radix*), so its progressions are traced in the reigns of Henry VIII and onwards. Certain crucial events for crown and country, such as the Gunpowder Plot and the execution of Charles I, are also considered, as are the transits of Uranus (not then discovered), the planet of change. There is also an interesting analysis of William's nativity.

A. L. K.

Note: Dates are expressed in New Style. Unfamiliar terms will be found in the Glossary.

It was at Brixham, in the county of Devon, that William landed with his army at noon on 5 November 1688, 'His Highness the Prince of Orange whom it hath pleased Almighty God to make the glorious instrument of delivering this Kingdom from Popery and Arbitrary Power'.

Edgar, son of Edmund the Magnificent, was king of the English between 944 and 975. On the death of his brother in October 959 Edgar became king of a united England. His coronation was delayed till 973, when it took place with much ceremony at Bath, and was followed by the submission of eight kings, including the kings of Scotland and Strathclyde. It is the chart for this coronation which I consider to be the foundation chart for the British monarchy – the first great chart of England (Figure 13); the second great chart of England (Figure 14) is for the coronation of William on Christmas Day, 1066. Certain degree areas of these charts have persistently demonstrated their potency throughout our history. I shall concentrate upon the chart for the coronation of Edgar, because I have some affection for it.

Will charts of such antiquity respond to secondary progressions, and also to transits?

In a lecture some years ago, I demonstrated the relevance of the transit of Uranus combined with syzygies, to the 973 chart at the time of the Battle of Britain. In this study I have experimented with several different methods of progressing the angles of the 973 chart, and I have opted for solar arc in longitude; *all dates will be expressed in New Style*.

THE 973 RADICAL CHART

Consider the 973 Saturn/Jupiter square in Figure 13. The Tenth House of a national chart has dominion over the highest authority in the land, Jupiter has a natural association with monarchy, and the Fifth House (I have found) is also connected with that institution. Saturn occupies the Tenth House and is ruler of the Fifth. Jupiter is regal by nature, and these two are in square radical aspect. We may therefore conclude that this square will be involved at times of crisis or importance for the monarchy.

If this is the foundation chart of our monarchy, then it must be a

FOUNDATION CHARTS OF ENGLAND

Edgar crowned
11 May 973
Noon
51N22 2W22

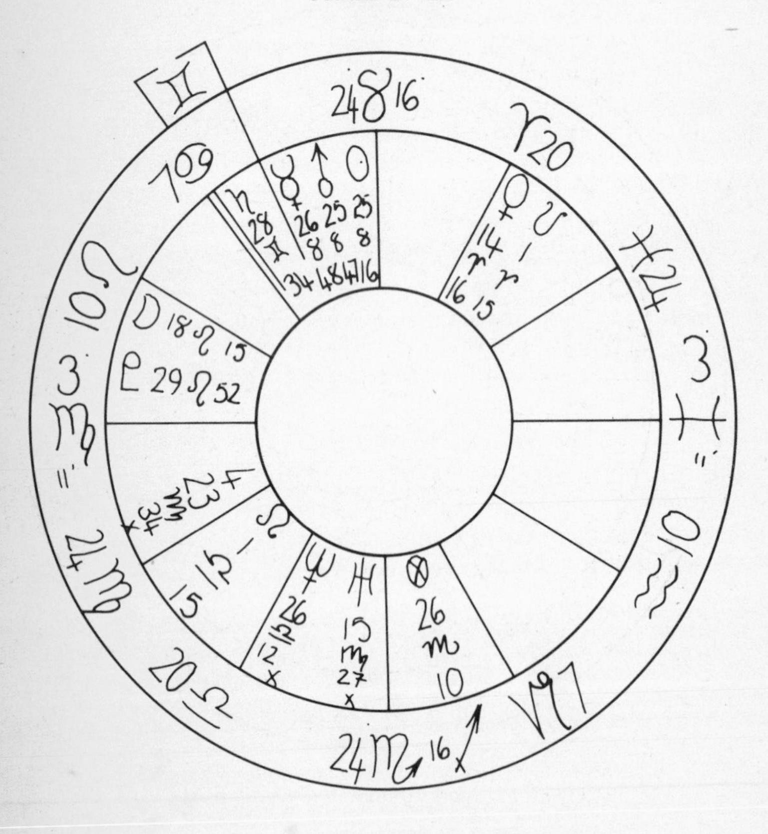

Figure 13 *Coronation of Edgar (973)*

William crowned
25 December 1066
Noon
Westminster

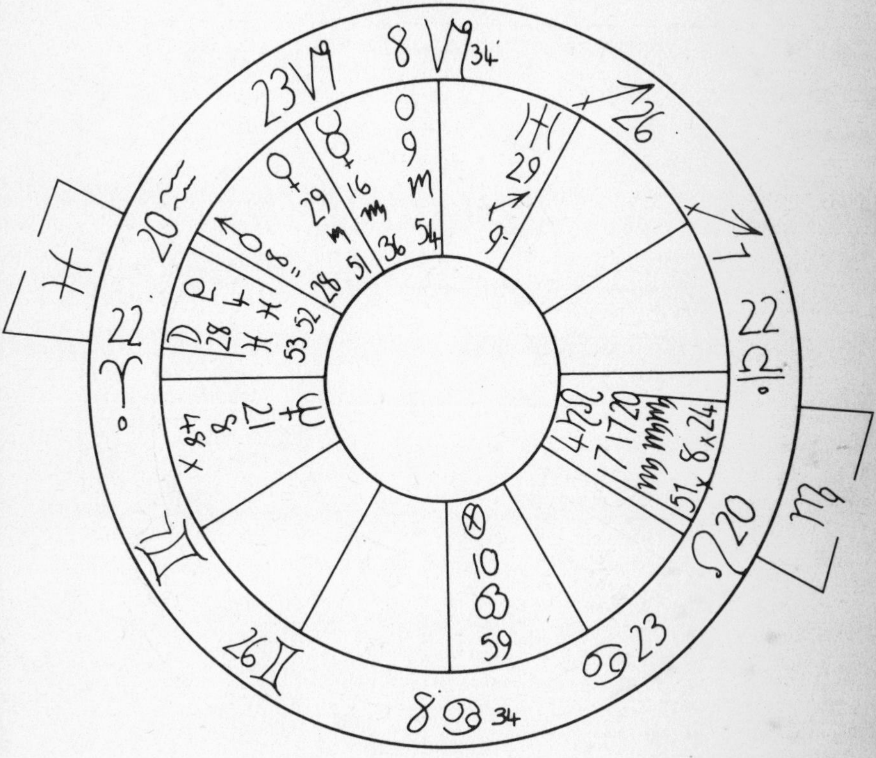

Figure 14 Coronation of William I (1066)

very powerful inception, for the institution has proved remarkably durable. You may think this is reflected in the combination of stability represented by Taurus and adaptability shown by Virgo. Popularity is shown by Venus (lady of the Tenth) trine moon (the common people). Note the mutual receptions between Sun/Moon, and Venus/Mars. A good Moon increasing in light, and a good aspect or reception between the lights is virtually indispensable to a successful inception.

THE 973 CHART PROGRESSED

Let us see what the progressed angles were doing at the greatest period of crisis experienced by monarchy (Figures 15 and 16).

On 1 September 1642, when Charles I unfurled his standard at Nottingham – PMC (progressed mid-heaven) was opposing Jupiter; when his head was chopped off on 9 February 1649 and monarchy was extinguished (temporarily) PMC had moved to square Saturn. Thus, during the Civil War, PMC was moving between each point of the radical square.

The Restoration of the Monarchy occurred on 18 May 1660, and

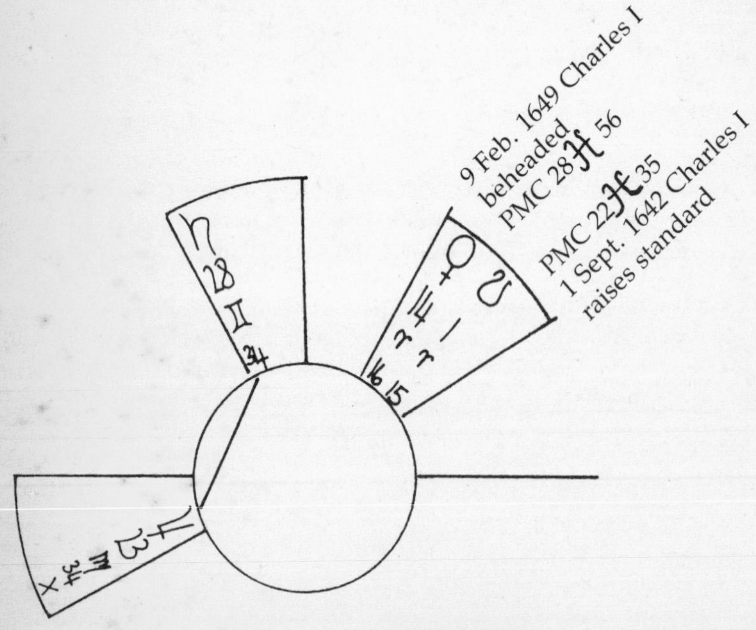

Figure 15 The AD 973 chart progressed

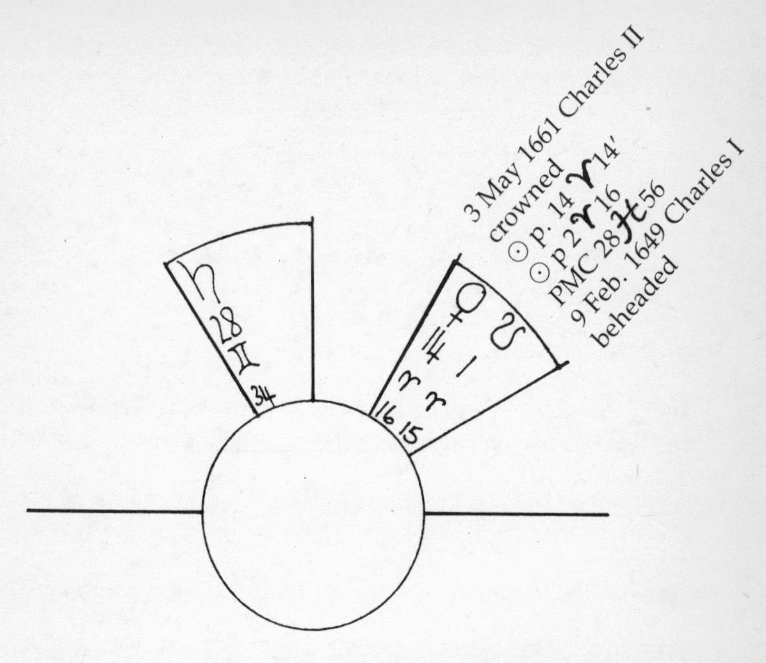

Figure 16 The AD 973 chart progressed

Charles II was crowned on 3 May 1661. By this time Jupiter had progressed to 4 degrees 27 minutes Sagittarius and PASC (progressed ascendant) was closing to a trine; meanwhile progressed sun conjunct the south node when Charles I was executed had arrived at a conjunction with radical Venus (lady of the tenth) at the coronation of Charles II.

You may feel that these contacts are highly appropriate to the events, and although they are not sufficient on their own to justify the concept of progressing national angles by solar arc, they provide a convincing starting point.

THE PROGRESS OF MARS

The Ninth House of a national chart has dominion over religion and the church, and Mars is ruler of the 973 Ninth. Perhaps the progress of Mars (Figure 17) through the chart will give indications of religious climate over the centuries. We are working on a year-for-a-day, so Mars will take some 686 years to return to its natal place.

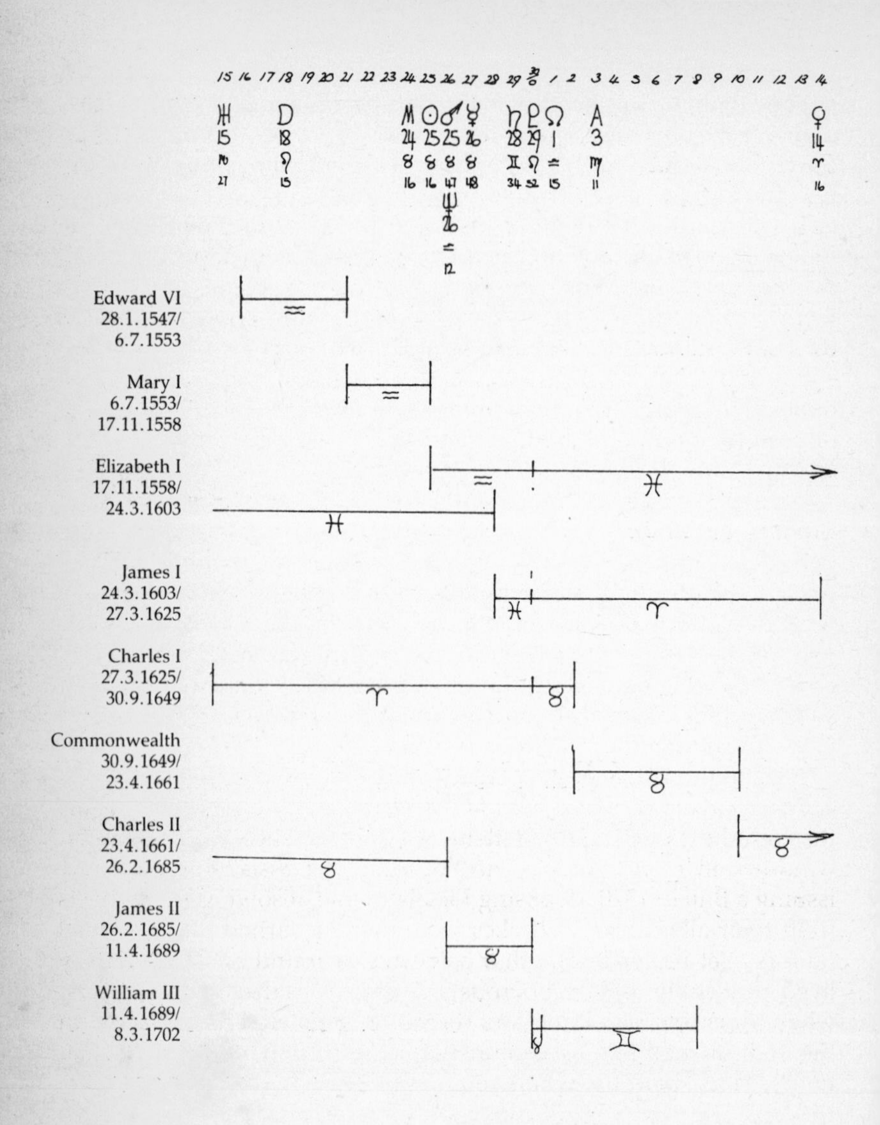

Figure 17 The progress of Mars

It was in the reign of Henry VIII that Mars progressed into Aquarius; but he was hardly a Protestant, rather in favour of a papacy without the pope. On the one hand he burned those who denied transubstantiation, and on the other lopped off the heads of those who denied the royal supremacy. It would have been easy in his time to find oneself in a no-win situation!

It was during the reign of his son Edward VI (a minor) that the Reformation really took hold; the Council of Regency was dominated by reformers. An English liturgy and a Protestant confession of faith were introduced, the clergy were permitted to marry, and in 1548 deliberate iconoclasm was encouraged. Mars was passing in opposition to radical moon, in fact he had got half way between the opposition point of the moon/mid-heaven square, and almost to the opposition mid-point of the moon/sun–Mars square; then came 'Bloody Mary' (1553–58).

As Mars swung into the later half of the aspect, Mary – a devout Catholic – brought the country back into the papist fold and violently persecuted Protestants. The common people, sympathetic to Protestantism from the first, became more so as the queen desperately increased efforts to stamp out deviation from the 'true faith'. Mars had also been moving in opposition between the radical moon/Pluto conjunction 21 degrees 05 minutes – 24 degrees 24 minutes Aquarius, so that when Elizabeth I came into her inheritance on 27 November 1558, it was standing square radical sun.

Elizabeth did her best to create an atmosphere of tolerance and sought to avoid the extremes of both her brother's and sister's reigns through the 'Reformation Settlement'. She said she would not 'open windows in men's souls'. The Pope did not assist this policy by issuing a Bull in 1570, deposing Elizabeth and absolving her subjects from their allegiance. Catholics were thereby turned into potential traitors. Yet under Elizabeth a balance was found and the country lived peacefully and prosperously. Apart from the first few years, when Mars opposed Pluto and therefore completed its contact with the radical moon/Pluto conjunction (completion of the Reformation?), Mars spent the whole reign in Pisces.

THE GUNPOWDER PLOT

It could be argued that it was the Papal Bull of 1570 which culminated in the Gunpowder Plot of 15 November 1605 in the reign of James I (Figure 18). At this time Mars was conjunct the south node at 0 degrees 20 minutes Aries. The progressed mid-heaven was in square

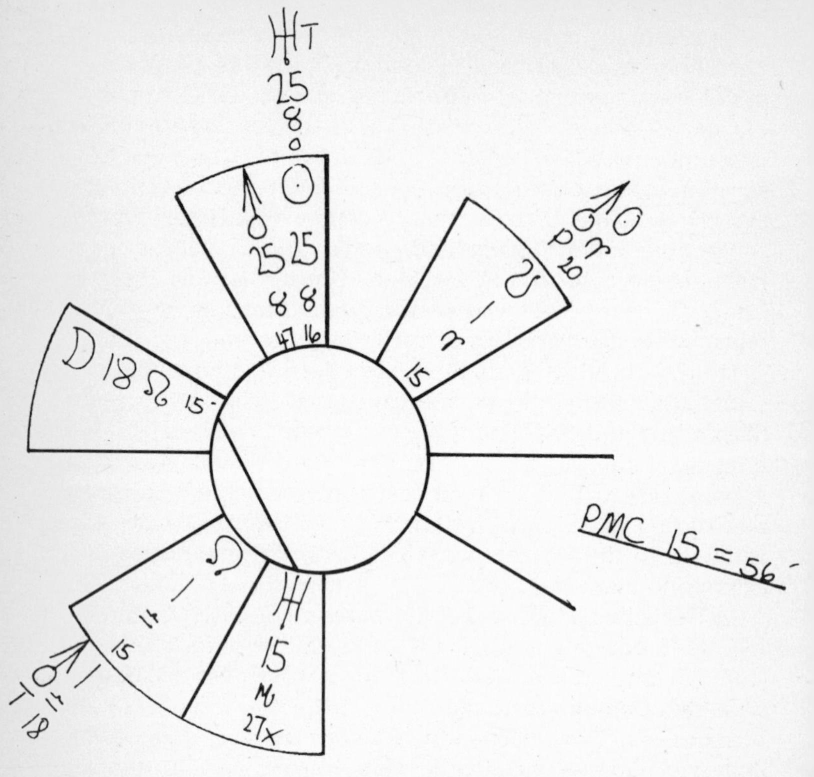

Figure 18 The Gunpowder Plot

aspect with radical Uranus, transitting Uranus was conjunct radical sun, and transitting Mars was exactly opposed to progressed Mars at the north node.

Throughout the remainder of James' reign Mars (powerful in Aries) was moving between the south node and the radical Venus in the Eighth House (see Figure 13). James entered into alliances with the German Protestant Union and regarded himself as the Protestant champion of Europe. He also believed in witchcraft and many poor souls met a fiery end during his time, although he later repudiated the belief.

Mars was conjunct Venus when Charles I came to the throne (3 April 1625), and at his death it was 1 degree 30 minutes Taurus, opposed to progressed Neptune. Charles had been brought up a

Calvinist, but promoted clerics who favoured the Catholic ritual, and he was strongly influenced by his Catholic wife, Henrietta Maria.

Mars entered Taurus at the end of Charles' reign, and was in the first decanate of that sign during the years of the Commonwealth.

Charles II (crowned 3 May 1661) spent much of his reign in contention with Parliament, and attempting to stave off severe sanctions against Catholics; he was received into the Catholic church before his death. Mars was at 10 degrees 4 minutes Taurus at his coronation, and at 26 degrees 25 minutes Taurus at the accession of James II (16 February 1685). Thus, during the last three years of Charles's reign, Mars had struck the mid-heaven, sun, and Mars, returning to its natal place by progression for the first time.

James II, brother of Charles II, was surrendered to the parliamentarians at Oxford in 1646, but escaped to the continent. He served in the French and Spanish armies at various times. He returned to England at the Restoration, an experienced and able soldier, and was appointed lord high admiral and warden of the Cinque Ports, in which capacity he modernized the Royal Navy. He had success in battles with the Dutch, and was a good commander as well as an excellent organiser.

In December 1660 he secretly married Anne Hyde (1637–71). In 1672 he made public his conversion to Catholicism. The Test Act (1673) required denial of the doctrine of transubstantiation – impossible for a Catholic – and James was obliged to resign his offices. On 10 October 1673 he married the Catholic princess, Mary of Modena. Both his daughters by Anne Hyde, Mary and Anne, had been brought up as Protestants, and in November 1677 Mary married William of Orange. Strong anti-Catholic feeling among the people obliged James to return to the continent; meanwhile the Exclusion Act (May 1679) threatened to exclude him from the succession.

When Charles fell ill in August, James was recalled, but he was kept from the court by being made high commissioner in Scotland. When Parliament finally excluded James from the succession in 1681, it was dissolved by Charles II.

James returned to court in 1682, became very powerful, and the exclusionists were finally vanquished. He became king on the death of Charles II. He survived the rebellions of Argyll and Monmouth, but the severity of the reprisals, in particular the 'bloody assize' of Judge Jeffreys, caused widespread revulsion. James further aggravated the nation by publicly celebrating mass, pressuring judges, obtaining the power to dispense Catholics from the Test Act, and bringing Catholics into important positions in the army and admin-

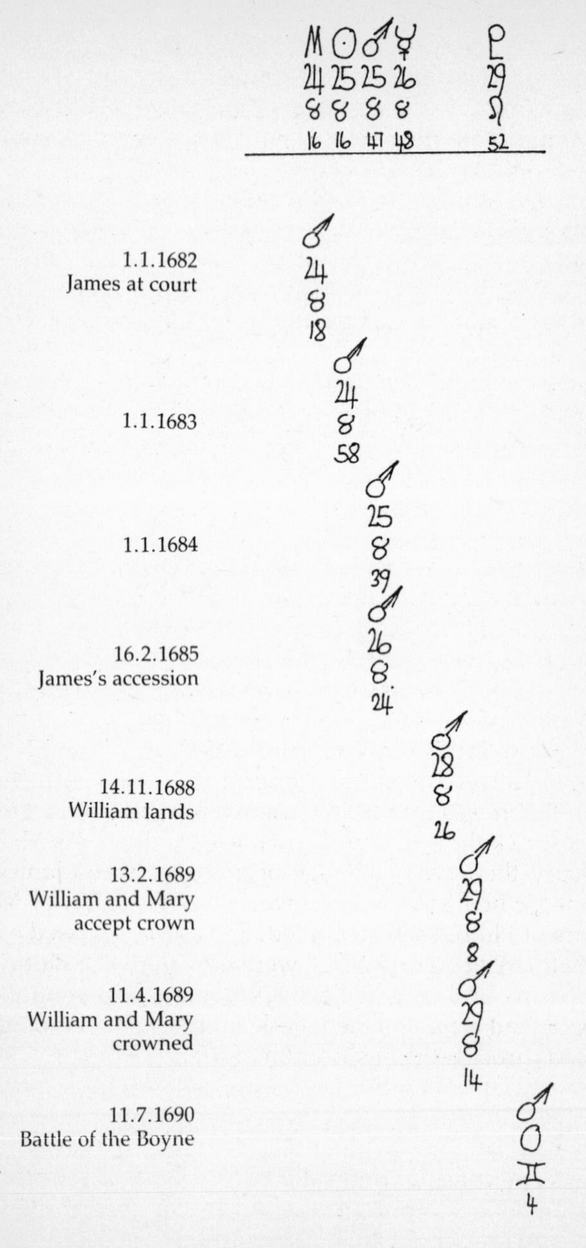

Figure 19 Progressed Mars in close-up

istration. He also increased his army to 20,000 and had it stationed within easy reach of the capital. James persisted with his pro-Catholic declarations and proclamations and then, in June 1688, his wife gave birth to a son, which promised a Catholic succession. In the wake of this alarming event, the 'immortal seven' sent their famous invitation to William of Orange.

William landed on 15 November 1688 and eventually swept all before him; James was finally allowed to escape to France. He landed in Ireland on 22 March 1689, went to Dublin and summoned a Parliament, but was defeated at the Battle of the Boyne on 11 July 1690. Two more serious attempts to regain his throne (1692 and 1696) were thwarted.

Now the English monarchy was staunchly Protestant, Parliament established in its right and privileges and the bloodless and so-called Glorious Revolution was complete!

PROGRESSED MARS IN CLOSE-UP

This specific set of problems had begun when James returned to the court of his brother in January 1682 as privy councillor, on the committee of foreign affairs and lord high admiral. (It was remarked at the time 'the Duke of York did chiefly manage affairs, but with great haughtiness' for that was when he began to bring Catholics into important positions of power and influence.)

As James came to court, progressed Mars (Figure 19) was conjunct the mid-heaven, religion became an issue in government – one might say religion was interfering in government – and so it continued as Mars struck the sun and its own radical place. As Mars closed with Mercury there was a change of monarch when James came to the throne. When Mars was between a conjunction of Mercury and a square of Pluto, William landed, and as Mars passed over the square of Pluto, William and Mary were crowned, the Battle of the Boyne was won, and a great revolution/transformation had occurred. Popery had been pushed back and the power of the monarchy limited through the Declaration of Rights.

THE REVOLUTION

Now let us consider the major events in detail (Figure 20). The bold horizontal lines represent the radical degrees of the important 973 pattern. Throughout 1688/90 the progressed ascendant was moving between the conjunction of moon and square of sun; we see again the

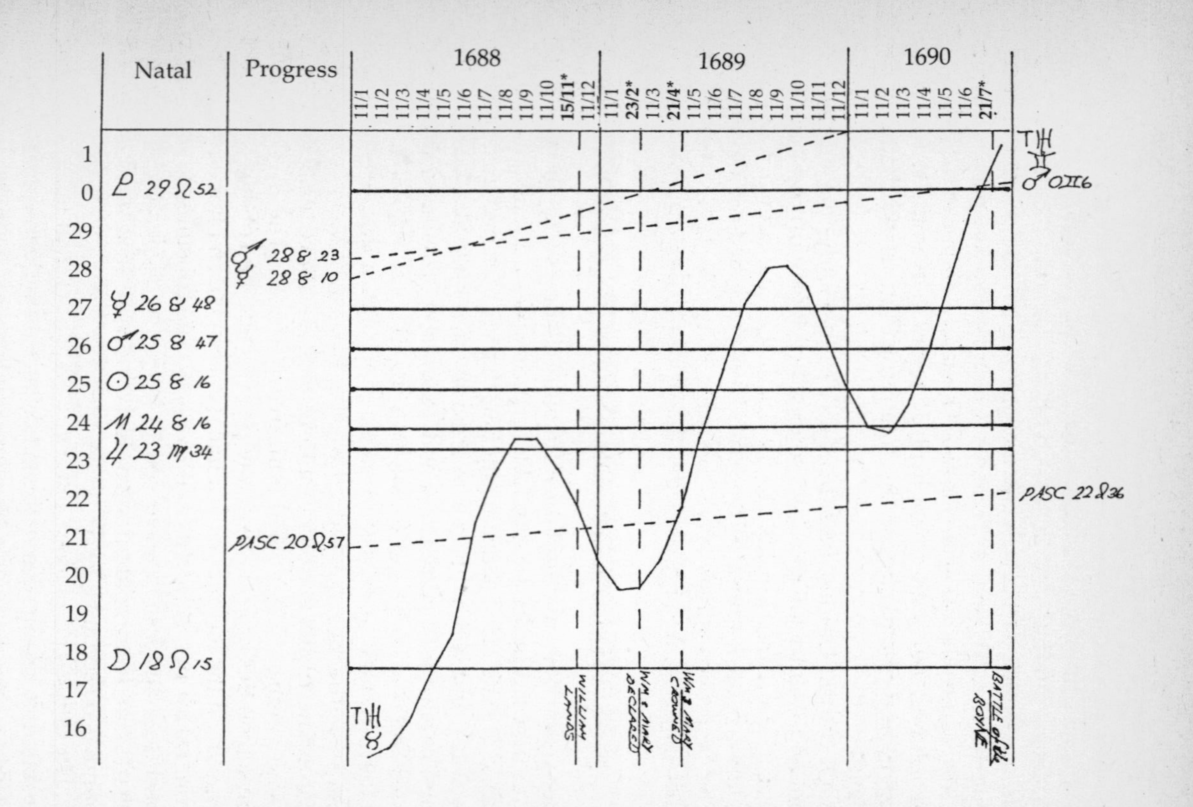

Figure 20 The Revolution

movement of progressed Mars; progressed Mercury started off conjunct progressed Mars, squared Pluto around the time of William's landing, and then sped off into Gemini. It is the transit of Uranus which particularly fascinates: square PASC when the invitation went to William and then off to trine Jupiter, back to square PASC again when William landed. During the course of the 'Glorious Revolution' he made contact with all the planets in the tenth House twice, and finally cleared the square of Pluto at the Battle of the Boyne.

Of course, Uranus does this dance every eighty-four years or so, but on this occasion he was partnered by Mars returning to his natal place by progression for the first time. On the previous occasion Uranus made a transit of the tenth House, we had the Gunpowder Plot, the subsequent cycle coincided with the latter part of the Crimean War, and the one after that with the Battle of Britain.

WILLIAM OF ORANGE'S NATIVITY

Born eight days after his father's death, William of Orange (Figure 21) was brought up by a formidable grandmother until he was made a 'child of state'. He was asthmatic and slightly hunched, reserved and taciturn, but well educated, a good linguist and, like Mary, a fine connoisseur – a competent and successful general and devoted husband. He had a gift for discovering able (but not always loyal) administrators; he was mad on hunting, and a devout Protestant. Such an attractive man indeed was he, that when Mary was told she was to marry him she wept for three days. We have the birth data as 14 November 1650, at 8.30 p.m. in The Hague. The first task I set myself on this project was to attempt a rectification of the birth time; I employed the technique of prenatal epoch, which I hoped would be confirmed by 'accidents'. It was a time-consuming and risky business, and I shall leave you to judge the likely accuracy of the chart, but I am content with 14 November 1650 at 19 hours 54 minutes 30 seconds GMT.

His father had attempted a *coup d'état* which had failed, with the result that on his death the office of stadtholder was abolished. William grew up among enemies, and learned to conceal his feeling behind a mask of immobile, almost repulsive, coldness. It was said of him that, like Charles XII of Sweden and the younger Pitt, he was a wonderful example of premature mental development.

In 1672 Louis XIV of France, in alliance with Charles II of England, suddenly invaded Dutch territory. The Dutch people turned for help

William III, 1689–1702
4 November 1650
19.54.30 GMT
52N7 7E14

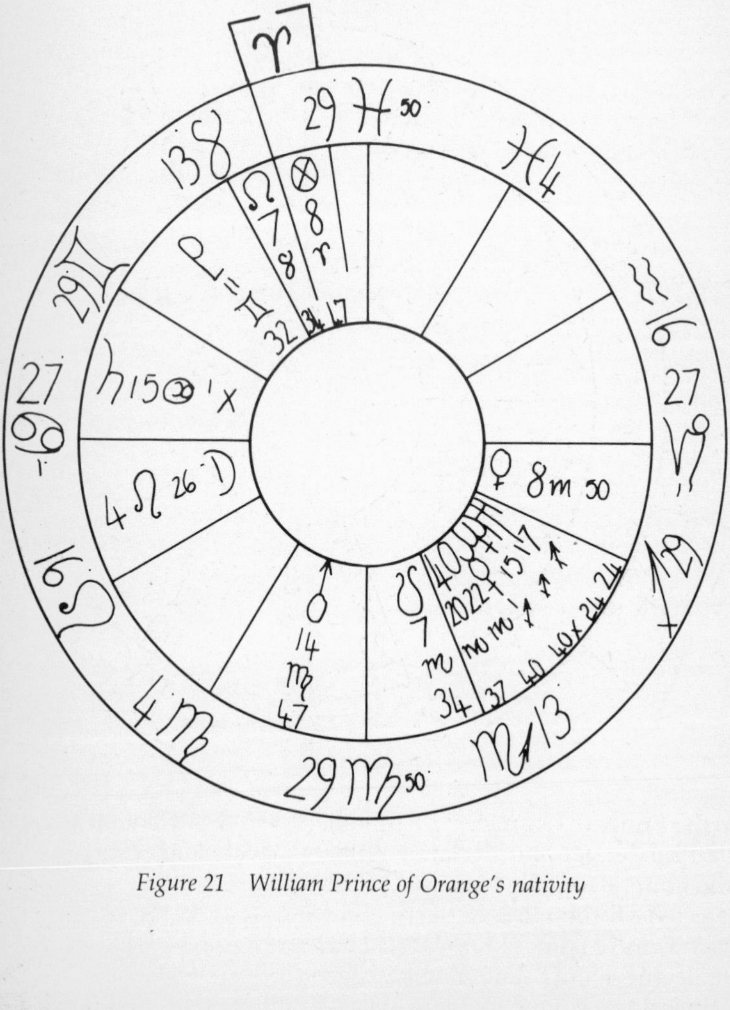

Figure 21 William Prince of Orange's nativity

William's pre-natal epoch
27 February 1650
5.16.0 GMT
52N7 7E14

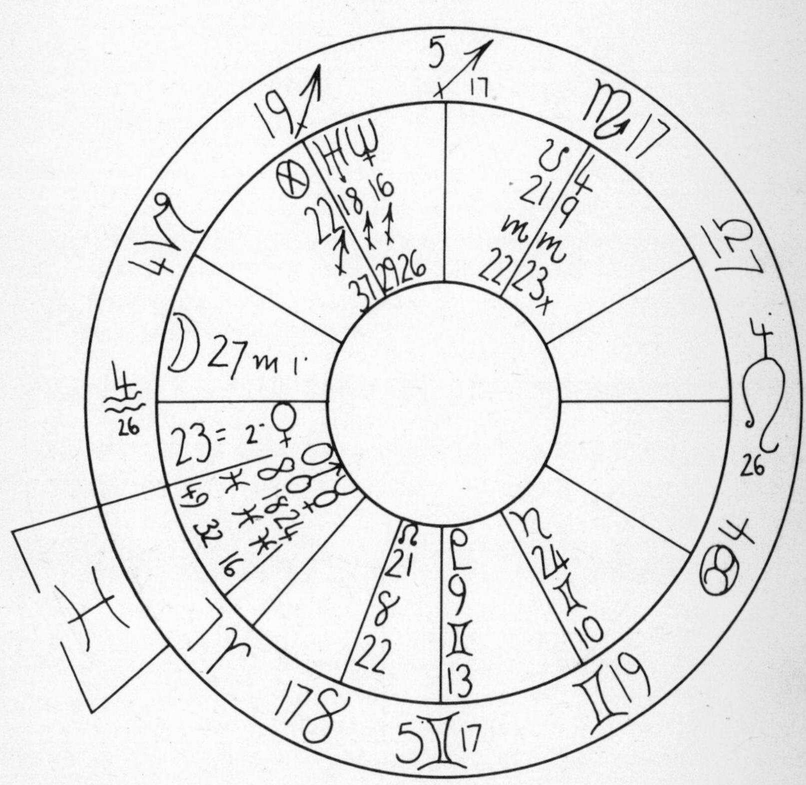

to the Prince of Orange. On 8 July 1672 the States-General revived the stadtholderate, and declared William stadtholder, capitain-general and admiral for life. William confronted Louis with heroic obstinacy, rejected all thoughts of surrender, and opened the sluices, laying vast tracts of land under water. The French army could not advance, while the French and English fleets were defeated by the Dutch Admiral De Ruyter. William successfully resisted the French for six years, his marriage to Mary in 1677 was a diplomatic victory, and as a result of negotiations with England the following year, Louis was forced to make terms and sign the Treaty of Nijmegen in August 1678, under which the Dutch did not have to make any concessions. William was regarded as the Protestant champion of Europe.

William started a new coalition against Louis in October 1681 by making treaties with Sweden, the Empire, Spain and several German princes. But even when Louis absorbed Strasbourg (1681), invaded Spanish Flanders and took Luxembourg (1684), the new league would not fight and allowed Louis to retain his conquests by the Treaty of Regensburg (1685); but these events provoked a more closely knit and aggressive coalition, which was organized in 1686 and known as the League of Augsburg.

After his marriage William kept a careful eye on politics in England. On the accession of James II he tried to bring him into the League of Augsburg. When he saw that James would not join the league against Louis, he turned for support to the English opposition. He caused his chief minister, Fagel, to write a letter expressing his disapprobation of the religious policy of James, which was published in November 1687. But he made it clear he would not interfere unless he received a definite invitation. On 30 June 1688 Admiral Herbert, disguised as a sailor, set out from England with a letter from the 'immortal seven' asking William 'to bring over an army and secure the infringed liberties' of England. Obligingly, William landed at Torbay on 'Guy Fawkes Day', 1688 (15 November NS).

The moon rising in Leo would give William a youthful appearance, but, in the terms of Saturn, a dark complexion. Proud, and doubtless haughty, he would naturally command public attention, yet with the last decanate of Cancer rising, as well as the moon, very sensitive nonetheless. That sensitivity might well have been expressed in the appreciation of the arts, for we are told he was a fine connoisseur. Also, if I may add, any man with a powerful first House moon really needs the company of women. William would have been attracted to glamorous and strong-minded women (such as may be described by Leo), and easily flattered by them, and herein lies a weakness. And it is not difficult to see in that moon a reflection of his autocratic grandmother. Contrast this with what he actually got, for his wife is described by Saturn in Cancer retrograde in the twelfth – a timid woman, dutiful and serious, but tall and beautiful.

With Mercury in Sagittarius in the fifth, of course he enjoyed hunting, of course he was a good linguist; Virgo Mars in the third might suggest that he was a compulsive talker, but we are told otherwise; he was, apparently, a very good listener and when he spoke it was to the point, yet he must have been quite witty with a gift for repartee.

Venus is awkward in Capricorn, so he does not easily display his very deep and intense emotions; he is somewhat clumsy in this regard but extremely ardent.

The focal point of the chart, of course, is the sun/Jupiter conjunction in the fifth House in Scorpio. Here is a man of deep and broad vision, someone who can see long-term consequences of events, almost a psychic. The link with a Saturn sensitized by Cancer adds the ability to plan and give form to the visions stirred by Jupiter. Virgoan Mars is also drawn into the pattern and adds an analytical dimension. Here is a man who, through the moon and through Saturn, is highly sensitive to every change in his environment, an expert at recognizing signs and signals, and also at reading and analysing them. Jupiter, then, is able to project all these indications on to a wider screen and to see the broad picture.

The fifth House is a regal House, and the sun – part ruler of the first and ruler of the second – combined with Jupiter, lord of the tenth, does speak of great gains through speculative enterprises, and achievement of high status (a promise backed by moon trine tenth House Fortuna). No wonder he gained a kingdom. Consider also Jupiter's rule of religion: William might have gained the English crown partly because he married the right person at the right time, but mainly because he was a champion of the Protestant religion. All these things relate to sun/Jupiter in the fifth, but that combination confers on a native an additional benefit without which all else could fail, and that is plain old-fashioned luck! Lucky William – Jupiter the regal, Jupiter the visionary, Jupiter the rich, Jupiter the famous, Jupiter the religious, and Jupiter for luck!

But whatever else this or any nativity might contain, never forget or underestimate the core of the chart; William was a Scorpio! An intense, devoted, determined, ruthless, unforgiving Scorpio – the best of friends and the most dedicated of enemies.

From the moment when Louis XIV attacked Holland in 1672, William devoted all his efforts to the overthrow of the predominance of France and the restoration of the 'balance of power'. When peace was concluded at Ryswick in September 1697, Louis restored all his acquisitions since 1678, except Strasbourg, and recognized William as king of England. The Scorpio had triumphed, but the loss of Strasbourg must have stuck in his gullet.

Declaration of Rights
23 February 1689

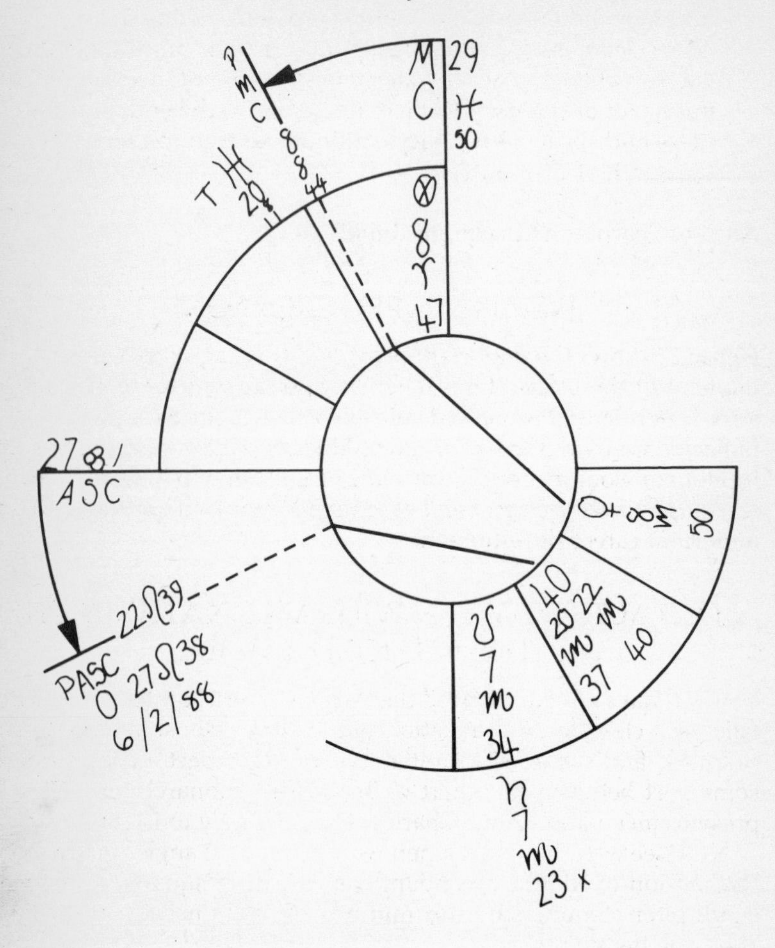

Figure 22 William's progressions for the Declaration moment

Encyclopaedia Britannica (1926) gives a most apt description of William's Sun/Jupiter conjunction:

> His essential greatness lay in his European policy. The best proof of his real powers of statesmanship is that the Peace of Utrecht was subsequently made on the broad lines which he had laid down as the only security for European peace nearly

> a dozen years before its conclusion. While he lacked in diplomacy the art of a Louis XIV, or the graces of a Marlborough, he grasped the central problems of his time with more clearness, or advanced solutions with more ultimate success, than any other statesman of his age. Often baffled, but never despairing, William fought on to the end, and the ideas and spirit of his policy continued to triumph long after the death of their author.

All very Scorpionic you might think!

WILLIAM'S PROGRESSIONS

Figure 22 shows the important progressed contacts for William at the moment of the Declaration, when he and his wife were proclaimed joint sovereigns: progressed mid-heaven was in trine aspect with radical Capricorn Venus; progressed ascendant was activating the Jupiter/sun conjunction; meanwhile, the full moon before the event fell close to the progressed ascendant. Not bad patterns for an important career development.

CONTACTS BETWEEN WILLIAM'S NATIVITY AND THE 973 HOROSCOPE

You will have already noticed that William's sun/Jupiter conjunction falls very close to an opposition of 973 tenth House and all that it contains, and sextile 973 Jupiter. We would expect a connection of some sort between the chart of an English monarch and 973 (the present queen and Prince Charles relate strongly to it) (Figure 23).

Now see what happens when we progress the angles of 973 to the Declaration of Rights: ascendant comes within square of William's sun/Jupiter conjunction, and mid-heaven conjunct his north node and trine his Venus.

Now let us remind ourselves of William's progressed angles at the same date: they are doing exactly the same thing! Thus, for these few years in our history, at a critical time for the monarchy, the angles of the foundation chart of the monarchy and the angles of the monarch are moving as one.

The transits for the Declaration neatly link in with the pattern.

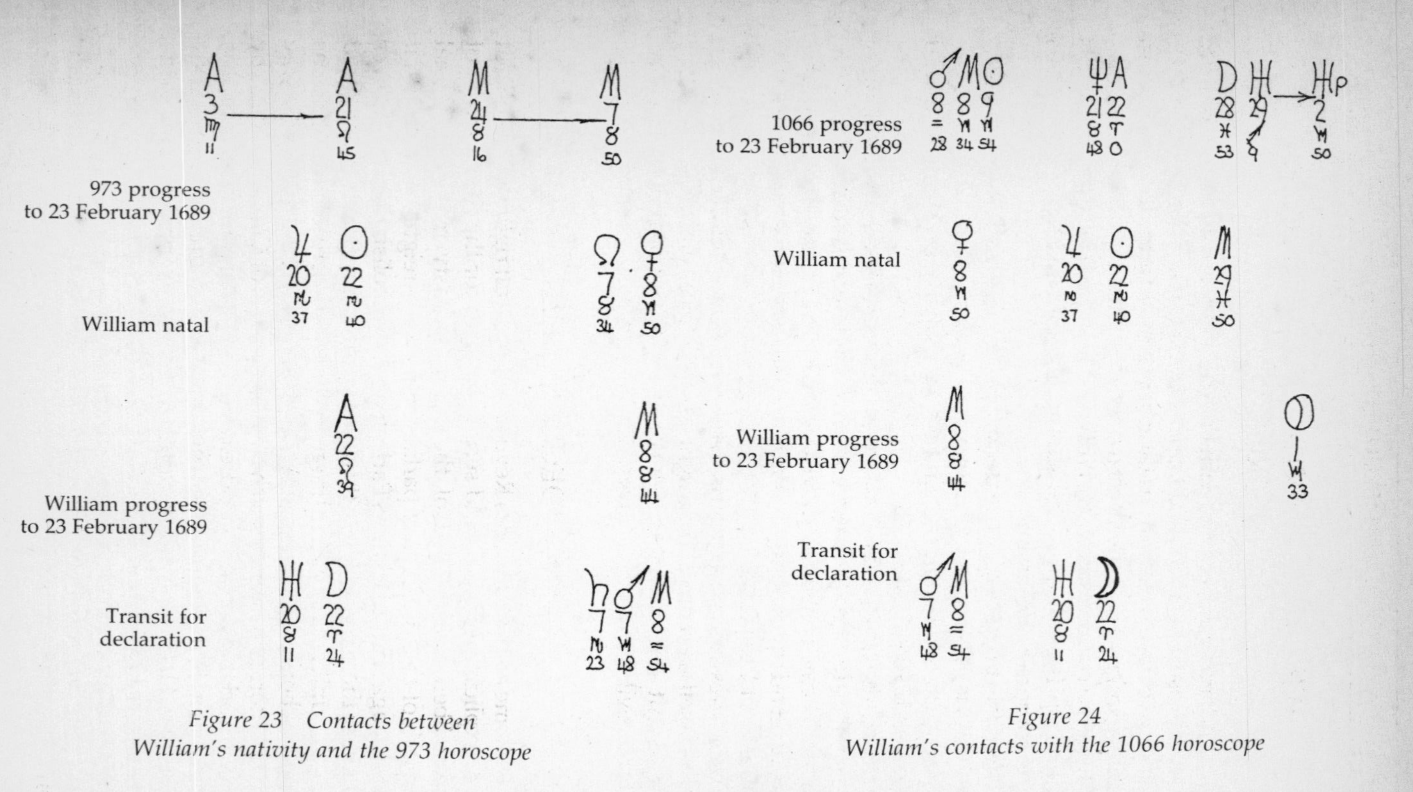

Figure 23 *Contacts between*
William's nativity and the 973 horoscope

Figure 24
William's contacts with the 1066 horoscope

WILLIAM'S CONTACTS WITH THE 1066 HOROSCOPE

Now William's connections with the 1066 chart are just as remarkable as with those of the 973, and I can't resist showing them (Figure 24).

First we have relevant radical positions from 1066, but with Uranus progressed to the declaration moment.

Next the connections with William's radix. See how his Venus sits right upon 1066 MC, how his sun/Jupiter opposes Neptune, and his MC is conjunct 1066 moon.

Then his progress for the declaration brings his PMC to trine his own Venus, 1066 mid-heaven/sun and square Mars. Also, his progressed sun/moon conjunction falls exactly between the radical and progressed 1066 Uranus.

Finally the transits for the moment of declaration show fascinating links right through the pattern, the most impressive being declaration mid-heaven conjunct 1066 Mars, and declaration Moon conjunct 1066 ascendant, which, if nothing else, seems to testify to the accuracy of both charts.

From these cosmic patterns there can be little doubt that almighty God herself appointed His Highness the Prince of Orange to be the instrument of delivering these islands from the dangers of 'popery' and the evil of arbitrary power.

THE DECLARATION

At the time of 'The Glorious Revolution', the full rights of Parliament were explicitly declared, and securities taken for the maintenance of public liberties. The end of the Stuart dynasty marked the final triumph of the principle of parliamentary sovereignty; henceforth it is never again disputed that Parliament may abolish the prerogatives and alter the common law. It was the beginning of a long hard road towards universal adult suffrage. Perhaps the greatest change was brought about by the Reform Act of 1832, which effectively did away with the corrupt system which allowed control of Commons seats by the territorial aristocracy, and enfranchised a greater section of the population in the boroughs; but it was not until 1867 that the agricultural labourer was enfranchised. By the Representation of the People Act 1918 women over 30 years of age were given the vote for the first time, and in 1928 the age restriction was removed, so that all adults enjoyed equal voting rights some 240 years after the declaration (Figure 25).

Declaration
23 February 1689
10am 30
London

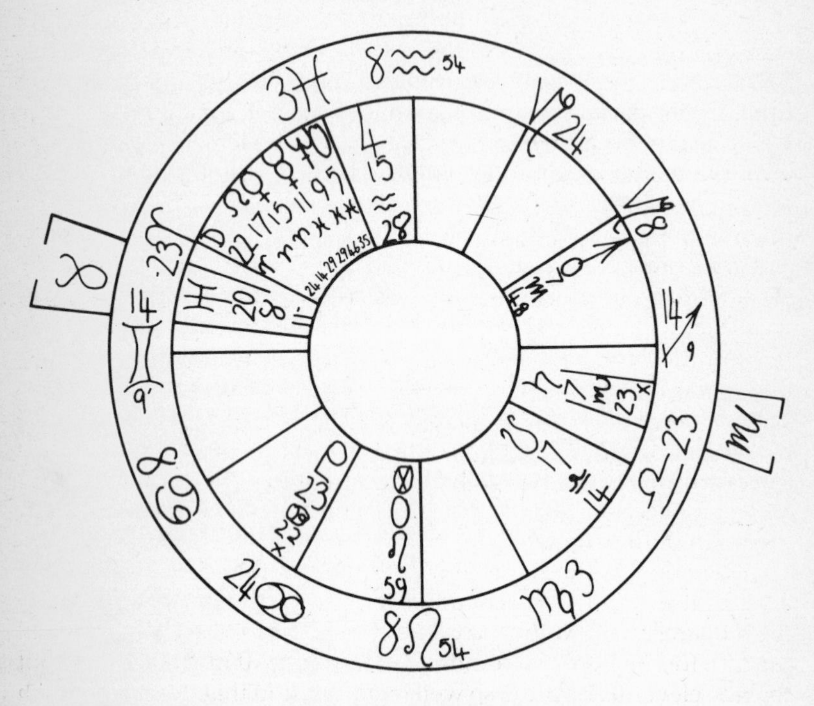

Figure 25 The declaration

After the monarchy had been brought into line, Parliament became concerned with the relative power of Lords and Commons. Victory for the Commons (if victory it was), came on 15 November 1910, when Asquith advised the king to dissolve Parliament but accompanied this advice with a request (which was granted) that the king should pledge himself beforehand to create a sufficient number of peers to carry the Parliament bill into law if the Liberal Party were returned to power. The Liberal Party was returned, the Parliament act became law, and established the legislative supremacy of the Commons over the Lords.

Since that time we have seen the gradual increase in power of the Cabinet over the Commons, so that now some of us might feel that we no longer vote for a Member of Parliament, but for one of two possible Cabinet teams, which has rapidly become a choice between two possible prime ministers; and that might stir in some of us the suspicion that we are adopting willy nilly some kind of presidential system.

It is not an easy chart to unravel; initially it is a matter of signification. Parliament consists of the monarch, the Lords Spiritual and Temporal, and the Commons; without each element fulfilling its particular role, Parliament cannot function. Deciding which planet and/or House represents which element is, to a large extent, a matter of art and opinion. The task is not made easier by the outer planets, none of which would have been present in the original chart.

There can be little doubt about the monarchy which must be shown by the tenth House and, given the nature of the event, it is reasonable to find Saturn (the monarch) retrograde in the sixth House in Scorpio, yet in harmonious trine with the sun and Mercury. The monarch had really become the servant of Parliament, but his influence was powerful as is suggested by Scorpio, and even more so by the Saturn/Mars reception. The monarch is head of the armed forces which stresses the sixth House and the connection with Mars; he is also head of the Church of England, and the Sixth House is the ninth of the monarch.

Where do we find Lords and Commons in this chart? There is an argument for giving the Commons to the fourth House, opposed to the monarch, but tradition says the eleventh is for the Commons and the fifth for the Lords in mundane judgements. It must be significant that the eleventh House is so well tenanted, and that the ruler of both fourth and fifth are found therein.

Now, it will take a long period of very careful study of the history of Parliament since 1688 to make final decisions about correct signification. Meanwhile, just as a taster, allow me to point to a couple of interesting progressions.

THE DECLARATION AND THE 1832 REFORM ACT

This, the most important and far-reaching development since 1689 (Figure 26), was marked by the progressed sun conjunct radical and progressed Pluto, on the 143rd anniversary of the Declaration, with the progressed moon poised to pass over that conjunction. At the same time transitting Uranus spent the year passing to and fro over radical Jupiter.

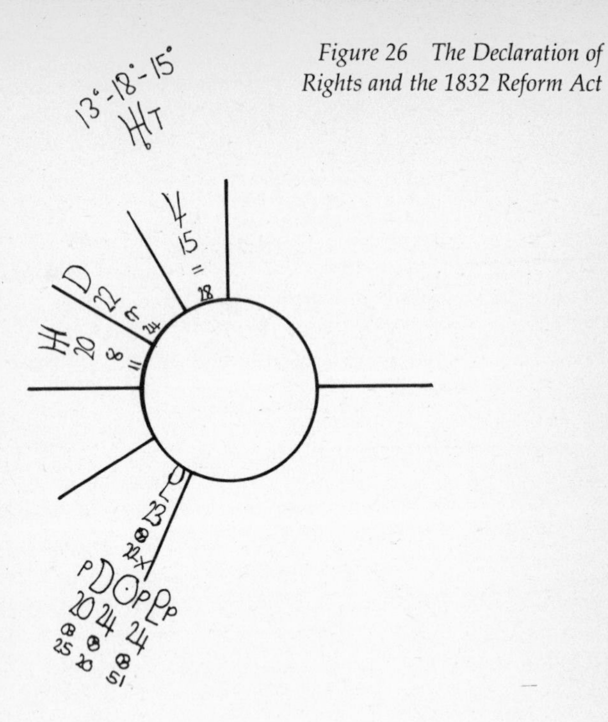

Figure 26 The Declaration of Rights and the 1832 Reform Act

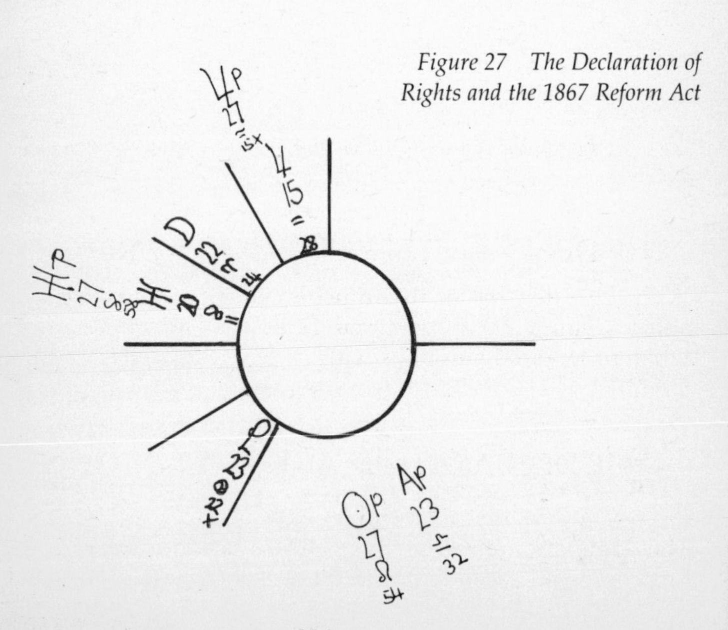

Figure 27 The Declaration of Rights and the 1867 Reform Act

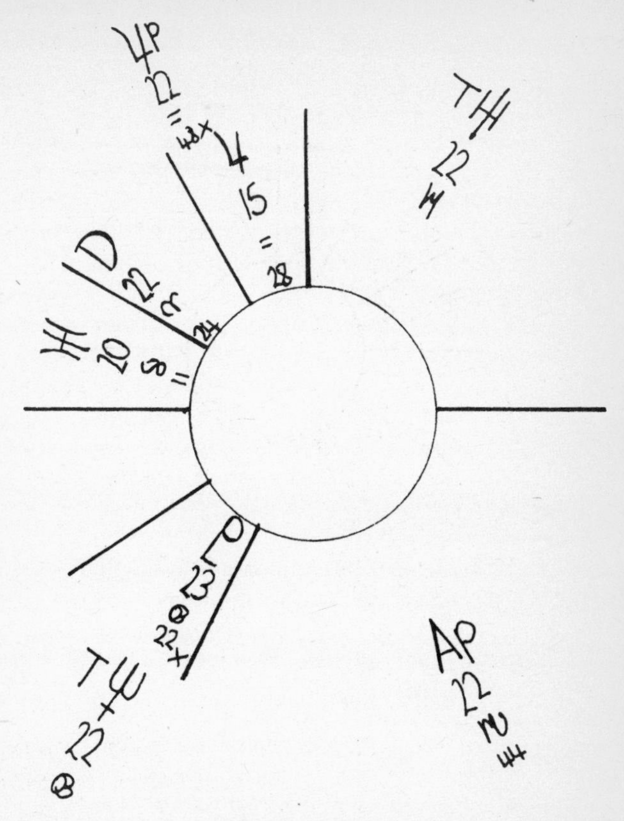

Figure 28 The Declaration and the Lords versus Commons on 15 November 1910

THE DECLARATION AND THE 1867 REFORM ACT

With the extension of the franchise to the labouring classes of the shires (Figure 27), progressed ascendant is square radical Pluto, while progressed sun links with progressed Jupiter and progressed Uranus.

THE DECLARATION AND THE LORDS VERSUS COMMONS IN 1910

The dominance of the Lords by the Commons (Figure 28) is marked by progressed ascendant trine Pluto and square progressed Jupiter, while the transitting Uranus/Neptune opposition falls across the degree of Pluto and squares the moon.

Thus, at every major transformation Pluto was involved, although it had not then been discovered.

Taking the chart as a great historic moment, which limited the powers of monarchy and ensured the Protestant succession, perhaps I can make some final observations.

This moment did not at a stroke transform our nation from an autocratic monarchy to a democracy; it took several hundred years for the common man and woman to become enfranchised; yet, within the moment, the potential for such development must be shown. Jupiter in Aquarius probably symbolises that potential, its elevation and power in the angle mark it out as the dominating influence of the moment; its good aspect with Venus and the moon does perhaps give some indication of eventual benefit to the common people, but the square with Uranus describes the long struggle to achieve it.

The chart shares with the 973 one three elements important to any successful inception: the MC is fixed showing stability, the ascendant is mutable, giving adaptability; the moon is above the earth and increasing in light. I should also mention that the moon of this chart is the ascendant of 1066, and the mid-heaven is the Mars of 1066 (ruler of the ascendant).

POSTSCRIPT

I must resist the temptation to veer off towards '1992'. We are living in interesting times. Since 1973, when Britain became part of a latter day Franco–German Empire, Parliament has been gradually ceding power to Brussels. Margaret Thatcher has already fired the first shots in what I am sure will turn into a battle to preserve the integrity of our most precious institution. However, 1992 and beyond must wait for another time.

Bibliography

Zee, Henry and Barbara van der (1988) *William and Mary* (Harmondsworth: Penguin).

X

JOHN WORSDALE AND LATE EIGHTEENTH-CENTURY ENGLISH ASTROLOGY

Patrick Curry

Commentary

Patrick Curry notes that Worsdale rejected horary astrology as irrational, but probably used it himself. This is interesting in relation to the detection of thieves, for which he had a great reputation. There is a very long tradition of detecting thieves by horary astrology; this is mentioned in Chapter 1 in connection with Greek texts.

William Lilly also had a great reputation for discovering thieves and lost objects by horary methods. His book, *Christian Astrology* (see especially pp. 336–66) deals with every imaginable aspect of thieves or theft: the age of the thief, whether man or woman, one thief or more, his clothes, his names, whether of the house or no, a stranger or familiar, where he is now, whether he still has the goods, whether it is his first theft or not, his age and appearance, where the knave is. Haly and Guido Bonatus are quoted as authorities.

It would be very interesting to know if, secretly, Worsdale used Lilly's methods, if only to detect theft.

Dr Curry also mentions Worsdale's rather grisly expertise in predicting the nature and time of clients' deaths, and the terms *apheta* and *hyleg*, which are used as synonyms by Lilly, who explains how to find the 'planet or place of Heaven' meant by them (see *Christian Astrology*, p. 527–8) in nativities, according to complicated rules. He says *hyleg* is a Chaldean word. It is defined as 'the giver of life', 'from which we judge of Life or the state thereof', by directions of the natal chart.

John Worsdale was born on 2 December 1766. His birthplace, Fulbeck, is 10 miles north of Grantham in Lincolnshire. I do not know a time of day but his horoscope might be of interest. It seems that one of his clients, a Lincoln hairdresser called Richard White, annoyed Worsdale by speaking disrespectfully of astrology. On Monday 8 September 1817, he asked for his nativity to be calculated. Worsdale predicted that White would die, seven years later, at the age of 33. 'He died on the 18th April, 1825, at noon, aged thirty-three Years nearly.' This incident is related by Worsdale in his *Celestial Philosophy* (1828), quoted by Ellic Howe in *Urania's Children*. Richard White was born at Lincoln on 25 April 1792 at 3.45 a.m. (*Note*: The date falls after the change of calendar in 1752 and so is in New Style.)

On the question of predicting death for a client, Augustus in the year AD 11 issued an edict forbidding any predictions about dates of death for anyone, not just a ruler. He published his own horoscope at the same time. Firmicus, in the passage on the behaviour of an astrologer quoted on page 25, writes: 'Do not give a response about the condition of the Republic or the life of the Emperor – that is illegal'; while Lilly (page 25) writes 'Give not judgment of the death of thy Prince . . . ' Cardan, who came to England to cast a horoscope for Edward VI, a sickly boy, said he would live to be 55. When taxed with his mistake he said he had failed to do an extra hundred hours of calculation, and that he was glad of this – a rather reasonable attitude.

A. L. K.

I would like to discuss a major, but relatively little known, English astrologer: John Worsdale (1766–c. 1828), of Lincolnshire. I will also try to use Worsdale to gain some understanding of English astrology as a whole at that time.

Just to set the scene a little, the eighteenth century in England was a quiet, not to say low, time for astrology, especially after the heady days of the mid-seventeenth century. Among the labouring and semi-literate or illiterate people, relatively primitive astrological beliefs clung on tenaciously. These mainly concerned the moon, and applied to matters of physic, agriculture and husbandry, and omens for personal guidance. Sales of Moore's *Vox Stellarum* continued to rise (to over 300,000 copies a year by 1800), but overall sales of almanacs were down, in a population whose literacy was rising, and whose active readership was doubling.

In terms of the more sophisticated sort of astrology, involving horoscopic maps or 'figures', just six textbooks teaching astrology appeared in the entire eighteenth century, of which only three were new. There were certainly excellent astrologers – particularly from and/or in Leicestershire and Lincolnshire, from among whom Henry Andrews (1744–1820) stands out – but they were much less publicly prominent and influential than their seventeenth-century predecessors. So someone like Worsdale, an astrologer well established in his part of the country and with several books to his name, was unusual. Apart from Andrews, the only other such astrologer in the late eighteenth-century was Ebenezer Sibly, to whom I will return later.

Worsdale was born in Fulbeck, near Grantham. After living in Helpringham, Spansby, and Donington Northorpe, he eventually settled in Lincoln, 'near the Cathedral'. He was the upholder of a venerable tradition which he felt others (such as Sibly) had betrayed: that is astrology as a rational science, but one based not on modern science but on the principles of Aristotle and Ptolemy. In this, predecessors whose lead he acknowledged were John Partridge and the Italian astrologer–monk, Placidus.

Like them, he viewed the science of Galileo and Newton as at best irrelevant, and at worst destructive; accordingly, he viewed the past efforts of John Gadbury and others to place astrology on a more scientific footing as merely clumsy meddling with tradition. But he was *equally* opposed to a magical or occult astrology, which offended his view of astrology as a rational discipline, with formal canons laid down by Ptolemy and refined by Placidus. He also regarded the magical tradition as offensively populist (that is 'vulgar') and unorthodox from a religious point of view.

Worsdale (again, unlike Sibly) was an unrepentant élitist. The dedication of one of his books (to Henry Andrews) remarks: 'I do not require the Vulgar and Illiterate to busy themselves with a subject of this nature; it is to you, Sir, and those that are learned in the Sydereal Mysteries, I only appeal in this case.' And he emphasized that a great deal of study is necessary in order to become 'qualified to decide, whether a planetary influence operates among mankind, or not'.

In keeping with this tendency, Worsdale's judicial astrology involved highly detailed mathematical calculations, particularly concerning directions, and arcane interpretive points – without any possible physical rationale – such as the *apheta* and *hyleg*. These two terms – concerned with predicting a subject's longevity, and the date and, if possible, nature of his or her death – particularly interested Worsdale. In several of his books he remorselessly recorded their apparent accuracy and reliability, with his subjects invariably meeting the astrologically appropriate death. This was his favourite 'proof' of astrology, and comprised the entirety of (for example) *A Collection of Remarkable Nativities . . . Proving the Truth and Verity of Astrology, in its Genethliacal Part* (1799). While it gives his work a somewhat macabre air, in this respect Worsdale was undoubtedly typical of many medieval and Renaissance astrologers.

Perhaps it was also partly his revenge on the clients who supplied him with most of his livelihood, but for whom he clearly had little respect. Worsdale rejected horary astrology on principle, as rationally indefensible; but equally, it is unlikely he scrupled over its usefulness in practice. He was not the only astrologer in the area, the others being 'illiterate pretenders, who too often deceive the ignorant and unwary'. Indeed, 'There are many of this tribe in several places, and there are some also that reside in the City of Lincoln, who, in alehouses and other noted places, prate about calculating Nativities . . . ' (1819, p. 44). But he certainly seems to have been the best known, and John Worsdale or Worsdall, 'the Lincoln Wiseman or Astronomer', survived well into the nineteenth century as a figure of popular folklore. In this capacity he had uncanny powers of knowledge, detecting thieves and lost objects for farmers, gamekeepers, etc., who regarded him with uneasy respect. He was even invariably accompanied by a familiar spirit, usually a cat or a blackbird. Thus did the common folk he despised get their own back!

In addition to his *Collection*, Worsdale published *Genethliacal Astrology* (1796), an analysis of *The Nativity of Napoleon Bonaparte* (1805), and (echoing Placidus) *Astronomy and Elementary Philosophy* (1819). In the last, he claims to have predicted the fall of Napoleon in his preceding book – another vindication of his astrology, as opposed to the 'Vulgar Astrology' of 'illiterate pretenders' (9, 44).

Unusually, he also struck a (Whiggish) note in common with Sibly: the 'elevated and dignified' positions of the planets at the time of American independence, he thought, 'most clearly forebode, that the time will arrive, when THAT EMPIRE shall give laws to all Nations, and establish FREEDOM and LIBERTY in every part of the habitable Globe'.

Worsdale's last and lengthiest book, published posthumously, was *Celestial Philosophy, or Genethliacal Astronomy* (c. 1828). In it, he reaffirmed his unwavering faith in Ptolemy, and lashed past and present astrologers who fell short of his particular and demanding standards: Gadbury, Coley, and Parker ('pirates'), and the new work of Sibly ('has done incalculable harm'), Thomas White ('a wretched compilation of borrowed, and stolen trash') and James Wilson. Lilly is admitted to be 'the greatest professor of the Mundane, and Horary departments of this science', but only John Partridge – strict Ptolemaic that he was – receives unstinting praise (v–vii). The *apheta* and *hyleg* are affirmed as the bulwark of true astrology, against the scorn of 'the Infidel, the Deist, the Atheist, and the critic', (39). By now, Worsdale had at least won some acclaim among other astrologers. The editors of *The Conjuror's Magazine* favoured him over the 'faulty and erroneous' work of Sibly, and one C. E. Wynne of Portland

Place, London, published an adulatory *Address to Mr. John Worsdale . . .* (1816).

To understand Worsdale, you really have to know something about his near contemporary, and astrological adversary, Ebenezer Sibly (1751–99). I will concentrate on his astrology, rather than his life. To put it in a nutshell, Sibly was not only a southern and metropolitan counterpart to Worsdale; he represented a different and competing astrological tradition.

Sibly was a leading freemason, proponent of mesmerism, and able physician. He was well read in the scientific literature of his day, and in his writings he freely mixed Newton, Priestley and Lavoisier with Paracelsus, Hermes Trismegistus, and earlier astrologers. Sibly believed in the value of *both* modern scientific knowledge and the vitalism and spirituality of the natural magic tradition. Only by combining the two, he felt, would it be possible to preserve the crucial connections between man (the microcosm) and the universe (the macrocosm), and their equal dependence on divinity.

Sibly was also a prolific writer, and his *A New and Complete Illustration of the Celestial Science of Astrology* (1784–8) – sometimes appearing as . . . *of the Occult Sciences* – was the finest major public statement of astrology for many years. It appeared in four parts, and ran to over a thousand pages; by 1817, it had already gone through twelve editions, and continued to be reprinted until 1826.

The *Illustration* was a comprehensive restatement of judicial astrological doctrine, and none the less so for being largely derivative of seventeenth-century material. It covered astrology in its genethliacal (that is natal), horary, political, and meteorological branches, interspersed with current knowledge, miscellaneous observations of interest, and predictions. It also reveals Sibly's assumption that natural philosophy should be supplemented by occult knowledge. This resulted in a treatment of astrology that, on the one hand, defined his subject naturalistically, as a science, and, on the other, emphasized its magical elements: macrocosm/microcosm, sympathy and antipathy, the doctrine of signatures, etc. Sibly also asserted that astrology 'is a science which all may attain to, by common diligence and application . . . '

In all important respects, then, the astrologies of Worsdale and Sibly were opposed; for the latter, astrology was part of an advance into the future, extended by modern scientific discoveries and ancient magical tradition finding new applications – what I will take the liberty of calling the Astrological Association of Great Britain position in the 1980s. Furthermore, it was knowledge open, in principle, to everyone. For Worsdale, on the other hand, modern science and old magic were equally corruptions of the true astrology, which was the rational, non-occult but also non-scientific or materialistic discipline instituted by Ptolemy. Furthermore, its difficulty was held to be such that only a very few ever succeeded in mastering it. These different traditions have endured up to the present day.

The antagonism between a magical astrology (such as that of Lilly, d. 1681), a scientific astrology (represented by Gadbury, d. 1704), and Ptolemaic astrology (represented by Partridge, d. 1715) was already well established. But Sibly's successful combination of popularized science and natural magic was a new development. What made it possible was an unprecedentedly large and independently minded middle class, consisting of what Adorno has called 'the semi-erudite', who provided an appreciative audience for this new breed of ideas.

Succeeding Victorian astrologers like Zadkiel and Raphael essentially followed the same pattern as Sibly, and their relative success after 1830 is further evidence that the kind of astrology embodying this combination had indeed found an enduring middle-class audience.

Worsdale, on the other hand, it is difficult to see as other than a remarkable – and remarkably late – heir of the Ptolemaic tradition of Partridge and Placidus. His uncompromisingly 'traditional' and technically complex astrology was too demanding, too intellectually unorthodox, and too narrowly internal to appeal to the new constituency for judicial astrology, which appeared in the 1830s and 1840s. Of course, the very same things have meant, and may continue to mean, that individual astrologers find him a more congenial and even inspiring model than more 'popular' or 'successful' astrologers, either now or then.

Note: For fuller references, see my PhD thesis (University of London, 1986), chapter 8. Published references include Ellic Howe, *Astrology and the Third Reich* (Wellingborough: Aquarian Books, 1984), pp. 26–8; and James Obelkevitch, *Religion and Rural Society: South Lindsey, 1825–1875* (Oxford: OUP, 1976), pp. 288–9. All Worsdale's books discussed above are in the British Library.

ASTROLOGICAL LITERATURE IN LATE EIGHTEENTH-CENTURY ENGLAND

Patrick Curry

Commentary

Dr Curry discusses late eighteenth-century astrological literature and mentions the periodical *The Conjuror's Magazine* (later *The Astrologer's Magazine*). Volumes of this are now rare so I have reproduced some pages by way of illustration.

The horoscopes are drawn up with the squares-within-squares arrangement – very convenient once one is used to it; it emphasizes the angles, whose cusps are at the mid-points of the four sides of the outermost square. My first example is the nativity of Nicholas Culpeper, who is of special interest to students of medical astrology.

Culpeper (1616–54) was the son of a clergyman, educated at Cambridge and then apprenticed to a London apothecary; later he had a large practice in Spitalfields. He was much opposed to the monopoly held by the Royal College of Physicians. He had great sympathy with the poor and taught that anyone could have herbal remedies for a few pennies. He had radical ideas and fought for Parliament in the Civil War. Culpeper was a popular translator and compiler of medical writings; he published astrological almanacs in the 1650s.

The analysis of Culpeper's horoscope which I quote here was dated 3 December 1792, and signed 'Peter', of 49 Liquorpond Street. It appears on page 193 of the January 1793 issue of what was then still *The Conjuror's Magazine, or, Magical and Physiognomical Mirror*. NOTE J. Harris pointed out in the June issue that this horoscope was filched from Gadbury's 'Collection', and was said by Partridge to be false.

NATIVITY OF NICHOLAS CULPEPER

'A General Judgment on this figure'

> The sign ascending the horoscope is Capricorn, a sign of brevity; and Saturn, lord of the ascendant, is in Taurus, a sign of brevity also, the Moon in the sixth house, decreasing in light; all which are arguments of a middle stature, and somewhat of a spare, lean body,

NATIVITY OF NICHOLAS CULPEPER.

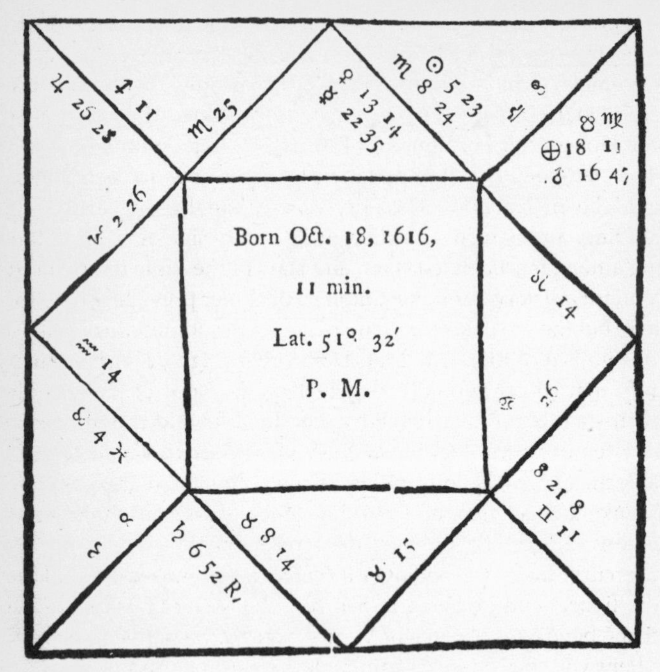

A GENERAL JUDGMENT ON THIS FIGURE.

THE ſign aſcending the horoſcope is ♑, a ſign of brevity; and Saturn, lord of the aſcendant, is in ♉, a ſign of brevity alſo, the Moon in the ſixth houſe, decreaſing in light; all which are arguments of a middle ſtature, and ſomewhat of a ſpare, lean body, complexion darkiſh, or ſwarthy, hair dark brown, viſage more long than round, eyes quick and piercing, &c. and the perſon of this native was exactly ſuch; and he was alſo full of agility, very active and nimble, which I preſume was occaſioned by the Moon's poſition in the houſe of ☿ in ✶ to ♂ and ♄ in the houſe of ♀, having South latitude.

His temperature, according to aſtrologers, ſhould be melancholy, choleric, as is plain by an earthy ſign aſcending, and ♄'s poſition in an earthy ſign alſo, and ☽ being among martial fixed ſtars, and ſtars of the ſame nature in the aſcendant are very ſtrong teſtimonies of choler prevailing over this native; but the greateſt argument of choler predominating, I take to be the Sun's reception with Mars from violent ſigns, which ſeems to ſignify that choler ſhould overpower the humour of melancholy, notwithſtanding an earthy ſign aſcending, &c. He was indeed of ſuch a temperature, that melancholy was an extraordinary enemy unto him, ſo great at ſome times, that wanting company he would ſeem like a dead man; and at other times

VOL. II. C c would

Figure 29

complexion darkish, or swarthy, hair dark brown, visage more long than round, eyes quick and piercing, &c. and the person of this nativity was exactly such; and he was also full of agility, very active and nimble, which I presume was occasioned by the Moon's position in the house [sign] of Mercury in sextile to Mars and Saturn in the House [sign] of Venus [=Taurus], having South latitude.

His temperature [temperament], according to astrologers, should be melancholy, choleric, as is plain by an earthy sign ascending, and Saturn's position in an earthy sign also, and Moon being among martial fixed stars, and stars of the same nature in the ascendant are very strong testimonies of choler prevailing over this native; but the greatest testimony of choler predominating, I take to be the Sun's reception with Mars from violent signs, which seems to signify that choler should overpower the humour of melancholy, notwithstanding an earthy sign ascending &c. He was indeed of such a temperature, that melancholy was an extraordinary enemy unto him, so great at some times, that wanting company he would seem like a dead man; and at other times would his choler afflict him very strangely, even more than melancholy.

Mercury, the patron of ingenuity, &c. is the most potent planet in the figure, and he being in Scorpio, the house of Mars, and so near the benevolent beams of Venus, argued the native to be of an excellent wit, sharp fancy, admirable conception, and of an active understanding.

For proof of this let his many worthy works extant be summoned to give in evidence . . .

He was very eloquent, a good orator, spoke both freely and fluently; and if I should speak the truth he was very conceited [=full of ideas], and full of jests as the square of Mars to Mercury denotes . . .

The fixed sign Aquarius is on the cusp of the second house [of money], and the Moon and Jupiter casting their friendly rays thither and the Moon's North Node in the house of Jupiter, viz Pisces, intercepted there; there are testimonies of a competent fortune naturally, according to Haly, Bonatus, &c . . .

It is most true, that he was always subject to a consumption of the purse, notwithstanding the many ways he had to assist him. His patrimony was chiefly consumed at the University. – He had a spirit so far above the vulgar that he contemned and scorned riches . . .

Had he not had Caput Draconis [the Moon's North Node] in the second, he would have been perpetually poor.

> Now Mars, Lord of the eleventh, in square to four planets, denotes the native's friends, or at least such as pretend friendship unto him, to be hypocritical and deceitful . . .

Comments upon the 'General Judgment' of Nicholas Culpeper's Nativity

The writer in 1792 seems to claim a close acquaintance with Culpeper's appearance and temperament, although he had died in 1654 (see note on p. 243). The first two paragraphs make an interesting comparison with the self-description of Kepler (see page 152). There is a good deal of emphasis on fixed stars and their effects.

Mercury, 'the patron planet of ingenuity', is also the planet ruling medicine. Caput Draconis (the moon's north node), in the second House, is often cited like this as a saving grace that mitigates hostile effects.

As the printing of the original is faulty I give below the cusps, Houses and positions of the horoscope.

Ascendant: Capricorn 2:26. 2nd: Aquarius 14. 3rd: Aries 8. 10th: Scorpio 8:24. 11th: Scorpio 25. 12th: Sagittarius 11.
Sun (9th) 5:23 Scorpio. Moon (6th) 21:8 Gemini. Mercury (10th) 22:35 Scorpio. Venus (10th) 13:14 Scorpio. Mars (8th) 16:47 Leo. Jupiter (12th) 26:23 Sagittarius. Saturn (3rd) 6:52 Taurus retrograde. Moon's north node (2nd) 4 Pisces. Fortuna (8th) 18:11 Leo.

LOUIS XVI

In January 1793 *The Conjuror's Magazine* published the nativity of 'The Unfortunate Louis XVI', with a commentary signed by '"Mehmet", Tenbury, Nov. 2, 1792'. I quote:

> The cusp ascendant is beheld by sextile Moon and trine Saturn and body Sun and Mars with an evil fixed star of the nature of Saturn, and all debilitated; shews him to be at one time furious and head-strong, another time melancholy and stupid, regretting his former wilfulnes, always at extreme, immutable in all his actions, to his great prejudice.
>
> In person strong, well-set, of a sanguine complexion, little bent in the knee, with a sandy curling hair. – Mercury retrograde conjunct Jupiter both combust of sun in the 12th House, declares powerful enemies and imprisonment; the two infortunes angular,

THE

CONJUROR's MAGAZINE.

FOR JANUARY, 1793.

NATIVITY OF THE UNFORTUNATE LOUIS XVI.

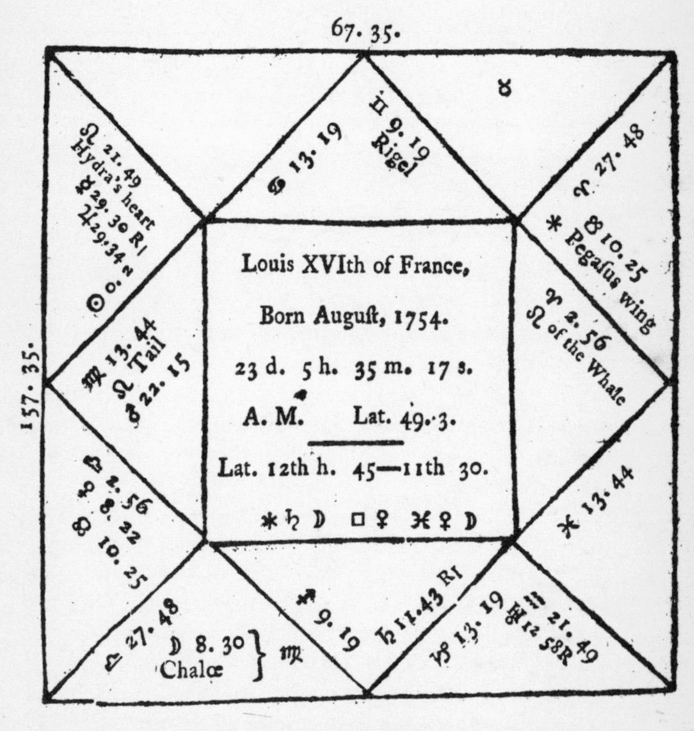

B b 2 LAT.

Figure 30

> the fortunes cadent with a violent fixed star of the nature of Saturn, denotes the same; the cusp of 8th house adorned with evil fixed star and South Node all these declare untimely death: Saturn retrograde though in house and angular cannot be but of an evil tendency, it being retrograde; a planet retrograde is by no means benevolent.
>
> *The Conjuror's Magazine*, January 1793, p. 188

It is interesting that Uranus, which had been discovered as recently as 1781, is marked on the horoscope for Louis' birth in 1754 but with no comment on its being exactly inconjunct the ascendant.

By the time the February issue was being prepared Louis had been executed and 'W. E.' published his horoscope for the event with a long commentary showing his hostility to the revolutionaries.

THE 'CONJUROR'S MAGAZINE' FOR FEBRUARY 1793

This issue began with 'W. E.'s' observations on the event map of the 'Murder of the King of France'. Readers would be able to compare this with Louis' nativity in the issue of the preceding month. The writer claims the event map is set 'for the precise time on which that unfortunate monarch, Louis XVI late king of France, was solemnly murdered on a scaffold erected for that purpose. – Agreeable to the cruel and unjust sentence passed on him at his sham-trial by a junto [*sic*] of sanguinary regicides . . . ' (*Note*. Given the precision of the data, the astrologer probably rectified the horoscope.)

There are mistakes in the printed horoscope. It must have been done in great haste in order to 'scoop' the event on the 23rd for the February issue. (The cusp of the 7th should be Libra, not Cancer; the cusp of the 8th should be Scorpio, not Virgo). However, the commentary is right: 'The cusp of the 8th in the radix [nativity] of Louis ascending the horizon [of the execution].' Also 'The lord of the ascendant [Mars] being lord of the 8th [with Scorpio on the cusp]'.

> And, as to the manner of it [death], it was wonderfully decyphered by the Moon, who we find posited in the sign Taurus and in the second house, both of which governs the neck, the very part doomed to receive the fatal stroke that was to give this unfortunate potentate his passport from a life of insult, wretchedness and misery, to a glorious and blisful eternity. She is there with the Pleiades, violent fixed stars of her own nature, and of the nature of Mars, from whose square she is just separating, and from the opposition of Jupiter also . . . What can be more strikingly descriptive of this sad event, than their positions?

THE

CONJUROR's MAGAZINE.

FOR FEBRUARY, 1793.

W. E.'s OBSERVATIONS UPON THE MURDER OF THE KING OF FRANCE.

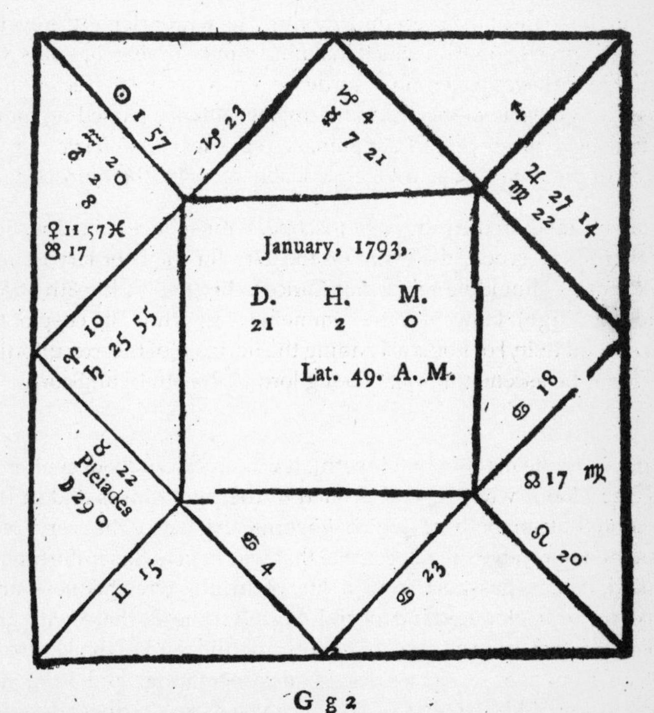

G g 2

THE

Figure 31

'W. E.' goes on to predict the outcome for the Bourbon family: 'royalty is still to remain with the house of Bourbon, who shall once more ascend the throne of France; . . . but it will be a limited monarchy . . . ' This because the 'cusp of the 5th in the radix culminating [in the event chart]'.

Interpretations at this time laid great stress on fixed stars and also upon very complicated interrelationships between nativities and event horoscopes.

Note: Modern authorities give the time of execution as 10.20 a.m. on 21 January 1793. This horoscope is set for about two hours before noon and, allowing for time difference etc., is based on 10.20 a.m. News sheets about executions were on the streets of London within a few days.

To emphasize the special interest in political matters which is characteristic of this magazine, I should mention two horoscopes for the moment when George III 'Delivered the Minister's Speech from the Throne' (13 December 1792, at 2.50 p.m.) and the moment on the same day when it was 'Received' by the House of Commons (6 p.m.). This is a reminder of the astrological importance attached to Charles II's similar speech on 27 October 1673, when Elias Ashmole and William Lilly were his advisers. In the two issues, January and February 1793, which have been referred to here, roughly one-third is devoted to astrology.

A. L. K.

I would like to consider English astrological literature, and in particular the first periodical publication written by astrologers *for* astrologers – something that is taken for granted today. First, I will look at the literature itself, then at what it can tell us about astrologers of the past, and even of the present.

This periodical started life as – to give it its full name – *The Conjuror's Magazine, or, Magical and Physiognomical Mirror*. It appeared in August 1791, and was based in London. It was published monthly. In 1793, it became *The Astrologer's Magazine; and Philosophical Miscellany*. The last issue was in January 1794.

Its contents were a mixture of astrology, magic, and natural philosophy (or what we would call science). The astrology included items such as discussions of birth charts, from ancient (for example, Naibod) to contemporary ones (for example, George, Prince of Wales), examples of horary and mundane astrology, a judgement on a solar eclipse, and discussions of the merits of Placidean House division.

In between and among these were articles on the interpretation of dreams and visions, Nostradamus, Boehme, palmistry, physiognomy, mesmerism, Swedenborgianism, alchemy, talismans, and the principles of occult philosophy.

Finally, there were also discussions on cosmology; Newtonianism was a particularly delicate subject, with one contributor declaring sternly that

> Sir I. N[ewton], may keep his nonsense of vacuum and attraction out of the way, for we are not indebted to mythology and superstition for life and presiding genii in the sun, planets, and all creation, but to sound reason, genuine theosophy, and the oracles of GOD.

He went on to argue the soundness of Jacob Boehme, and the inadequacy of both astrology and morality without spiritual guidance such as Boehme had shown. Or as he put it, 'the powers of the natural heaven must be shaken with the spiritual man . . . '

This writer was one William Gilbert, a professional astrologer and occultist. Gilbert apparently lived in Queen Square. He raised most of his money from classes in the manufacture and use of talismans, for which he charged high fees: between £20 and £150 per annum.

What was the significance of this curious publication? To understand that, you have to appreciate the contemporaneous situation in British astrology. Popular almanacs, written not for astrologers but for the person in the street (or field), were selling well. The leader, *Old Moore's*, was rising to a peak it reached in 1839 of 560,000 copies a year. The contents of these combined simple astrology with popularized science, biblical prophecy, and political comment.

But by the mid-eighteenth century, able and well-known judicial astrologers – practising and writing in the higher reaches of the art – were much thinner on the ground than they had been fifty years earlier. In particular, they were absent in London; the flag was kept flying mainly in Lincolnshire, Rutland, and Leicestershire.

In the 1780s, however, Ebenezer Sibly's massive *New and Complete Illustration of the Celestial Science of Astrology* appeared. Despite its size – over a thousand pages – it was a success, going into twelve editions by 1817. Combined with *The Conjuror's Magazine*, this was a signal of major changes in astrology and its audience.

In both cases, the content was something new. Formerly, the major split within the astrological world had been between those advocating magic and populism (like Lilly), and those favouring natural philosophy and élitism (like Gadbury). As it became increasingly dangerous to advocate the former position, it was replaced by the Ptolemaic astrology of Partridge – still anti-scientific, but claiming to be equally (or more) 'rational'.

But Sibly and *The Conjuror's Magazine* freely mixed natural philosophy, natural magic, and (although the magazine did so less) populism – that is, the assumption that astrological truth is available, in principle, to all who want it, rather than restricted to a few who are qualified.

Why was it possible at just this point – the end of the eighteenth century – to present this mixture. The short answer is that only now were the English middle classes beginning to break away from the social and intellectual dominance of their 'betters'. (The stirrings of this independence were evident in other ways at the same time.) Thus could astrologers feel impelled to lash Newtonianism – by this time, a centrepiece of gentry ideology – while drawing on the bits of natural philosophy they felt they could use. Thus they also felt emboldened to talk about and advocate magic, breaking a taboo that only a very few (and well-placed) people had broken in the century before, outside the pale of 'the vulgar mob' with which magic had been identified by the authorities and to which they had largely confined it. And most of all, they felt able to try to present and discuss astrology without admitting any contradiction with being educated and Christian citizens.

The Conjuror's and *Astrologer's Magazine* lasted four years; no less, but no more, either. Such long-term social and intellectual changes are never very rapid in human terms. The next attempt at a periodical for astrologers (*The Urania*) fell flat in 1814. But the more realistic project of an annual almanac aimed at a literate, urban, and more astrologically sophisticated audience than Moore's, including but not restricted to astrologers, was a success. Raphael's and Zadkiel's almanacs, beginning in the late 1820s and 1830s, soon reached a circulation of 10,000 copies each per annum.

A century on, after the Industrial Revolution had irrevocably established modern society, no fewer than seven periodicals for astrologers appeared. They all lasted at least a few years. The survivor was Alan Leo's *Astrologer's Magazine*, started in August 1890, whose title he changed to *Modern Astrology* in 1895.

GLOSSARY

Note: This glossary is an attempt to provide at least minimal definitions for those who do not understand astrology as well as for those who do. Differences between traditional and modern terminology are indicated.

ACCIDENTS: Events in the life by whose dates a more exact birth time may be determined or 'rectified'.
ANAPHORA: Beginning or rising; the coming over the horizon of a star or constellation. (See Firmicus Maternus, *Mathesis*, 3, 3.)
ANGLES: The cusps of the first, fourth, seventh and tenth Houses; ASCENDANT, IMUM COELI, DESCENDANT and MEDIUM COELI (qq.v.).
ANGULAR planets: those close to these cusps.
APHELION: That point of a planet's orbit at which it is farthest from the sun.
ARTIFICIAL DAY: The time from sunrise till sunset on a given day, varying throughout the year; hence:
ARTIFICIAL HOUR: That period divided by twelve, also varying. (See NATURAL DAY, NATURAL HOUR, DAY.)
ASCENDANT: (Usually 'ascend*e*nt' in early texts, but variable spelling); the degree of the ecliptic rising over the eastern horizon at the moment of birth; the cusp of the first House (of great importance in interpretation.) Also called the 'horoscope'.
ASPECT: An angular distance made at the centre of the earth between a line from one planet and a line from another planet, measured in degrees along the ecliptic. See MAJOR ASPECTS and MINOR ASPECTS.
AZIMUTH: A line of sight, measured across the visible horizon from observer to observed, expressed in degrees clockwise from celestial north.
CADENT: Cadent Houses are the third, sixth, ninth and twelfth; traditionally not favourable, particularly the sixth and twelfth.
CAERAU: Welsh for enclosures, usually fortified.
CAPUT DRACONIS: See DRAGON'S HEAD.
CARDINAL SIGNS: Aries, Cancer, Libra and Capricorn. See MOVABLE.
CAUDA DRACONIS: See DRAGON'S TAIL.
CHART: See HOROSCOPE.
COMMON: Traditional term for MUTABLE (q.v.).
CONJUNCT: See MAJOR ASPECTS.
CONJUNCTION: See Nicholas Campion's note on 'Mundane Astrology' (p. 89).

DAY: Each day of the week has its own planetary ruler; so has each hour, whether NATURAL or ARTIFICIAL (qq.v.).
DECANATE: One third part or 10 degrees of a zodiacal sign.
DESCENDANT: The cusp of the seventh House.
DRAGON'S HEAD: Caput Draconis; traditional term for the MOON'S NORTH NODE (q.v.). Favourable for affairs of the House where posited.
DRAGON'S TAIL: Cauda Draconis; traditional term for the MOON'S SOUTH NODE (q.v.). Unfavourable.
DIGNITIES: Each planet has signs (of dignity and exaltation), TERMS, FACES (qq.v.) and a triplicity which strengthen it; also signs (of detriment and fall) where it is weak. Signs of dignity and exaltation are also, confusingly, referred to as a planet's 'House'.
ELECTIONS: Choices made, on astrological principles, of the most auspicious moment for an event or the inception of a project.
ELEMENTS: Fire, earth, air, water; there are three signs in each triplicity (or trigon): Aries, Leo, Sagittarius; Taurus, Virgo, Capricorn; Gemini, Libra, Aquarius; Cancer, Scorpio, Pisces.
ELEVATED: A position near the MC (q.v.).
EVENT: (horoscope, map or chart): Horoscope for the time of an event, not a birth.
EXALTATION: a sign in which a planet is strong, for example, the moon in Taurus. See DIGNITIES.
EXTA: Entrails.
EXTISPICY: Inspection of entrails for purposes of augury.
FACE: A 10 degree division of a sign; it has a planetary sub-ruler. See DIGNITIES.
FALL: A sign where a planet is weak, being opposite the sign of its exaltation.
FIGURE: See HOROSCOPE.
FIXED: Fixed signs are Taurus, Leo, Scorpio and Aquarius; associated with stability and long duration.
FORTUNA, or the Part of Fortune: A point calculated by adding the longitude of the moon to the longitude of the ascendant and subtracting the longitude of the sun. Traditionally beneficial for the affairs of the House where it falls. One of the Arabic parts.
HORARY: A question the answer to which is interpreted by erecting a horoscope for the moment of that question.
HOROSCOPE: (Also called figure, nativity, scheme, map and – modern usage – chart.) A diagram of the sky showing positions of planets and luminaries in the twelve Houses and signs of the zodiac for a given moment.

HOUSES: Sections of the sky arbitrarily determined by various methods. Like planets and signs, each of the twelve Houses is traditionally associated with certain categories of human affairs. The word 'House' is sometimes used to refer to a planet's own sign.

IMUM COELI (IC): Point opposite the MID-HEAVEN (q.v.). Cusp of the fourth House. (Classicists prefer 'coelum'.)

IMMORTAL SEVEN, THE: The seven men who signed the invitation to William of Orange to come and take the throne with his wife; three were Tories, three Whigs, and Dr Henry Compton represented the church.

INCONJUNCT: Minor aspect of 150 degrees. /Quincunx/(Cap)

LADY OF THE . . . : moon or Venus when ruling a House.

LIGHTS, LUMINARIES: Sun and moon. For the sake of brevity, often included in 'planets'.

LORD OF THE . . . : Sun or other planets ruling a House. See LADY OF THE . . . .

MAJOR ASPECTS: Conjunction (0 degrees), sextile (60 degrees), square (90 degrees), trine (120 degrees), and opposition (180 degrees).

MARTIAN: Here adjective indicating the astrological attributes of Mars. ('Martial' has specialized associations.)

MEDIUM COELI (MC), MID-HEAVEN: The point of the ecliptic on the meridian.

M-HOUSE: Division of the celestial sphere by equal sectors of the plane of the ecliptic, starting from the MC, which is taken as the cusp of the first House. In this system, the ascendant is not identical with the cusp of the first House but is merely a sensitive point in the chart's eastern hemisphere.

MINOR ASPECTS: Quintile (72 degrees), biquintile (144 degrees), sesquiquadrature (135 degrees), inconjunct (150 degrees). See 'Kepler's Belief in Astrology', n. 11, in this book. /quincunx

MOON'S NORTH NODE: See DRAGON'S HEAD. The nodes are points at which the moon's orbit intersects the ecliptic as it goes from north to south latitude and vice versa.

MOON'S SOUTH NODE: See DRAGON'S TAIL.

MOOT HILL: natural or artificial hill on which local legislative assembly was held in Saxon times.

MOVABLE: Traditional term for CARDINAL (q.v.).

MUNDANE ASTROLOGY: See p. 89.

MUTABLE SIGNS: Gemini, Virgo, Sagittarius, Pisces; the traditional term is 'common'.

MUTUAL RECEPTION: Two planets are in mutual reception when each is in a sign ruled by the other. Beneficial.

NATIVITY, NATAL HOROSCOPE: Horoscope for the birth of an individual (the 'native'). Hence 'natal' and 'natally' are applied to conditions obtaining at birth.
NATURAL DAY: Twelve hours. See ARTIFICIAL DAY.
NATURAL HOUR: Sixty minutes. See ARTIFICIAL HOUR.
NEW STYLE: Dates according to the Gregorian calendar adopted by Roman Catholic countries in 1582 and in England in 1752, variably elsewhere. William III arrived in England on 5 November, Old Style, which was 15 November, New Style. George II's Act of 1751 provided that 1 January should be the legal beginning of the year instead of 25 March.
OLD STYLE: Dates according to the Julian calendar, still used by the Orthodox Church. See above.
OPPOSITION: See MAJOR ASPECTS.
PASC: Progressed ascendant. P prefixed to the abbreviation for a celestial point denotes that that point is progressed.
PERIHELION: Point in a planet's orbit which is nearest the sun.
PMC: Progressed MC or MID-HEAVEN (q.v.). See PROGRESSIONS.
PRE-NATAL EPOCH: A point about 273 days before birth when the degree of the ascendant and the longitude of the moon interchange with those points in the nativity.
PROGRESSIONS: Progression is a system whereby the celestial positions in a horoscope are advanced in the zodiac to a predetermined ratio, taking account of the number of years which have elapsed since birth. The new positions are compared with the originals to give indications of future events. (See SOLAR ARC progressions.)
QUERENT: The person who poses a question, whether horary or electional.
QUESITED: The matter asked about in a horary question.
RADICAL HOROSCOPE: The one cast for the birth of a person or for the inception or event from which others are seen to flow (for example the coronation of William I in 1066).
RADIX: As above.
RAGNAROK: Literally, 'twilight of the gods'; a great battle between Aesir and their enemies, described in *Gylfaginning*, which will end the old world order and precede a new one.
RECEPTION: See MUTUAL RECEPTION.
RECTIFICATION: Correction of an uncertain birth time by various methods. (See ACCIDENTS.)
RETROGRADE: A planet is said to be retrograde when it *appears* to be moving backwards in the zodiac from a geocentric point of view.
SATURN, SATURNIAN, SATURNINE: Saturnian (here) adjective denot-

ing the astrological attributes of Saturn. ('Saturnine' now specialized.)

SCHEME: See HOROSCOPE.

SECONDARY PROGRESSIONS: A method of PROGRESSION (q.v.).

SEXTILE: Benign. MAJOR ASPECT (q.v.).

SIGNS: Each belongs to one of the ELEMENTS (q.v.) and one of these qualities: cardinal (movable) – Aries, Cancer, Libra, Capricorn; fixed – Taurus, Leo, Scorpio, Aquarius; mutable (common) – Gemini, Virgo, Sagittarius, Pisces. (Traditional terms in brackets.)

SOLAR ARC: PROGRESSIONS (q.v.) using exact distance travelled by the sun along ecliptic since time of RADIX (q.v.) to create a new position for the mid-heaven and thence for the new ascendant. The method is based on the symbolic measure: one unit of daily motion equals one year of life.

SOLSTICE: One of two days in the year, currently 21 December (winter) and 21 June (summer), when the sun appears to stand still having reached its lowest (highest) noontime altitude and its southernmost (northernmost) intersection with the local horizon.

SQUARE: Difficult. MAJOR ASPECT (q.v.).

SYNASTRY: The comparison of nativities to see if the natives are compatible.

SYZYGY: Conjunction or opposition of sun and moon, that is new or full moon.

TERMS: A certain portion of each sign; groups of degrees where certain planets are powerful.

TRANSIT: The passage of a celestial body over natal positions, interpreted (as are progressions) as signalling events or conditions.

TRINE: Favourable. MAJOR ASPECT (q.v.).

VENUSIAN: Used here as an adjective indicating the astrological attributes of Venus (because 'venereal' has limited associations).

VOID OF COURSE: The moon is 'void of course' when it is seen that she will make no major aspects before leaving the sign she is in.

WAGGONS: Early English names for Great and Little Bears: Little Bear equals Our Lady's Waggon; Great Bear equals Woden's/Charles'/Arthur's Waggon.

YEAR FOR A DAY: When a horoscope is progressed to unfold its radical potential, the symbolic measure commonly used is known as 'a year for a day'. The planets are advanced along the ecliptic one day for every year of life. (PASC (q.v.)=progressed ascendant; PMC (q.v.)=progressed mid-heaven.)

INDEX